SMARTER SOLUTIONS

The finance pack

# The Finance Manual for Non-Financial Managers

The power to make confident financial decisions

PAUL McKOEN and LEO GOUGH

Prentice Hall

London • New York • Toronto • Sydney • Tokyo • Singapore
Madrid • Mexico City • Munich • Paris

PEARSON EDUCATION LIMITED

Head Office:
Edinburgh Gate
Harlow CM20 2JE
Tel: +44 (0)1279 623623
Fax: +44 (0)1279 431059

London Office:
128 Long Acre
London WC2E 9AN
Tel: +44 (0)20 7447 2000
Fax: +44 (0)20 7447 2170
www.business-minds.com

First published in Great Britain 1997

© Pearson Education Limited 2000

The right of Paul McKoen and Leo Gough to be identified as Authors of this Work has been asserted by them in accordance with the Copyright, Designs, and Patents Act 1988.

ISBN 0 273 64493 9

**British Library Cataloguing in Publication Data**
A CIP catalogue record for this book can be obtained from the British Library.

10 9 8 7 6 5 4 3
Typeset by Northern Phototypesetting Co. Ltd, Bolton
Printed and bound by Antony Rowe Ltd, Eastbourne
Transferred to digital print on demand, 2003

*The Publishers' policy is to use paper manufactured from sustainable forests.*

# Contents

# The MCI Middle

If you are studying for one of the NVQs on which the MCI standards are based, this book can help. Here's how some of the topics in this book relate to particular units.

## Middle Management Standards

**Unit 1   Initiate and implement change and improvement in services, products and systems**

Element 1.1   Identify opportunities for improvements in services, products and systems

Element 1.2   Evaluate proposed changes for benefits and disadvantages

**Unit 2   Monitor, maintain and improve service and product delivery**

Element 2.1   Establish and maintain the supply of resources into the organisation/department

Element 2.2   Establish and agree customer requirements

**Unit 3   Monitor and control the use of resources**

**Unit 4        Secure effective resource allocation for activities and projects**

**Unit 9        Seek, evaluate and organise information for action**

# Senior Management Standards

# Acknowledgement

Thanks to Steve Morris of the Burton Morris Consultancy for his initial support and encouragement.

# Key to margin symbols

**!**      Key thoughts for the section

**▶**      Example / case study

**✔**      Checklist

**☞**      An exercise

     A reference to another relevant section of the book

     A book reference

# CHAPTER ONE

# Reporting to the outside world

- Company background

- The framework

- The report

- The financial statements

- The profit and loss account

- The balance sheet

- The cash flow statement

- Published accounts and the stock market

## Company background

In this chapter we will look at the financial interface of a company with the outside world, which is its reporting of financial results.

These are typically referred to as 'annual reports', with listed companies filing interim half-year reports as well. Companies' annual reports are prepared to the end of that company's financial year, which is not necessarily either the calendar year or the April to March 'fiscal' year.

To understand the context of this reporting we must explore some of the background and history, since it is easy today to take the concepts entirely for granted.

The term 'company' is now used to describe a company registered under the

Companies Act. Today's Companies Acts, revised and updated by Parliament, continue to refine the laws relating to companies.

 The fundamental principles that follow from incorporation and registration of a limited company, are that:

■ the company has its own distinct legal existence, separate from that of its owners, and

■ the owners are protected by the concept of limited liability, which means that in the event of the company failing, they stand to lose only their investment in that company, and not any other assets which they may own.

Historically, the first Companies Act allowed business people to create companies instead of trading as a sole trader or partnership, with the benefits mentioned above.

In the landmark case of Salomon vs. Salomon Ltd 1897, the courts upheld the legal distinction between the company Salomon Ltd and Mr Salomon, confirming the separate legal existence of the Limited Company.

Additionally, the concept of shares and shareholders allowed stakes in such companies to be traded freely between individuals.

The quid pro quo for these commercial benefits was the stipulation of certain requirements and restrictions on the company in the form of: registration with Companies House, the maintenance at Companies House of up-to-date records, including particulars of directors, and the filing of annual reports of the financial affairs of the business.

Probably designed originally simply to protect existing and potential shareholders and creditors of the company, the law and best practice has since shifted to recognise the concept of a stakeholder in a company.

 A stakeholder is defined as someone with an interest or stake in the future of the company, and includes the following:

■ shareholders – these can be private individuals, other companies, pension funds or other financial institutions

■ creditors of the company (those to whom the company owes money)

■ those trading significantly with the company

■ employees of the company

■ the public at large.

With the growth in size of companies to the point where some of today's companies are substantially larger and arguably more powerful than many smaller nations, there has been a discernible shift toward more open management of companies. This is generally referred to as corporate governance.

A marked increase in the amount of information required in the annual reports, mainly of listed companies, has been one result of this trend. Increased legal responsibility of company directors has been another (*see pages 146–147*).

So *all* companies have the requirement to make annual returns to Companies House and to circulate these to shareholders. This book will assume that you work for a 'listed' UK company, but much of the information will be useful if you work in a private company. Most listed companies recognise that the annual report is not just a routine filing of financial information, but also the opportunity to inform shareholders of general information about the company's affairs and prospects, and so to increase the 'feel-good' factor among private shareholders.

Increasingly, the best corporate practice is to disseminate at least a summary of the annual report to all the employees of the company.

Do you have a copy of your company's annual report? If not, do obtain one; as we work through this section it will be very useful to refer to **your** organisation's report. If you have a copy but don't understand it, you've bought the right book. The fun starts here!

# The framework

The contents of the annual report follow a pre-set pattern that is similar for all companies. This is not a coincidence. The contents of the annual report are prescribed in some detail in the Companies Acts. The acts set out the requirements for directors' reports, which must include a fair review of the company's activities throughout the year and of its position at the year end. Additionally, detailed formats are provided for the financial information which must be supplied.

Further detail as to the preparation of company accounts in general, and the annual report, are included in FRSs, or Financial Reporting Standards (previously SSAPs, Standard Statements of Accounting Practice). These are developed and issued by the ASB (Accounting Standards Board) and cover areas which are developing, or which require additional clarification and standardisation within the profession in order to ensure that the accounting treatment of certain areas is consistent between companies.

The ASB has been authorised by the Secretary of State for the purpose of issuing such standards, and these statements become 'Accounting Standards' as referred to in the Companies Acts. There is generally substantial consultation within the accountancy profession before a new standard is issued.

The combined effect of the legislation, the standards and current best practice is, of course, enormously detailed, and way beyond the scope of this book. In the sections that follow, we will be describing the basic principles of reporting to the outside world, which takes place in the annual report.

## Directors are responsible

Although in practice non-financial managers and directors leave the preparation and filing of financial reports to their finance directors, if you are a director you have a duty to ensure that appropriate accounting records are maintained, prepared and submitted. As a director you *cannot* leave or delegate this responsibility to your Finance Director, you are jointly liable. If you are a director, I can recommend the Coopers & Lybrand publication *Being a Director* as an excellent 'user friendly' guide to the responsibilities of the post.

If you're a senior manager, particularly in a smaller company, ask yourself 'Do I act as a director?' If so, the law might treat you as one! Consider taking professional advice.

# The report

Having discussed the framework which stipulates the contents of the report, let's look at the report itself. Every report will contain:

- a directors' report
- a statement by the auditors
- the financial statements.

We will take a brief look at the first two before examining the financial statements in more depth.

Read through the annual report and accounts of your company – you'll find the report of the chairman/directors contains a full review of the year and some description of the current position and outlook. There'll be a section on directors' contracts, corporate governance, and dissemination of the report to employees. All this information is required.

> Often companies add to the reports in order to produce a document that will impress potential investors and/or customers, but you'll find that much of the content is mandatory.

The picture of the chairman smiling confidently in front of his newest most glamorous product will also feature in your company's report. This isn't mandatory, but might as well be!

There will also be a report of the auditors saying that 'in our opinion the accounts give a true and fair view'. There is currently an interesting debate on the role of auditors, and the extent of their liability when they miss something. In an entirely unconnected development(!), some of the big audit firms either have, or are considering, moving to limited liability companies from their current status as unlimited liability partnerships.

In the real world, an audit can never check the validity of every transaction in every part of the largest companies, and hence the terms used in the auditor's report: 'reasonable assurance' and 'material mis-statement'. The audit can only ever provide a high-level review of the company's policies and controls together with more detailed spot-check reviews of new and/or more critical operations. Indeed the responsibility for managing internal controls remains with the directors.

5

# The financial statements

Let's now move on to look at the financial statements of the company. These are broken down into three main statements as follows:

- profit and loss account
- balance sheets
- cash flow statement.

Most large companies are now actually groups of companies, and their glossy annual report will cover the 'top' company, or ultimate holding company of the group.

The profit and loss account and cash flow statement will be for the group as a whole, while the balance sheet is provided for the consolidated group and for the holding company alone. For the purposes of this description I will ignore the holding company balance sheet, and concentrate on the consolidated statements.

The first thing to note is that the profit and loss and cash flow will state 'for the year ended ...', while the balance sheet will state 'as at (the year end)'.

Profits and cash are earned throughout the year, whereas the balance sheet is a snapshot at the point in time which is the year end.

| **profit and loss/cash flow** (Year 1) | balance sheet | **profit and loss/cash flow** (Year 2) |
|---|---|---|

## Consolidation (group accounts)

Note that a 'group' of companies will probably include some companies which are not wholly owned. The method of consolidation of these companies depends on whether they are managed or controlled by the group.

The basic test here is whether the ownership and/or control is over 50 per cent. The standards are actually quite complicated in this area, and are full of anti-avoidance measures. What follows is, therefore, a simplification.

The basics are as follows:

- **Subsidiary** – when a group owns a majority of the rights of another company, or exercises dominant control, the company is deemed to be a subsidiary of the group. Normally if 50 per cent+ of the shares of the company is owned by another company, the former is a 'subsidiary' of the latter.

- **Associate** – when a group owns a participating interest with a significant influence, the company is an associate. Normally if 20–50 per cent of the shares of a company is owned by another company, the former is an 'associate'.

- **Investment** – at less than 20 per cent of shares, the holding would be treated simply as an investment.

In the case of associates and investments, consolidation is simply shown by recording the group's share of profits and assets as 'one-liners' on the profit and loss account and balance sheet.

Subsidiaries are dealt with by including the whole of the subsidiary's results in the group accounts, and then excluding the minority interests separately.

## Example

For example, the results for a simple parent company with one 75 per cent owned **subsidiary** would be as follows:

|  | Parent | Subsidiary | Group |
|---|---|---|---|
| Sales | £100 | £100 | £200 |
| Profit | £100 | £100 | £200 |
| *less* minority interests |  |  | (25) |
| Total Group profit |  |  | £175 |

NOTE: sales and profits are shown gross, with the profits due to minority shareholders shown near the bottom of the profit and loss account.

Now let's consider the shape and content of annual reports, starting with the profit and loss account.

# The profit and loss account

Conceptually the most readily understood, the profit and loss is the statement of profits or losses in the year, or other stated period. The layout is prescribed in FRS3.

Profit is the surplus of revenue over costs attributable for that period. It is *not* cash flow. Profit can and often is earned despite strongly negative cash flow, particularly in fast-growing companies.

The treatment of stocks (or inventories) and capital investments can illustrate the generation of profit data.

## Example: Stocks

A company sells 50 pieces of machinery, but has manufactured 100 in the year.

| | |
|---|---|
| Costs 100 units @ £500 each | Total £(50,000) |
| Sales 50 units @ £750 each | Total £37,500 |

So the cash impact on the trading company is £50,000 out and only £37,500 in, or a cash outflow of £12,500. What is the profit?

At the end of the year the company still has 50 units of stock in hand, and may even have orders for delivery in the following year, so it has an asset worth at least the replacement cost of the units, or £25,000.

The accounting profit for the period would be developed by looking at the sales figures, and then deducting *the cost of those sales*. This is known as **matching**, and would be as follows:

| | |
|---|---|
| Sales 50 units @ £750 each | £37,500 |
| Cost of sales 50 units @ £500 each | (25,000) |
| Profit for the period | £12,500 |

NOTE: the difference between the cash outflow (top) of £12,500 and the profit of £12,500 is £25,000, which just happens to be the replacement value of the stocks at the year end. Look at your own company's accounts and find the note that is called 'reconciliation of trading profit to cash flow'. Find the line that reads 'increase/decrease in stocks'.

### Example: Capital Investment and depreciation

A company purchases a capital asset for £1 million with an estimated useful life of 10 years. In pure cash terms, it is down £1 million assuming outright purchase (i.e. not leased). What is the effect on profits?

As you might expect, there is a technique to 'spread' the cost of the asset, or, to be more accurate, to spread the charge to the profit and loss account, over the useful life of the asset. In that way you might think that you would take the cost of the asset, divide it by its useful life to give an annual amount, and charge this against each year's profits. This is called depreciation. There are two main kinds: 'straight line' depreciation which is very common, and 'declining balance' where a percentage of the remaining value is charged.

What is your company's depreciation policy? Look at your company's annual report for the answer. Try note 1, accounting policies if you're stuck.

For an asset with a three-year life, the charges would be as follows (declining balance assumes 50 per cent write off):

|  | Straight line | Declining balance |
|---|---|---|
| Purchase | £300,000 | £300,000 |
| Year 1 | (100,000) | (150,000) |
| Year 2 | (100,000) | (75,000) |
| Year 3 (final) | (100,000) | (75,000) |

Which method is 'right' or 'wrong' depends very much on the type of asset, the industry sector, whether there is a residual or scrap value at the end of the period, and on other variables. Other depreciation techniques also exist, but you'll find these two are the most common.

You can see why you might want to depreciate different assets different ways by considering the causes of depreciation:

- **Obsolescence.** Your company may have a substantial amount of high-tech equipment. This may have many years of working life left in it, but if new equipment comes out which works better, or can do more, the company will have to replace its old equipment in order to stay competitive. Companies in the media, for example, are constantly having to purchase new technology because of the rapid pace of improvements.

- **Wear and tear.** Assets wear out when they are used, but are also affected by the environment. Equipment located in harsh conditions overseas may well wear out faster than equipment at home.

- **Copyrights, patents and leases** are all assets, but they have a fixed life which is set either by law or by contract. This makes their remaining life predictable. This kind of depreciation is called 'amortisation'.

- **Growth.** If a company increases in size, some of its assets may no longer be useful. Suppose it operates ski-lifts in a resort which suddenly becomes popular – it will have to install new, improved ski-lifts which can carry more people and, perhaps, are more comfortable. The old ski-lifts may have to be scrapped if the company can't find a buyer for them.

Here are two important points about depreciation:

**1** Depreciation looks as if it is just a paper transaction. You don't actually pay out cash when you depreciate, although it reduces the profit figure. One day, though, the company's machines and other fixed assets are going to wear out and will have to be replaced. At that point, the company will have to pay out for new machines, so if it hasn't prepared itself by depreciating, it will have an unpleasant surprise.

**2** This might lead you to think that it is sensible to depreciate assets as quickly as possible – that way, the assets will have years of useful life left in them after they have been depreciated to nothing. The trouble with this is that it makes the percentage return on the capital you are using in the business look better than it really is. The same thing happens if you fail to revalue assets that have actually increased in value. A salutary example of this took place in the '60s and '70s, when many old-fashioned companies had the value of their buildings on their books at the price they were purchased at many years before; a company in this situation might think it was getting a return of, say, 16 per cent on its assets when, if the property had been revalued, it would really be getting a return of, say, 8 per cent.

Let's look now at the standard format of the profit and loss account in the annual report.

- The standard profit and loss account statement shows turnover, or total sales, gross profits, net profits, and other items.

- Turnover is shown as it reached the company, i.e. after deduction of all discounts, etc. and after deduction of sales taxes such as VAT.

- An interesting issue on turnover arises from long-term contracts. The classic example is the shipbuilder whose bespoke product may take several years to build. Sales 'receipts' may not reflect the progress of the ship. Here the accounting standards allow turnover to be recognised either on a sales-based or cost-based approach. This would allow one-third of the total turnover to be recognised if one-third of the ship had been completed, even if not all of these amounts had been received or were due.

- You will note that turnover is split between continuing operations, acquisitions, and disposals. This is to allow for year-on-year analysis in the company which has bought and sold part of its businesses during the year.

- Cost of sales is then deducted to show gross profit. This is the gross profitability of the business before administration, financing, etc. and is important for trend and margin analysis, of which more later.

- The next category is operating profit, which is the net profit of the business after administration costs but before financing charges. Like turnover this must be split by operations showing continuing operations, acquisitions, and disposals.

- Income from holdings in associate companies is then shown. (See 'Consolidation' above.)

- The company's interest charge or income is shown separately, to give PBT or Profits Before Tax.

- The tax charge for the year is shown, followed by PAT or Profits After Tax. Note that typically the charge for the year is an estimate since the completion of a company's tax affairs for the year is generally not finalised until long after the report is filed.

- Only then is the minority interest removed from the group's profits. (See 'Consolidation' above).

- Dividends are then shown, leaving a retained profit for the year. This represents the amount of PAT retained in the business to support future growth.

- EPS or earnings per share is then shown (this will be discussed later).

## Example

Here is an example of a profit and loss statement:

| XYZ plc | |
|---|---|
| **Profit and Loss Account for the year ending 20—** | |
| | *£m* |
| Turnover | |
| Continuing operations | 70 |
| Acquisitions | 20 |
| Disposals | 10 |
| | Total 100 |
| Cost of sales | (50) |
| Gross profit | 50 |
| Selling and distribution costs | (12) |
| Administrative expenses | (8) |
| | Total (20) |
| Operating profit | 30 |
| Interest receivable | 2 |
| Profit on ordinary activities before taxation (PBT) | 32 |
| Tax | 10 |
| Profit on ordinary activities after taxation (PAT) | 22 |
| Minority interest | (2) |
| Profit for the financial year | 20 |
| Proposed dividend | 8 |
| Amount transferred to reserves | 3 |
| Retained profits carried to next year | 9 |
| Earnings per ordinary share | 7p |

It is important to get an understanding of what a profit and loss statement *doesn't* tell you.

For example, it doesn't tell you:

■ how, exactly, your company's costs relate to sales – there is no detailed breakdown of profits between different products and services,

■ how much capital is invested in the business, or what the return on that capital is,

■ whether there were losses in previous years,

■ how much cash you have available right now,

■ what expenditure you must make in the future, and

■ the trend of profits over a period of years.

To discover the answers to these questions, we will need to examine the balance sheet and cash flow statement, to compare them with previous years, to apply ratio calculations to the figures and also to have access to other internal accounts. People outside the company, such as investors and bankers, will not have access to any internal information, but will have to rely on the published accounts.

# The balance sheet

As discussed above, the balance sheet is conceptually different from the profit and loss account and the cash flow statement in that it represents a 'snapshot' at a point in time, rather than the trading picture over a period of time. It shows, at the balance sheet date, the assets and liabilities of the company.

Since the net assets of a company are effectively 'owned' or 'due' to the shareholders, or owners, of the business, then the net assets of a company must always be equal to the shareholders' stakeholding, and the statement must always balance, i.e. net assets equal shareholders' assets equals the amount 'due' by the company to shareholders. Because these amounts must always balance, it is known as the balance sheet.

## Example

Let's use a simple example: an investor starts a company by subscribing £100 in share capital:

| | |
|---|---|
| Assets – cash | £100 |
| Share capital | £100 |

It balances!

The company trades and earns £10 profit.

| | |
|---|---|
| Assets – cash | £110 |
| Share capital | £100 |
| Profit and loss account | 10 |
| Total shareholders' funds | £110 |

It declares a dividend to be payable after the year end.

| | |
|---|---|
| Assets – cash | £110 |
| Dividend payable | (5) |
| Net assets | £105 |
| Share capital | £100 |
| Profit and loss account | 5 |
| Total shareholders' funds | £105 |

We'll examine some of the mechanics of this in more detail in Chapter 2, but for now, accept that the net assets of the company always equal the shareholders' funds.

Let's now look at the balance sheet items in detail. Again the format is prescribed in legislation and standards, so your company's balance sheet should look very much like this one.

*See the section on consolidation (page 6) for details of the treatment of subsidiaries.*

## Fixed assets

These are those assets which a company uses to provide goods and services – they are not traded routinely by the company.

- **Intangible assets** – these might include goodwill arising on the acquisition of another company (see 'Acquisitions' later). Amounts spent on developing specific products or patents can be 'capitalised', i.e. treated as expenditure on an asset instead of written off to profit in the current year. This has previously been a dangerous practice for some companies, and there are substantial restrictions on it.
- **Tangible assets** – buildings, machinery, etc. Shown in the balance sheet after deducting the charge for depreciation. The details are in the notes.
- **Investments** – this might include details of any investment properties together with the value of non-consolidated smaller holdings in other companies.

## Current assets

- **Stocks** – the inventory currently being carried by the company. These will include raw materials as well as finished goods. Also included here is the valuation of any part-finished long-term contracts (*discussed on page 57*). Again, check note 1, accounting policies for the valuation method used in assessing stocks.
- **Debtors** (or receivables) are the amounts due into the company from other parties. This, primarily, will reflect those sales made for which payment is still outstanding.
- **Cash** is the final current asset. You will also see cash equivalents described. These are normally liquid investments used by corporate treasurers to increase interest income on cash holdings.

It is worth noting here that the effect of the sales process, in balance sheet terms, is to reduce stocks as the goods leave the factory, and to increase debtors or cash by the amount on the sales invoice. We'll describe the detail of this process in Chapter 2.

Next on the balance sheet is current liabilities. These are amounts due to third parties in the 12 months from the balance sheet date.

You then find a sub-total 'net current assets', which is also known as working capital.

Falling after this are the long-term creditors, due more than 12 months after the balance sheet date, and provisions. Long-term creditors are typically financing loans from banks and others while provisions are those amounts set aside to cover potential future claims and losses which are reasonably foreseeable.

The final total is called **net assets**. Let's simplify all this:

**Fixed assets** (e.g. premises, factory buildings and equipment)

*plus*
**Working capital** (net current assets including stocks and cash)

*less*
**Funding and provisions**

*equals*
**Net assets**

The net assets of the company must also be equal to the shareholders' stake in the company, because ultimately the shareholders 'own' the company.

## Shareholders' funds

They consist of:

- **Called up share capital** – this is the nominal amount of the shares in issue. All shares carry a 'nominal' value, often £1, and this is the amount described here.

- **Share premium account** – shares are often issued at a premium, that is a company may issue additional shares after establishing a trading record and sell shares with a nominal value of £10,000 for £100,000. In this case, the called up share capital would increase by £10,000, and the share premium account would increase by £90,000.

- **Revaluation reserve** – is created when assets are revalued because their market worth has increased.

## Example

Let us now start an example. A company issues shares with a nominal value of £1, as above. The balance sheet is as follows:

**Barking Traders Ltd – Balance Sheet – 31st December 1996**

| | |
|---|---|
| Fixed assets | £0 |
| Current assets | |
| – cash | £100,000 |
| Net current assets | £100,000 |
| Net assets | £100,000 |
| Shareholders' funds | |
| – called up share capital | £10,000 |
| – share premium account | 90,000 |
| Shareholders' funds | £100,000 |

The company trades successfully for a month, ending the month with profits of £10,000 and some stocks. The company also buys a building for £50,000. The balance sheet is as follows:

**Barking Traders Ltd – Balance Sheet – 31st January 1997**

| | |
|---|---|
| Fixed assets | £50,000 |
| Current assets | |
| – stocks | £50,000 |
| – cash | 10,000 |
| Net current assets | £60,000 |
| Net assets | £110,000 |
| Shareholders' funds | |
| – called up share capital | £10,000 |
| – share premium account | 90,000 |
| – profit and loss account | 10,000 |
| Shareholders' funds | £110,000 |

The profits shown are those that are 'realised' or achieved. That is they relate to goods which have been sold. (The exception here relates to long-term contracts, which were discussed above.) Notice how the profit is added to 'shareholders' funds' and reflects the increase in value of the firm as a whole.

Let us now suppose that the company's building increases in value by £25,000, to £75,000. In order to give a true and fair view of the assets of the company, the balance sheet value should be increased to reflect the increase in value of the building. But where should the corresponding balancing entry go?

Had the building been sold, it would indeed be recognised as profit. In this case, however, there is no intention to sell the building, it remains as a fixed asset of the company. We therefore create a 'revaluation reserve' and the balance sheet looks as follows:

### Barking Traders Ltd – Balance Sheet – 31st January 1997

| | |
|---|---|
| Fixed assets | £75,000 |
| Current assets | |
| – stocks | £50,000 |
| – cash | 10,000 |
| Net current assets | £60,000 |
| Net assets | £135,000 |
| Shareholders' funds | |
| – called up share capital | £10,000 |
| – share premium account | 90,000 |
| – revaluation reserve | 25,000 |
| – profit and loss account | 10,000 |
| Shareholders' funds | £135,000 |

Information on the revaluation of fixed assets in this way must always be disclosed in the notes to the accounts.

> NOTE: of the shareholders' funds, only the profit line is distributable as dividend. Companies may not pay dividends out of capital, revaluation or other reserves, without applying to the court for a capital reduction, which is rather unusual. Going back to the early history of company law, the amount of owner's capital that is 'locked in' the business is important for the protection of the company's creditors.

# The cash flow statement

The main purpose of the cash flow statement is to enable interested parties to judge the reasons for a rise or fall in the amount of cash in the business during the relevant period. This sheds light on the information contained in the balance sheet and profit and loss account. For example, the statement serves as a check on whether the company is actually collecting its debts and whether the company's cash is being absorbed in replacing fixed assets – neither of which actions are revealed by the profit and loss account.

There are strict rules about the categories that must be used in the cash flow statement, but before we look at these, let's examine the way that cash comes in and out of a company:

**1** If a business is trading at a profit, the amount of cash in the business might be expected to rise over the year. Equally, if it is making a loss, the amount of cash might be expected to fall. (*See Chapter 10, page 190 on overtrading, though.*)

**2** If a company buys a fixed asset, such as machinery or a building, the amount of cash it has will fall. Conversely, if it sells a fixed asset, cash will come into the business.

**3** If the amount of stock a company holds is falling, its cash should increase, since it is not buying so much. If it buys more stock than normal, its cash holding will decrease.

**4** The same principle applies to debtors of the company. If you were suddenly able to force your customers to pay only in cash, for example, you would get much more cash in than normal, and if you suddenly gave all your customers 90 days' credit instead of the normal 30 days, you would have less cash than normal.

**5** If shareholders decide to invest more money into the business, the amount of cash will increase, and if they take money out by way of directors' drawings or shareholders' dividends the cash in the company will decrease.

**6** If the company borrows money, its cash will increase; when it pays the money back the cash will decrease.

**7** If the company orders more goods on credit than normal its cash will increase if it sells the goods before it pays for them, and if it reduces its debts to its creditors its cash will decrease.

Now let's look at the categories that actually appear in cash flow statements:

- **Operating activities** – cash generated in the normal course of trading. This is *not* the same as profits, and a reconciliation of this category to the profit and loss account follows the cash flow statement. The single largest items are the addback of depreciation, together with changes in working capital. The addback of depreciation often confuses – put simply, the profit and loss account is charged a share of the usage of fixed assets (see above). As this is a non-cash item that does not affect cash it is reversed in the reconciliation.

- **Returns on investments and servicing of finance** – this shows dividends received together with interest paid and received.

- **Taxation** – payments and repayments of taxes on sales revenue and capital gains are shown here, but not VAT, which comes under the 'Operating Activities' heading.

- **Investing activities** – shown here are the amounts of investment in fixed assets, including any disposals and the acquisition of subsidiaries (of which more later). Current asset investments, such as cash held at a bank, are also included, as are loans to and from companies in the same group.

- **Net effect** – the amount is then sub-totalled to show the net effect of all activities in the year before any additional financing has been raised.

- **Financing** – the amount of new money borrowed to finance the business is shown separately here. Only the receipt and repayments of the principal sum borrowed are included – the interest payments go under the 'Returns on investment and servicing of finance' heading. Cash flow relating to shares, bonds and other types of corporate financing are all recorded here.

The final total shows the absolute change in cash levels between the two balance sheet dates. This won't tally with the cash levels shown in the balance sheet because:

**a)** the short-term creditors will include overdrafts which are included in net cash, and

**b)** there will be a change of exchange rates which will impact on the cash flow.

# Published accounts and the stock market

Although the published accounts of a private limited company are public documents which anyone can obtain from Companies House, they are generally not subject to the amount of scrutiny from outsiders as are the accounts of companies listed on the stock market. Listed companies, because their shares are widely held by outside investors, must expect a great deal of attention when they produce their accounts each year.

All companies are subject to conflicting pressures when they produce their accounts, and despite the new accounting standards there is still some leeway in deciding how to present the figures. Outside investors know this, and scrutinise published accounts very carefully. The annual report and accounts of a listed company is generally a glossy publication which is designed to impress. Professional investors, though, will often skip over these sections and start reading the report from the back.

- They will look at the AGM resolutions to try to gain an insight into the intentions of the directors, and the manner in which the company is governed. In particular this will include compliance with the accepted best practice, now including Cadbury and Greenbury.

- They will read the notes carefully, and relate any significant matters to the figures in the balance sheet and profit and loss statement. For instance, if the company has sold a business but has give some financial guarantees to the purchaser, this will appear in the notes. Investors will take a view on the likelihood that the company may have to fulfil these guarantees in the future, and will mentally adjust its profit figures accordingly.

- They will apply various ratios (*see Chapter 2*) to the figures in the balance sheet and profit and loss statement. For instance, if the company is reporting a much greater profitability than are other companies in the same business, investors will want to know why. The professional investors are a shrewd bunch, and will calculate the overall return on all the capital being used in the business as well as the return obtained by the shareholders. These figures are then compared with the return investors could get by, say, simply leaving their money in a building society at virtually no risk, and if the return is not good enough, some investors will pull out, causing the share price to fall.

- They will compare the cash flow statement with the profit and loss figures – the figure for operating cash flow ought, logically, to be similar to the figure for operating profits. If they aren't, investors will wonder if the company is being optimistic about its profit figures, and will investigate further.

- They will look at the amount the company is paying in tax as a percentage of its profits. Corporation tax is currently 33 per cent, so if the percentage paid in tax is a lot lower than this, it could mean that profits are being exaggerated, so they will want to understand the reason for the divergence.

- They will compare the annual accounts with those of previous years, looking for changes in policy, not all of which have to be reported, but will show up under analysis. When they find a change in policy, investors will try to work out the effect the change has on reported profits.

Despite the careful attentions of outside shareholders and potential investors to the annual report and accounts, however, the share price of a company may rise and fall far beyond the true value of its business. The story of Asil Nadir, founder of Polly Peck plc, illustrates this.

| CASE STUDY | POLLY PECK |

In 1968 Asil Nadir owned Wearwell, a clothing company which was not listed on the Stock Exchange. It was a small business, with a turnover of £370,000 and a low profit of £10,000, but by 1973 it had grown to a turnover of £4 million and its annual profits were £672,000. Nadir had made it as a businessman, working grim 15-hour days throughout the 'Swinging Sixties'.

In 1973, Nadir took his company public and sold 40 per cent of his equity on the stock market for £1.47 million. By September Wearwell's shares had risen from 46p to 78p – a 70 per cent profit in two months.

Soon, however, Wearwell was threatened by competitors. Nadir went into mail order, losing some £650,000 during the 1974 oil crisis. Dividends on Wearwell's shares were suspended. Nadir gave up mail order and retrenched into his core 'cash and carry' wholesale business. Wearwell's profits returned in 1976–77, but he had to find a way to expand.

He soon found the answer; the newly rich oil producing countries of the Middle East had money to spend, and soon Nadir was exporting school uniforms and other unfashionable clothing to Libya and Iraq. It was a big risk; as one of his associates has remarked, 'God help you if you have a bad debt'.

Wearwell was seriously in debt and highly leveraged; in 1976 Nadir was forced to give a supplier 10 per cent of its equity and a seat on the board to keep going. At the same time he was forced to sell shares to repay a loan of £86,000 which he had taken from the company in contravention of the Companies Act.

Wearwell's exports paid off in 1979, when the company resumed dividend payments and increased profits. For the first time Nadir returned to his roots, opening factories in Northern Cyprus and making cost savings of more than 70 per cent, despite the increased costs of transport.

## The boom

Determined to expand, Nadir bought a shell company, Polly Peck, in 1980, and decided to enter the fruit business. The 1974 Turkish invasion of Northern Cyprus had left its economy in ruins; its main product, citrus fruit, was rotting on the ground, and the tourist industry had dried up. As a Turkish Cypriot, Nadir saw a perfect opportunity to become a hero in his homeland and make substantial profits at the same time.

Within a few months Polly Peck's shares rose by 85p; on his £270,000 investment Nadir had made a profit of £2.25 million by June 1980, even though the company had not made any concrete announcements about its future. Asil Nadir's reputation was growing.

In July 1980, Polly Peck raised £1.5 million through a rights issue to buy Unipac Packaging, a company owned personally by Nadir which had a lease on some concrete sheds in Famagusta, Cyprus. The plan was to turn the sheds into a cardboard box factory, giving the citrus farmers the boxes they needed to save their rotting fruit.

As well as Polly Peck and Unipac, Nadir bought 57 per cent of another shell company, Cornell Dresses. As soon as Nadir's involvement was known, Cornell's shares shot up from 26p to over 100p, despite no firm announcement of its plans. In a single year, Nadir had become a multi-millionaire on paper, effectively controlling three new companies, none of which had begun trading in Turkey and Cyprus. All Nadir really had was Wearwell, clearly a good business, but hardly a justification for the speculative frenzy in his other companies.

The rest of the 1980s saw the spectacular rise of Polly Peck, despite the occasional hiccup. Nadir moved into mainland Turkey, taking advantage of Turkish Premier Ozal's new Thatcherite policies. He bought a spring water company, Niksar, a large consumer electronics company, Vestel, and began building luxury hotels in Turkey and Cyprus.

Despite doubts about Polly Peck's true profits – the Turkish lira is a soft currency and inflation was raging in Turkey throughout the decade – investors in London were still keen to invest substantial sums in the company. At the same time, Nadir's borrowings across all his companies rose massively. By the late '80s, Nadir was buying large companies across the world, including Sansui, a Japanese electronics business, Fruco, a German fruit importer, Russell Hobbs, the British white goods manufacturer, Noble Air, an airline, and finally, the biggest catch of all, Del Monte, the huge international fruit distributor.

## The crash

In early 1990 Nadir was on top of the world. Polly Peck was worth some £2 billion on its market valuation, and its latest profits were £161 million. He was a media star in Northern Cyprus, Turkey and the UK, rated as the 36th richest man in Britain and widely acclaimed as a new Onassis.

Then Iraq invaded Kuwait. Turkey was immediately plunged into a recession, and Polly Peck's share price plunged with it. Disturbed by the fickleness of the stock market, Nadir made a bad mistake; he decided to take Polly Peck private. He had some good role models for doing so – both Richard Branson and Andrew Lloyd-Webber had done the same recently – but under Stock Exchange rules Nadir could not back out after making the announcement, and it was not clear where he would find the cash for the purchase and the refinancing for Polly Peck's £1.3 billion of debt.

A few days after his announcement, Nadir abandoned his offer. There was an immediate Stock Exchange investigation, Nadir was censured, and the report was passed to the Serious Fraud Office; if it could be established that Nadir had known at the outset that he could not afford to buy Polly Peck back, he might be open to a prosecution for creating a false market in Polly Peck's shares.

Meanwhile Polly Peck's share price collapsed, and its bankers became rather nervous. The press had a field day, with wild stories competing with each other for headlines. It was, however, a sign of the times. The wild and wonderful economic boom of the 1980s was definitely over.

By September the Serious Fraud Office was using its very great powers to investigate Nadir's public and private operations. On the 25th, Polly Peck missed its first debt payments; it was the beginning of the end. In October the company was put into administration.

In December 1990 Nadir was arrested on specimen charges of false accounting and theft; bail was set at £3.5 million, the highest in British history. Suddenly it was all over; the company was forced to liquidate as much as it could, including millions of pounds' worth of antiques from Polly Peck's head office in Berkeley Square, Mayfair.

It is still unclear whether or not Polly Peck's accounts were ever substantially misleading. Throughout the company's dramatic rise in the 1980s there were constant criticisms of its heavy borrowings and methods of accounting for profits made in 'soft' currencies, but this did not prevent its share price rising – which is effectively a vote for the company by outside investors.

# CHAPTER TWO

# Analysing accounts
## Using ratios, corporate governance and the role of auditors

- Analysing company accounts

- Ratio analysis

- Applying ratios in credit control

- Corporate governance

- Auditors

## Analysing company accounts

Chapter 1 outlined the contents of the results that are published annually and bi-annually by large companies. These accounts give a good picture of the state of the company in isolation but we might also want to compare the performance of the company with:

- earlier years of the company's performance to determine trends, and

- other companies to ascertain comparative performance.

In these circumstances it is not very helpful just to know that, say, the sales of one company are greater than another, or that one is more profitable than another. These could be the result of any number of factors such as the relative sizes of the companies, or the different industries in which they operate.

> What is required is a set of common tools that can be used to compare companies, regardless of size, and to measure trends. These tools most often take the form of ratios and hence the widely used term of 'ratio analysis'.

So who needs to conduct this sort of analysis?

By far the largest group of corporate analysts are in the 'City' and include:

- Stock-brokers who make their living by buying and selling shares on behalf of their clients and by advising clients on companies' likely future share performance. You may have seen analysts' comments on your company advising investors to 'buy', 'hold' or 'sell'.

- Pension fund management whose job it is to invest large sums on behalf of our future pensions whilst optimising the trade-off between risk and return. They employ many professionals whose role is solely to analyse and project the future performance of companies in their portfolio or potential portfolio.

Other users of analysis tools might include:

- The individual investor who invests in their own portfolio, possibly through a PEP.

- YOU – you might wish to do business with a small company – are they credit worthy – how sound are they?

- YOU – suppose a head-hunter approaches you with an attractive job offer in a small company – you'd want to know they were on a sound financial footing.

# Ratio analysis

There are many ratios which are used and this book will explain only the most common and therefore, hopefully, the most useful of them. The familiarity and application of these ratios will allow the user to obtain a quick understanding of the financial state of a company. They can be grouped into different categories, although a meaningful analysis can only be achieved by the use of a number of the ratios from each category.

> **!** Don't even try to read this section without a set of your company accounts and a calcu-lator. These are straightforward tools which you can easily calculate for your company as you go. If you also have the accounts for your nearest competitor and a copy of the FT, even better.

Open up your FT to the inside back page of the 'Companies and Markets' section. Each listed company is shown with the previous day's share price, together with some inter-esting data. The 'Mkt Capn£m' is the Market Capitalisation in £millions. This is simply the share price multiplied by the number of shares in issue, or, put more simply, the market value of all the shares in circulation.

Also shown is the P/E. This is the first of our ratios.

## Price/Earnings ratio

Let's say your company has a P/E of 15. This means that the company has a market capitalisation (is worth!) 15 times its profits.

The formula is as follows:

$$\frac{\text{Market capitalisation (Shares in issue} \times \text{Share price)}}{\text{Latest profits after tax}}$$

gives the P/E ratio. To discover the number of shares in issue look at the balance sheet. At the bottom will be a line 'Called up share capital', and there will be a reference to a note. Under the note you will find the number of shares allotted and fully paid; this is the number of shares in issue.

A high P/E generally indicates stable profitability with an expectation of future growth. By contrast a lower P/E would indicate less prospect for growth with a greater volatility of earnings. Historically, high P/Es have been those of 15 or above.

# Gearing

Gearing and interest cover are considered together. The gearing is a measure of the way a company's long-term financing is structured. All companies require long-term funding through a mixture of shareholders' funds (i.e. share capital) and other sources, typically long-term loans. The formula is:

$$\frac{\text{Long-term loans} \times 100 \text{ (to give percentage)}}{\text{Total shareholders' funds plus long-term loans}}$$

Thus, if we have long-term debt of £60 million and total share capital, reserves and retained profits of £40 million, then the gearing would be 60 per cent. This is important for both long-term debt providers and for potential equity investors and is related to interest cover.

# Interest cover

This is the amount by which profits exceed the amount of interest due to be paid. The formula is

$$\frac{\text{PBIT (Profits before Interest and Tax)}}{\text{Interest due}}$$

Thus, if profits were £100 million and interest payments were £50 million, interest cover would be said to be 2. This is important because of the simple possibility that profits might go down. In such circumstances:

- the company with a lower gearing and high interest cover can reduce or suspend the payment of its dividends

- the company with a higher gearing and lower interest cover might find itself in a loss after payment of interest. Its long-term survival would be at risk much more quickly than a company with a more conservative level of gearing.

## Example

There is a balance to be struck when considering gearing, so let's consider a very simplistic example for illustration. An entrepreneur develops a cunning plan which requires £100 million of capital. Consider two possible outcomes:

|  | Low geared | | High geared | |
|---|---|---|---|---|
|  | Best case | Worst case | Best case | Worst case |
| Capital required | 100 | 100 | 100 | 100 |
| – share capital | 80 | 80 | 20 | 20 |
| – debt capital | 20 | 20 | 80 | 80 |
| Profits before interest and tax | 20 | 5 | 20 | 5 |
| Interest payments | -2 | -2 | -8 | -8 |
| Net profits | 18 | 3 | 12 | -3 |
| Return to shareholders | 18 | 3 | 12 | -3 |
| Percentage return on capital | 23% | 4% | 60% | -15% |
| Memo – | | | | |
| interest rate | 10% | | | |

Figure 2.1   Gearing

- best case with profits of £20 million,
- worst case with profits of £5 million.

In the low geared example the best case shows a return to shareholders after interest of £18 million, a percentage return of 23 per cent. Pretty good but it is dwarfed by the percentage return of 60 per cent earned by the high geared company.

In the worst case though, the low geared company can cover its interest costs, generating a small return for shareholders. The high geared company cannot cover its interest costs, and will be showing a loss. In this situation it will clearly be difficult to raise additional funding of any kind and the result could be a total loss for the shareholders.

This example assumes a constant interest rate. In practice the lenders are wary of the more highly geared projects or companies and expect a commensurately higher interest rate on their lending.

There is no one 'right' level of gearing, but the higher the level of gearing the higher the risk and the higher the volatility of earnings. The trade off is a higher return for investors when things go well.

## Profitability

ROCE – Return On Capital Employed – the formula for which is:

$$\frac{\text{Net profit} \times 100 \text{ (to give a percentage)}}{\text{Capital employed}}$$

This ratio has a number of applications. We have used the ratio in the above example on gearing to generate the return on equity finance. This is the most normal application. The formula can also be used to generate a return on incremental projects when undertaking project analysis, although it is best used here in conjunction with other tools (see separate chapter on projects).

Of course when used to analyse a company from the viewpoint of an investor or potential investor the P/E will tend to be used instead. The two ratios in this application are effectively the reverse of each other.

You will see in Chapter 11 – Acquisitions that when a company is purchased an amount of 'goodwill' is created. This is the surplus of the purchase price paid for the company in excess of the book value of the acquired company's assets. This amount is then written off against reserves, effectively reducing the amount of the purchasing company's capital base. There is a strong argument for excluding this write-off from the company's capital base. In this way you would calculate the ratio as follows:

$$\frac{\text{Net profit} \times 100}{\text{Capital employed (excluding goodwill written off)}}$$

Note that this will give rise to a larger capital base and therefore a lower return on capital. The resultant ratio is probably a truer reflection and more useful when comparing the performance of those companies who have made acquisitions against those which have grown organically.

## Profit as a percentage of sales

The ratio is:

$$\frac{\text{Profit} \times 100}{\text{Sales}}$$

This important ratio shows the margin or mark-up being achieved by the company or division. In effect it shows the added value being generated by the company for its customers.

> **!** The ratio is often calculated using either net or gross profit depending on the circumstances and clarity of the basic data.

# Liquidity

It is a truism to say that companies do not fail because they are unprofitable, they fail because they are unable to pay their bills. The measure of a company's continuing ability to trade by generating sufficient cash to meet its liabilities is known as liquidity.

First and foremost check the cash flow statement excluding items such as acquisitions. Is the company generating cash? Many profitable and fast growing companies fail to generate cash, and this in itself will not cause failure provided sufficient support is available from financiers. Continued failure of a company to generate positive cash flow is likely to be a problem though, irrespective of its profitability.

Aside from the cash flow statement there are a couple of ratios which can be applied to the balance sheet to determine current liquidity levels. These are the current ratio and the acid test ratio.

## Current ratio

The formula for this is:

$$\frac{\text{Current assets}}{\text{Current liabilities}}$$

The ratio compares the levels of debtors, stocks and cash to that of the current liabilities or short-term creditors. This important measure of liquidity is also referred to in the chapter on financing. Ensuring that long-term assets are financed by long-term debt, and that there is sufficient short-term cash and facilities to cover immediate bills and requirements, is known as 'term matching'.

## *Acid test ratio*

This is:

$$\frac{\text{Current assets (excluding stock)}}{\text{Current liabilities}}$$

Both these ratios are used to test the company's ability to pay its next set of bills. Once again there is no right level of ratio. Common sense might suggest that these ratios should exceed 1, but the large supermarkets, to take one example, survive and indeed thrive on remarkably low liquidity ratios. This is simply because the structure of their business allows them to utilise payment terms of, say, 30 days from suppliers while their sales are all for cash or pseudo cash. This, combined with the necessarily very high stock turnover, means that the liquidity ratio in this business is very different from many others.

# Investment for the future

How is the company being managed in terms of its longer term outlook? Remember from the first chapter that the depreciation charge to the profit and loss account is intended to be a measure of the amount by which fixed assets are 'used up'. The amount of investment in new fixed assets is shown in the cash flow statement. Compare these two amounts: are fixed assets being used (depreciation) more quickly than they are being replaced? Or is the company investing heavily in the future?

> Of course, simply spending lots on new assets does not mean that the investments are efficient, nor does an excess necessarily mean that the company is in decline, but this does form another indicator in association with other ratios.

# Ratios generally

Be very careful when using ratios to ensure that you are comparing like with like. When comparing one company with another, where they operate in different industries or even different markets, ratios will be of little assistance.

Ratio analysis is at its most useful when looking at **trends**. The same company when trading over several years will experience differences in its market environment, its relative strength in the market, and the skill of its management. Using ratio analysis will highlight the changes in the company over a period of years.

- Look at cash flow over a three-year period – is cash being generated? If so, how is it being used? If not, what is the structure of financing? Is gearing increasing?

- Look at profitability trends – are sales increasing only at the expense of margins?

- Look at other trends – investment levels, absolute sales and profitability. What is the trend of these items? If profitability is falling how far will it fall, and will it recover?

Ratio analysis is also useful to make a **comparison of companies in the same or similar market place**, such as your immediate competitor:

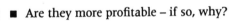

- Are they more profitable – if so, why?

- Look at operating profits to isolate interest and tax issues. Are they more profitable? Is it at gross margin level (commanding a price premium for a better product or a better distribution network) or through less overhead? Or is the manufactured cost lower?

- How are they financed? Do they have a lesser or greater interest burden?

- What are their investment levels – not just in fixed assets but also in R&D.

---

Using your own company's published accounts for the last two or three years, apply each of the foregoing ratios to them. What do they reveal about your company's financial position, and does it tally with what you already know?

Now get hold of the accounts of your major competitors, apply the ratios and compare them with the results you got for your own company. What are the differences? How do the differences from the ratio analysis correlate with what you know about the company and its products in the market?

Learn to look behind the numbers in the company accounts and try to relate them to what you know about the physical characteristics of the companies. In this way when you have to look at a new set of accounts you'll have a head start in terms of being able to develop a feeling for the business from the numbers.

---

Ratios are used both by managers within a company and interested outsiders, and have a very wide range of applications. Let's look at a practical problem within businesses which ratios can help solve: the problem of credit control.

# Applying ratios in credit control

When you supply other businesses, you generally have to allow them some time before they settle their bills. Invoices which you have issued but have not yet received payment for, are known as 'accounts receivable'. Accounts receivable often make up a significant proportion of a company's total current assets, and have an adverse effect on cash flow, so it is vitally important to keep firm control of them.

To keep control, you must know the answers to the following five issues:

**1** What are your credit terms? For instance, do you offer a cash discount for early or prompt payment, and how much time do you give your customers before the invoices become due?

**2** How do you collect evidence that the customer owes the money? Do they sign receipts for your goods and services, or do you use formal letters of agreement?

**3** What criteria does your company use to decide whether or not to issue credit to a particular customer? In general, the looser your criteria are, the higher the proportion of bad debts, but the number of customers and the size of their orders may be higher too.

**4** How do you decide on the amount of credit you will allow a particular customer? What records do you inspect before making a decision? Do you just ask for a bank reference?

**5** What are your procedures for collecting debts? How do you collect from reluctant debtors, and at what point do you stop extending credit to late payers?

In this section we will look at how you can use ratio analysis to answer questions in issues 3 and 4. There is often conflict between marketing people and accounting people over whether certain customers should be given credit – the marketing people want to get the sale, and the accountants want to make sure that they get paid! Clearly, both are right in their aims, but what is needed is an objective way of evaluating the creditworthiness of companies. With an understanding of how to use ratios, you will be able to argue your case more powerfully.

Many studies have shown that the financial ratios of companies which go bust are markedly different from those which survive and prosper, even five years before they fail. Compared with successful firms in the same industries, failed companies tend to have:

- high debt
- low return on capital
- high accounts receivable
- little cash.

Surprisingly, they also tend to have:

- low stock levels.

As the unsuccessful companies approach collapse, the difference between their ratios and those of healthy companies tends to deteriorate markedly. Here's a table based on a study which illustrates this.

 **Example**

| Ratio | | | |
|---|---|---|---|
| | *Years to failure* | | |
| | 5 | 3 | 1 |
| *Cash flow/total debt* | | | |
| Surviving companies | 0.45 | 0.46 | 0.45 |
| Failed companies | 0.15 | 0.05 | 0.15 |
| *Total debt/total assets* | | | |
| Surviving companies | 0.37 | 0.37 | 0.37 |
| Failed companies | 0.51 | 0.51 | 0.79 |
| *Working capital/total assets* | | | |
| Surviving companies | 0.41 | 0.41 | 0.41 |
| Failed companies | 0.30 | 0.30 | 0.06 |
| *Current ratio* | | | |
| Surviving companies | 3.4 | 3.3 | 3.3 |
| Failed companies | 2.5 | 2.5 | 2.0 |
| *Net income/total assets* | | | |
| Surviving companies | 0.06 | 0.06 | 0.06 |
| Failed companies | 0.04 | 0.00 | 0.20 |

Don't worry too much about the actual numbers in this table – they will vary according to industry and economic conditions. The important thing to notice is that it illustrates the idea that when you apply several ratios to a company, and compare the results with those of similar companies, the less stable firms will show up quite clearly as having markedly different ratios from stable firms, and if they slide towards disaster, the ratios will only worsen. If you are supplying such companies on 30-day credit terms you may well decide to continue doing business with them until they are quite close to collapse – the trick is in deciding when to pull out! By constantly monitoring their ratios, you can get an idea of when this may occur.

## Other credit analysis methods

Checking the ratios is only the first step; you will need to apply other tests as well. The main ways of checking the creditworthiness of companies are:

- Checking their past record with you and other suppliers. Good payers tend to remain good payers, but beware the firm that always pays small bills, then requests – and receives – a massive credit extension and then goes bust.

- Dun & Bradstreet is a well-established credit agency that provides detailed reports on the creditworthiness of large companies. There are numerous other credit agencies specialising in various fields.

- Checking the credit rating of a large company's bonds will give an indication of what others in the financial community think of the company.

- You can obtain published accounts from Companies House and then analyse them.

These methods may not be very useful with small companies and consumers, since their privacy is much greater. With these types of customer it is helpful to construct a 'credit index' against which you can compare an individual case.

### Example

Suppose you are a credit card company which seeks new customers by mass mailings to homes all over the country. You are not going to be able to investigate every applicant in much detail, but you can get a good idea of the chances that they will pay up on time by asking them a series of standard questions. Here is a much shortened list of the kind of questions you would ask:

Do you:

- own your own home?
- rent a house?
- rent a flat?
- rent a room?

Do you:

- have a bank account?

How long have you spent in your present job?

- less than 6 months
- 6 months – 5 years
- more than 5 years

Are you:

- single?
- married?
- divorced?

- What is your post code?
- What is your age?
- What is your occupation?
- How many children, if any, do you have?

Each possible answer will be given a number, based on the percentage of people giving that answer who have defaulted in the past.

Some of these questions do not appear at first glance to have any direct bearing on the loan, and may seem discriminatory. For example, why should someone score badly just because they live in a bad area (identified by their post code)? The fact is that this is a similar method to that used by insurance companies. You may be an extremely careful 17-year-old driver, but statistics show that 17-year-old drivers have a lot of accidents, so your age will count against you. By having a large number of questions, though, a good customer who happens to score badly on one or two of them should not be unfairly refused credit.

---

# Corporate governance

Studying the ratios of a business is no use if the accounts on which you have calculated the ratios are incorrect. You need to be confident that the company you are looking at has produced trustworthy figures in its accounts, and to do this a company must have an adequate system of 'corporate governance'.

Corporate governance simply means how a company is controlled, with the ultimate responsibility lying with its board of directors. In recent years there has been a lot of emphasis placed on raising the standards of corporate governance, particularly in large companies listed on the Stock Exchange.

Since listed companies (companies whose shares are sold on the Stock Exchange) are largely owned by shareholders who have no direct involvement in the business, they are heavily regulated to minimise the danger of shareholders and other interested parties being given misleading financial information about the company. Here is a brief list of the legal obligations of a listed company:

- they must keep proper accounts at all times
- they must produce accurate balance sheets and profit and loss accounts each year
- they must produce an annual report describing their business activities during the previous year
- the annual accounts must be audited by outside auditors.

Following the spectacular scandals of the late 1980s, such as the collapse of the huge international bank, BCCI, and Robert Maxwell and his misuse of company pension funds, a committee was set up to investigate how the financial aspects of corporate governance were being applied in large companies and how it might be improved to prevent such scandals happening in the future. In due course it produced a list of recommendations known as 'The Cadbury Report'.

1   The Board of Directors

1.1   The board should meet regularly, retain full and effective control over the company and monitor the executive management.

1.2   There should be a clearly accepted division of responsibilities at the head of a company, which will ensure a balance of power and authority, such that no one individual has unfettered powers of decision. Where the chairman is also the chief executive, it is essential that there should be a strong and independent element on the board, with a recognised senior member.

1.3   The board should include non-executive directors of sufficient calibre and number for their views to carry significant weight in the board's decisions.

1.4   The board should have a formal schedule of matters specifically reserved to it for decision to ensure that the direction and control of the company is firmly in its hands.

1.5   There should be an agreed procedure for directors in the furtherance of their duties to take independent professional advice if necessary, at the company's expense.

1.6   All directors should have access to the advice and services of the company secretary, who is responsible to the board for ensuring that board procedures are followed and that applicable rules and regulations are complied with. Any question of the removal of the company secretary should be the matter for the board as a whole.

**2   Non-Executive Directors**

2.1   Non-executive directors should bring an independent judgement to bear on issues of strategy, performance, resources, including key appointments, and standards of conduct.

2.2   The majority should be independent of management and free from any business or other relationship which could materially interfere with the exercise of their independent judgement, apart from their fees and shareholding. Their fees should reflect the time which they commit to the company.

2.3   Non-executive directors should be appointed for specified terms and re-appointment should not be automatic.

2.4   Non-executive directors should be selected through a formal process and both this process and their appointment should be a matter for the board as a whole.

**3   Executive Directors**

3.1   Directors' service contracts should not exceed three years without shareholders' approval.

3.2   There should be full and clear disclosure of directors' total emoluments and those of the chairman and highest-paid UK director, including pension contributions and stock options. Separate figures should be given for salary and performance-related elements and the basis on which performance is measured should be explained.

3.3   Executive directors' pay should be subject to the recommendations of a remuneration committee made up wholly or mainly of non-executive directors.

Figure 2.2   The Code of Best Practice

---

**4   Reporting and Controls**

4.1   It is the board's duty to present a balanced and understandable assessment of the company's position.

4.2   The board should ensure that an objective and professional relationship is maintained with the auditors.

4.3   The board should establish an audit committee of at least three non-executive directors with written terms of reference which deal clearly with its authority and duties.

4.4   The directors should explain their responsibility for preparing the accounts next to a statement by the auditors about their reporting responsibilities.

4.5   The directors should report on the effectiveness of the company's system of internal control.

4.6   The directors should report that the business is a going concern, with supporting assumptions or qualifications as necessary.

---

# The Cadbury Report

The Cadbury Report, known after the committee's Chairman, Sir Adrian Cadbury, sets out the following 'code of best practice', which all companies listed on the stock market are encouraged to adhere to. Although the code is voluntary, most companies are doing so.

As you can see, the Cadbury Code emphasises that the responsibility for the proper running of a listed company rests with the directors, and recommends safeguards to ensure that directors do not overpay themselves and that boards do not fall under the control of a minority of unscrupulous individuals. As we will see on page 48, the Maxwell case illustrates that determined wrongdoers have been able to abuse their positions as directors in the recent past.

Two other key recommendations in the Cadbury Report are that:

- Companies should set up 'audit committees' consisting of at least three non-executive directors with powers to investigate the accounting practices of the company and to ensure that finance directors and external auditors are properly heard by the board.

- Directors and auditors should explicitly report on the company's internal financial controls in the annual report, which is publicly available.

# Internal control

'Internal control' means the whole system that a company uses to manage the business according to its policies, including:

- the keeping of proper records
- protecting its assets
- preventing fraud
- ensuring that the business is running efficiently.

It covers a very wide range of different processes, and the larger a company is, the more complicated its internal control systems will be. These are the main types:

- A plan of the organisation. A large company needs to have a detailed plan, on paper, of the responsibilities, lines of reporting and definitions of authority for all the different activities it undertakes. The main object is to ensure that there is no aspect of the system where 'no one is in charge', and that individuals are accountable for their actions.

- To prevent error and fraud, companies will usually endeavour to separate different parts of the same transaction amongst different people and departments, so that no one person is in a position to control a whole transaction from start to finish.

- The location and safekeeping of valuable assets must be carefully controlled so that unauthorised individuals cannot have access to them.

- A system for authorising and approving its transactions. Authority levels will be defined; signatory limits will be set to allow, say, a secretary to purchase stationery up to £50 in value, while the procurement director's signature will be required for purchases over £5 million.

- A system for checking the accuracy of records, accounts, stock and documents.

- A system for checking that staff are competent and qualified to carry out their responsibilities.

- A system of day-to-day supervision of the internal controls.

- A system of management control over the operations of the business, including the comparison of management accounts with budgets and forecasts.

# Auditors

As you rise through the ranks in your career, you will become increasingly affected by the work of the auditors, whose job it is to check the accounts of your company.

Auditors must either be 'chartered' or 'certified' accountants in order to do their job. The most important point about their role is that they must be 'independent', which means that although the company pays their fees, the auditors must check the company's accounts in order to satisfy themselves that they are 'true and fair'.

There are a number of legal requirements for auditing which we will look at below, but before we do so, we should consider the genuine commercial benefits of having audited accounts, which are generally considered to be more objective than unaudited accounts. This gives more confidence to:

- lenders, such as banks
- investors (usually shareholders)
- the Inland Revenue and the Customs and Excise
- prospective purchasers of all or part of the business.

**Note:** interim (6 month) accounts issued by plcs are not normally audited.
In addition, auditors are useful internally:

- they provide another line of defence against mistakes and frauds
- they show up weaknesses in internal accounting systems
- they can advise on how to control the business during periods of rapid change.

## What is an audit?

Auditors don't simply recheck the sums in your ledgers and prepare a balance sheet – that's what your finance team does. Simply preparing accounts does not enable an accountant to say whether or not they are completely accurate. All he or she can say is that the accounts are in accordance with the company's books. If the company has cooked the books, then the accounts will be wrong.

Auditors don't actually prepare accounts – what they do is examine the profit and loss statement, the balance sheet and other financial statements so that they can give an opinion as to whether these documents:

- comply with the law, and
- give a 'true and fair' view of the company's financial affairs.

Notice that the auditor is only giving an opinion. As with the law and medicine, the deeper you go, the less and less sure you become that it is possible to make general statements with 100 per cent accuracy; all you can really do is to give a professional opinion.

Another point which can cause confusion is that auditors may, at other times, do other work as accountants. Thus, you may at one time meet an accountant who is doing an audit, and at another time meet the same person who is doing some other type of accounting work on behalf of your company, for example as a consultant on tax matters. *Don't confuse the task with the person!*

## The auditing process

A regular annual audit will normally start with a planning meeting. Senior managers meet the auditor to discuss how the audit will be conducted and to consider any particular points that need special attention. Normally it is the auditor who sets the agenda, which may include:

- any problems which have emerged since the previous audit
- a review of whether the managers implemented changes recommended in the last audit
- a review of the business's present circumstances
- a review of the company's internal accounting systems
- a timetable for the audit
- a discussion of the company's accounting policies
- a timetable for the checking of internal controls
- an agreement by the company to send letters to third parties giving them permission to release information to the auditor
- documents giving valuations of important assets, such as buildings
- documents giving details of shares, bonds, directors' fees, and employee loans
- deciding on the 'materiality limit', which is simply an amount below which an item is considered too small to bother with. This amount will vary depending on the size and state of the company.

Since auditing is a costly business, it is in the interests of managers to help to arrange the work so that it is done as quickly and efficiently as possible, and to make sure that any information required from the company is readily available. In many cases the auditor will bring in a team of staff to do much of the work. The team will:

- test the efficiency and accuracy of transactions and accounts
- verify and value the assets of the company
- verify the debtors and creditors, sometimes by writing to them
- verify the movement of cash through the company's bank accounts
- check the accuracy of the accounts for VAT, corporation tax, PAYE and National Insurance payments
- check that the pension scheme is being properly run
- check the efficiency of computer systems and their internal controls
- check the company's financial statements.

As you can imagine, this process of checking is a massive task in a large company, and may take several weeks to complete. The final aim of the audit is to produce a report which will be published along with the company's annual accounts. It is a very important document, since it is the main guarantee that shareholders, stock market analysts, bankers and the public at large have that the company's accounts are truthful.

## The auditors' report

Reports are of two kinds:
- Unqualified reports
- Qualified reports.

'Unqualified' reports are the most reassuring type; in effect, they mean that the auditors are satisfied that the accounts give a 'true and fair view', and that there are no nasty surprises looming on the horizon. Sometimes, however, auditors feel that they must 'qualify' their approval of the accounts. Qualified reports do not necessarily indicate that there is something seriously wrong with the company; it may simply be that a stock check at a particular site has not been carried out in time, for example. The auditor will specify exactly what his or her doubts are in the report. Here is a list of matters which might be mentioned in a qualified report:

**Not necessarily serious:**

- stock checks incomplete

- accounts not completely verified, but the management have assured the auditor that all is as it should be

- the company may be the defendant in a large court case

- a variation to standard accounting practice, as specified in the FRS standards (*see page 4*). The auditor would highlight the deviation from practice perhaps with his or her view as to whether it was appropriate

- the auditors are not certain that all the outstanding debts will eventually be paid

- information about sister companies overseas is missing.

**Could be serious:**

- some accounts or records are not being properly kept

- the auditors could not verify some cash transactions

- the auditors are unsure about the value of certain contracts

- the auditors disagree with the company on the valuation of the 'goodwill' of the business

- the auditors disagree with the amount allowed for (called 'provision') against expected future losses.

## The auditors' liability

As we have seen, the responsibility for producing accurate accounts lies with the directors, not with the auditors. However, the auditor can be liable to prosecution in the case of fraud, falsification of records, or the concealment of information. In general, though, an auditor will not be held responsible if a company has been managed fraudulently.

The UK Government is currently taking legal action against the auditors of the De Lorean car company previously based in Northern Ireland. The outcome of this case may well create further precedent in the issue of auditors' liability.

To examine the issue of auditors' liability as it currently stands let us consider the case of Robert Maxwell, which was a major factor in the introduction of the Cadbury Code.

## CASE STUDY · ROBERT MAXWELL

Ever since he started out in business in 1947, Robert Maxwell had taken a cavalier attitude towards the accounts of the companies he controlled. In 1954 he was criticised for trading while insolvent during the winding up of a large book wholesaler he owned. In the early 1960s he launched his publishing company, Pergamon Press, onto the stock market, but following a takeover some years later it was discovered that Maxwell had massaged the company's accounts to show high profits and conceal losses. A DTI inspection at the time reported that Robert Maxwell was 'not, in our opinion, a person who can be relied upon to exercise proper stewardship of a public company'.

Notwithstanding this setback, Maxwell continued to operate a large number of inter-linked companies, and in 1984 he was able to take over the Mirror Group of newspapers, which was listed on the Stock Exchange. For the rest of the decade he conducted a series of acquisitions that massively increased his debts to some £2.2 billion. To understand how Maxwell was able to commit fraud to the extent that he did, in spite of the presence of auditors and other directors, consider the corporate structure of his empire. The situation in early 1991 is depicted in Figure 2.2.

Maxwell exploited the fact that private companies have less stringent disclosure rules than publicly listed companies to compartmentalise his businesses in a complex and ever-changing scheme of ownership with a spider's web of cross-shareholdings culminating in Liechtenstein trusts. Since the trusts were protected by Liechtenstein's comprehensive privacy laws, it was not possible for auditors or others to verify any of Maxwell's statements regarding the ultimate ownership of the trusts and the value of their assets.

None of the other directors in this network of private and listed companies were able to penetrate the confusion that Maxwell deliberately cultivated – in effect, many of them often had to 'rubber stamp' financial decisions with only Maxwell's reassurance that they were complying with company law.

As his debts grew, Maxwell began to take huge risks to keep his wobbling empire from collapsing, the most well-known being his illegal use of assets from the Mirror Group's pension fund as security for his borrowings.

In normal circumstances such wrong-doing would have been discovered by the auditors or the other directors, but Maxwell's skilful compartmentalisation, a readiness to forge documents and his overpowering personality prevented this until after his death.

At a trial of his sons Kevin and Ian Maxwell in early 1996, auditors giving evidence admitted that although most of the auditors working on different branches of the Maxwell empire were employed by the same accountancy firm, they did not compare notes and so were unable to discover inconsistencies. They argued that they were not obliged to query much of the information given to them by the directors. In other words, if the directors said something was true, and the audit did not find any evidence to the contrary, then the auditors felt entitled to believe what they were told.

Maxwell was able to move assets belonging to pension fund members and shareholders around his empire at will and informally, in contravention of the obligations of a directors of a publicly listed company. It was to prevent directors from becoming unaccountable to their boards by improving corporate governance and internal controls and encouraging the use of non-executive directors in audit committees that the Cadbury Code was drawn up.

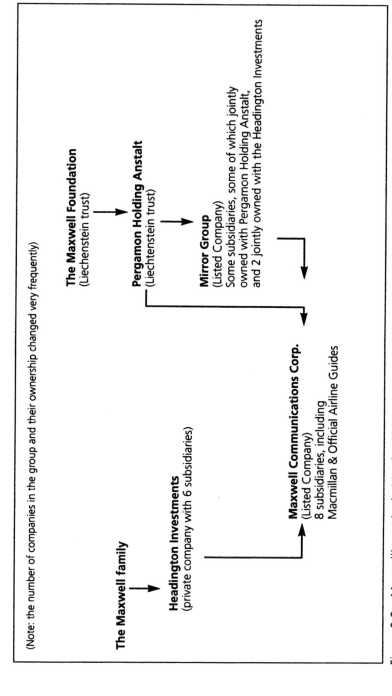

Figure 2.3   Maxwell's empire in March 1991

# CHAPTER THREE

# The basics of accounting

- Double entry bookeeping – the debits and the credits

- Accounting records

- Basic principles

## Double entry bookkeeping – the debits and the credits

Double entry bookkeeping is a simple method of recording business transactions. It is perfectly possible to understand every aspect of your business and be completely *au fait* with the published reports discussed earlier in this book without understanding double entry.

The chances are, however, that you will come across it, and contrary to the myth it's really not hard to understand.

We'll use examples; first you'll need a T-account, which looks like this.

Now add the debits and credits.

| *Debit* | *Credit* |
| --- | --- |

This system goes back to something like the sixteenth century, when the Venetian traders of the time, lacking Pentium processors and using the abacus instead, found it easier to add lots of numbers than to add, subtract, add and subtract.

A system developed whereby additions and subtractions were put in debit and credit columns, then each column of numbers could be totalled and only the net balance arrived at by subtraction.

 **Example**

Each item or account has a T-account, so for a simple company we might see:

- Shareholders' funds
- Cash
- Stocks
- Sales
- Cost of sales.

In our example the owners put in £1000 of cash. The company buys £500 of stock (100 units @ £5). The company sells half of this stock for £350 having incurred adminis-tration costs of £50.

This is what the ledgers will look like after the above trading. Ledgers are simply the books used to record the transactions, often for ease of dividing responsibilities, split into sales ledger, purchase ledger, etc.

**Shareholders' funds**

| Debit | | Credit | |
|---|---|---|---|
| | | Shares issued for cash | £1000 |

**Cash**

| Debit | | Credit | |
|---|---|---|---|
| Shares issued for cash | £1000 | Stocks purchased | £500 |
| Sales | 350 | Administration costs | 50 |

**Stocks**

| Debit | | Credit | |
|---|---|---|---|
| Bought cash (100 units) | £500 | Cost of sales (50 units) | £250 |

**Administration costs**

| Debit | | Credit | |
|---|---|---|---|
| Administration costs | £50 | | |

**Sales**

| Debit | | Credit | |
|---|---|---|---|
| | | Cash (50 units) | £350 |

**Cost of sales**

| Debit | | Credit | |
|---|---|---|---|
| Stocks sold ( 50 units) | £250 | | |

> NOTE: in double entry the books always remain balanced. Hence if we increase assets, e.g. stock, we also decrease assets, e.g. cash, or increase liabilities, e.g. payables. In this way the total of each transaction is always zero.

At the end of the period, the first piece of hugely complex analysis is known as the trial balance. This is the first exercise done by the finance department at the end of the year and involves adding up all of the numbers: all the debits and all the credits. From the above entries the result in the example will be:

| | | |
|---|---|---|
| Debits | Dr | £2150 |
| Credits | Cr | £2150 |

From this exercise we can determine that debits equal credits and the books therefore balance. If debit cash is positive and therefore good news, why are sales in the credit column?

> The only way to really get your head round this is to think of the balance sheet from the point of view of the shareholder. In this way, assets are shown as debits, while profits, once earned, are shown as credits since they are 'due' to shareholders.

This may seem a bit convoluted, so let's lay it out in a table:

The entries below assume an increase in monetary amount, so where it says 'assets' under the debit column, this represents an increase or a new asset. A sale of an asset would be a credit – with a corresponding debit to cash!

| Debit | | Credit | |
|---|---|---|---|
| Fixed assets | – premises | Shareholders' | – shares issued |
| | – machinery | funds | – profits |
| Current assets | – stocks | Liabilities | – amounts owing |
| | – cash | | – debt financing |
| Cost of sales | – all expenses | Sales | |

The next stage is then to close the books at the year end. This involves establishing the trial balance as above and then making the closing adjustments. These adjustments typically include ensuring that all the assets are in the right place, with depreciation properly accounted for, and a stock check to double check that the books match the physical inventory. Stock that has become old during the year may be written off as obsolete. Detailed accounts with each individual supplier are balanced off to facilitate consolidation. Expense accounts are balanced and posted to the profit and loss account. The final profit and loss account can then be created and the reports which provide the base for the annual accounts are produced.

# Accounting records

Tiny businesses can often keep all their records in just one book (also called a ledger) which is used, along with receipts, invoices and bank statements, to prepare the published accounts at the end of each financial year. With larger businesses, however, the basic ledger has to be broken down into different books, each with a different function. The actual quantity and organisation of these books will vary from company to company, but they will all be recorded in double entry form.

Here are the ledgers you are likely to come across:

## The Sales Ledger

This records sales and payments by individual customers, listed by customer. If you want to know how much a particular customer has bought from you during the last year, for example, you would be able to get the information from the Sales Ledger.

## The Bought Ledger (or Purchase Ledger)

This book records purchases from, and payment to, suppliers, listed by supplier. If you want to know how much business you are doing with a particular supplier – perhaps because you are thinking of changing to another supplier – you would find the information here. If a supplier hasn't been paid, he or she may telephone your company and ask to speak to the 'Bought Ledger' department, meaning he or she wants to speak to someone in charge of your purchase records.

## The Cash Book

Cash books record cash coming in and going out of the company. Normally they will also have a column relating to payments in and out of the company's bank accounts, since most of a business's cash normally passes through the bank accounts. Bank statements will be regularly reconciled against the Cash Book to make sure that neither side has made any mistakes.

## The General Ledger

In a small business, this would be where all transactions are recorded, which is fine for producing end-of-year accounts, but isn't very helpful when you need to extract management information, and is unwieldy in organisations of any size.

For this reason, there are usually a series of 'journals' which simply list transactions, and are not in double entry form. The main ones are:

## The Sales Journal

This is a list of all the invoices your company has issued, usually entered by date. Invoices are numbered to prevent unauthorised use of them, and the number will also be recorded in the journal, which helps you track down a particular invoice.

## The Purchases Journal

This is the opposite of the sales journal – each invoice you receive from your suppliers is listed here as it comes in, and transferred to the General Ledger periodically.

## The Returns Inwards Journal and the Returns Outwards Journal

These are simply lists of goods that customers have returned to you (Returns Inwards) and goods that you have returned to your suppliers (Returns Outwards). In each case, the company which has received the returned goods will issue a 'credit note' to confirm that the customer will not be charged for them. Your company will send a 'debit note' to the supplier to confirm to them that the goods have been returned.

> Most companies of any size rely on computer systems to maintain the accounting records. The methodology behind these is still identical in terms of the double entry concepts explained above. The development and implementation of these systems is complex and it is essential to ensure that the base data is classified and coded in such a way as to permit fast and flexible retrieval. A properly implemented computerised accounting system can form the base for a complete MIS (Management Information System) which will also include key non-financial data.

These basic records, whether they are on paper or in a computer, are essential to the business, and it is from these books that financial accounts are prepared. As a manager, however, you will need all sorts of information that has to be extracted from them in order to make your decisions. (*This information is called 'management accounting' and is discussed in detail in Chapter 4.*)

For now, think about how you might obtain the information you need to help solve the following problems:

- One of your small retail outlets doesn't seem to be doing as well as others in similar locations. What financial information do you need to help you to find out what is going wrong?

- A colleague keeps claiming at meetings that 'we cannot afford to offend' a large customer by taking certain actions. How would you check out just how large the customer is, and how profits might be affected if your company lost that account?

- One of your products is selling unexpectedly well, and a supplier of materials for it seems to be having trouble with quality control. You suspect that you are buying so much from the supplier that he is having trouble keeping up with your orders. Before confronting the supplier, you want to have all the facts at your fingertips so that you can make a judgement about the state of his business and decide whether or not to continue the relationship.

Financial accounts have two main deficiencies from the point of view of managers who want to control the day-to-day running of the business. They are:

**1** Financial accounts are about the past – they are 'historical'. Managers need to know what is going on now, in order to control what is going to happen in the future. If managers only used financial accounts, it would always be too late to take action. This doesn't mean, though, that financial accounts aren't useful to managers; many lessons can be learned by looking at what has happened in the past.

**2** Published financial accounts deal with the whole of the company's activities; they don't give detailed breakdowns of how particular products and services are doing. Managers need detailed information about particular aspects of the business for which they are responsible as well – and this information is often sensitive, so it is just as well that it doesn't appear in the published accounts, or your competitors would know far too much about how you are doing!

## Accruals

You might have heard of accrual accounting. Take the example of a supplier who undertakes a valuable project which starts in one accounting period and ends in another. Maybe he is repainting the exterior of your building. You are contracted to pay him at the end of the job, but at the end of the first period he has completed half of the work for which in normal circumstances you will be liable to pay. The amount 'due' at the end of the first period would be recognised as a cost to the business, even though it had been neither invoiced nor paid. This is known as an accrual.

> Non-accountants often misunderstand the accruals idea because there is a tendency to think of a company's expenses in a given period as being the same as the cash it pays out during that period. This is almost never the case, however: the cash that a company pays out during a given period will not match the amount of liabilities it incurs during the same period – the unpaid liabilities are the accruals, and there will also be other differences, such as money which is prepaid for goods and services not yet received.

Accrued income is also accounted for; this is money which has been earned by the company but not yet received. For instance, if the company is a landlord receiving rents, some rent may be earned during a period but not received until afterwards. This rent would count as having been earned, but is distinguished from rents actually received.

The 'reverse' of an accrual is known as a prepayment. A typical example of a prepayment might be the annual insurance premiums paid halfway through the accounting year and covering the business until midway through the following accounting year. The portion of this premium which related to the current year would be recognised as an expense, while the part that related to future periods would be shown as an asset on the balance sheet and not charged against profit until the following year.

## Provisions

A provision is a charge against the profits of the business for something which is inherently uncertain. An example might be a court action which could be won or lost. It would be prudent (see 'Basic principles' below) to assume that the case would be lost and to make a provision for the costs of losing the case. In the event that the case is won the provision is then 'released' in the following period, which has the effect of increasing profits.

There are two other important types of provision you may come across; again, they are essentially adjustments to your calculations of profit:

- bad debts
- discounts.

## Provision for bad debts

You don't know that a customer is not going to pay you when you supply them – or you would not do business with them! As you supply your customers, you issue invoices, which sets off other accounting processes, all of which initially assume that the invoices are going to be paid. As time passes, and a customer does not pay, your credit control department will no doubt make increasingly strenuous efforts to obtain the money due, and will be successful in many cases. There will come a point, though, when it is clear that some debts are simply never going to be paid – for example, if the customer goes bankrupt – so they become known as 'bad debts'.

> Once you know of a bad debt, you have to account for it in the profit and loss account. But past experience will have taught you to expect a certain percentage of bad debts each year on your sales overall, so you can make provision for bad debts in advance of knowing which particular invoices will actually go bad.

There are various ways of estimating a figure for future bad debts, some more scientific than others, and which one you use will depend upon your own company's experience. The main point to remember is that it is no good pretending to have made, say, a million pounds in profits if you know perfectly well that £200,000 of it will never be paid. Ordinary common sense, or 'prudence', tells us that we should provide for bad debts which we can reasonably foresee.

## Provision for discounts

Some companies feel that simply having provisions for bad debts doesn't go far enough, since there is another uncertainty affecting your profit calculations – the discount for prompt payment. You cannot be sure exactly how many of your customers will take advantage of the discount until they do so, but it makes sense to make provision for a proportion of them doing so.

As you can see, the decision of the timing and amount of a provision lies within the company.

There are unscrupulous people who go so far as to manipulate profits, by creating provisions in a good year to give them a head-start in the following year (*see also Chapter 11, page 224*).

Be aware that auditors (internal and external) are well aware of this effect of using provisions and will always want to audit provisions. You have been warned!

# Basic principles

Unfortunately there is no single, generally accepted, theory of accounting, either internationally or within the UK. Different companies and industries have widely differing methods of accounting; this is not too problematic for the managers of a business – they can get the information they need in order to make decisions – but it does make life difficult for outsiders who are trying to understand the published accounts. For this reason there have been various attempts to set standards which apply across the board.

There is an International Accounting Standards Committee (IASC) which tries to harmonise accounting practices across the world, and many of its recommendations have been adopted in the UK. There are still many inconsistencies, however, but companies are required to disclose any material deviation from the accounting standards in the notes to their published accounts.

Accounting has some general principles which are applied in cases of doubt and these are briefly discussed below.

## Cost

The assets that a company buys are normally shown in accounts at the price the company paid for them, although they may be revalued from time to time. The reason for valuing things at cost is that it is generally an objective measure. Everyone, both inside and outside the company, can agree that a purchased asset cost the company a given amount, although they might have widely different opinions on what it is currently worth. This practice is known as 'historic cost accounting'.

We know that the buying power of the pound will diminish through inflation, but historic cost accounting will produce distortions in the published accounts, particularly during times of high inflation. You may have purchased a building in 1919 for £1000, say, and today you may know that it is worth over a million, but it is still on the books at £1000! There are various ways of adjusting the accounts periodically to allow for changing values. Controversy rages about which is the best method of doing this.

## Realisation

Normally, accounts regard profits as being earned when the customer receives the products or services from the company and an invoice is issued. This is not the same time as the point when a contract is signed, or when the customer's payment is received. This practice implies the need for making provisions (*see pages 66–67*) for reduced payments and bad debts.

## Materiality

Materiality is an accountant's way of saying 'too small to worry about'. In this way, to be trivial, a box of pens is assumed to be used up the moment it is purchased. At the end of the year when assessing any provisions against bad debts, the larger debts might be assessed individually but the myriad of smaller debts might have a blanket, say 2 per cent, applied as a provision for non-recovery. External auditors will apply materiality tests when determining whether to audit an area of the accounts item by item or to apply cruder high level tests.

An interesting aspect of materiality is that it does depend on the size, and wealth, of the firm. A one-man band will not be allowed as much leeway on 'immaterial' amounts as a large plc will be. In addition, different firms of similar size will have different policies on what they call material. One company may have a threshold of £50,000, for instance, while another may have its threshold at, say, £1000 for some items and £1500 for others. In contrast, the one-man band's accountant might look askance at an attempt to consider sums of £50 as immaterial.

Since there is no statutory fixed limit on immaterial sums, it does depend on the judgement of the company's auditors and will be one of the first issues discussed between company and auditor when the year-end audit is planned.

## Prudence

Prudence, also known as conservatism, means that when in doubt an accountant will err on the 'safe' side. In this way losses are recognised as soon as reasonably foreseeable, while profits are only recognised when realised or actually achieved (*see 'Provisions' on page 58*).

Another good practical reason for prudence is that non-financial managers will tend to be optimistic about sales, values, and future income generally, so accountants generally prefer to err on the side of underestimating profits.

## Consistency

In the event that there is more than one treatment for a particular transaction, it should be treated consistently from transaction to transaction and from period to period. This is important, because if you constantly changed your accounting methods your published accounts might be misleading and it would be impossible to make meaningful comparisons between the performance in different years. Often there are new developments in a business, however, that do require a change of method, and in such cases it is perfectly in order to do so. If the change affects the profit and loss statement, then there should be a note, either in the profit and loss statement or in one of the accompanying reports, explaining what has been done.

## Going concern

Unless it is obvious that this is not the case, a company's accounts are always prepared on a 'going concern' basis. This simply means that it is assumed that the company will continue to trade in the future, which means, for instance, that you assume that its raw materials will be turned into finished goods, and its fixed assets will continue to be used in the business. If the company is about to go bust, its accounts would have to be prepared on very pessimistic assumptions about values, since all its assets would have to be sold off for whatever they could fetch, which is generally much less than you would hope for. The going concern assumption justifies the practice of valuing things at cost (see above). We are not interested in how much all the assets will fetch if they had to be sold in a hurry because we are assuming that they will continue to be used productively by the business.

## Substance over form

This is really accounting's version of the 'anti-avoidance' laws. Typical examples here might include assets that are leased or on hire purchase. Many such arrangements are considered by accountants to be purchases of fixed assets which should be shown as such with the financing shown separately. There are very strict rules that govern when  such financing can be shown 'off balance sheet' (*see Chapter 10*).

# CHAPTER FOUR

# Accounting *within* the organisation

- Internal versus external accounts

- The control cycle

- Structuring the plan

- Making budgets effective

- Cost centres

- Profit centres

- Measuring performance

## Internal versus external accounts

In the first two chapters we concentrated on the accounting reports that are published to all the stakeholders of the business including the general public and professional investors.

This section will focus on the information that is published solely *within the organisation*. It is characterised generally by the following features:

- available at all levels of the organisation from a single department up to the whole company
- published much more frequently – typically monthly
- used for internal decision making and control

- takes a wide variety of formats depending on the needs and style of the organisation
- confidential to the organisation and not published externally

There is one further fundamental difference between the internal reports and the published or external accounts which is that:

- published accounts deal with the previous period – they look backward
- internal accounts deal with *both* the recent past periods and typically *also include a forecast of future* periods.

You may have heard the terms 'financial accounting' and 'management accounting'. Financial accounting typically refers to the production of published accounts, while management accounting typically refers to the internal (or management accounts) of the business, and can also include other internal analysis such as project analysis, of which more later.

So management accounts are the latest internal data relating to the most recent past, together with the latest projection for the whole period, normally a year.

**Q** Why are they produced?

**A** Control.

---

Let's look now at the typical control and reporting cycle for a business, making the normal assumption that the business period is twelve months.

| Month | Planning activity |
|---|---|
| -4 (August) | FD starts to prepare for next year's planning process. This will require the collection of information from all the relevant departments. |
| -3 (September) | First responses are returned. The sales figures don't tally at all with the production volume figures assumed by the manufacturing areas. |
| -2 (October) | Various exciting meetings are held to thrash out a set of figures on which all can agree. Finance use these to produce the plan to present to the board. |
| -1 (November) | The board is never happy with the first plan – further exciting meetings ensue to squeeze more profit from the plan. |

| 0 (December) | Next year's plan is agreed and published. |
| 1 (January) | January's results are produced and compared to the year's plan. Variances to the planned figures are produced for management action where appropriate. |
| 2/3 (Feb./March) | The actual figures are produced for the periods and compared to the plan as above. A full year forecast is produced for comparison with the plan and action as required. |
| 3 (March) | The accounts for last year are published to the outside world. |

Note that 'actuals' in this context, and in many companies, refers to data for past periods and is distinct from 'forecast' data.

As the year goes on the actual figures are produced on a monthly basis, compared with the plan and provided to management who act on the information. As new actual data comes through it is used to keep the forecast for the full year up to date.

Typically, at the middle of the year, the most thorough analysis is held, with a detailed management review of the actual results from all areas of the company together with a close scrutiny of the forecasts for the year as a whole. This is done to ensure that the business is on track, but also because:

- it can then form the base for *published half year actual results*
- it is used as the base for the *following year's business plan.*

In many organisations the above process forms part of a larger longer ongoing process which might look as follows:

- ten-year strategic plan developed covering major structural, market, and competitive issues to be addressed. This would include the usual SWOT, market and product analyses, together with high level profit projections
- five-year business plan produced from ten-year planning process with more detailed plans and financial projections
- the following year's budget would be developed from the business plan.

Organisations do differ widely in the use of long-range planning, and this normally is consistent with the nature of the business. You would expect, and indeed find, that an industry with a product development time of several years, and a product life of five to eight years, would need to take much time and care over its long-term plans. A service industry by contrast, which is much more responsive to its environment, is more likely to focus on short-term planning and control.

# The control cycle

Having established the type of pattern used for planning we should briefly look at the means of control we are assuming when we look at planning, budgeting, and reporting. This would follow the pattern below:

- collect data (be it actual or forecast – production volumes or profits)
- compare with objectives
- understand reasons for any variances
- take actions as required to correct adverse variance or capitalise on favourable ones
- collect data on outcomes (step 1 above refers).

Figure 4.1 illustrates the classic feedback loop control cycle which is used at *all and every* level of decision making and control. Let's take a couple of examples:

**At board level:**

- request next year's business plan
- compare with objectives (last year's published accounts, this year's plan, city expectations, etc.)
- understand changes – external factors, size of market, competition, etc.
- direct and manage necessary enhancements to the plan, and request a revised consolidated plan
- review revised plan, etc.

**On the production line:**

- production is only 25 an hour
- plan is 50 an hour
- one of the two drilling machines has failed
- call maintenance to repair drilling machine

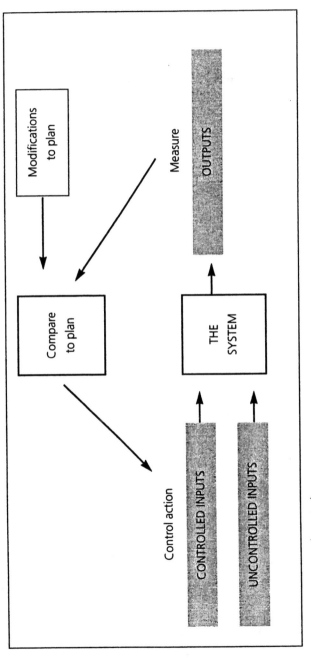

Figure 4.1    Internal control

- production returns to 50 an hour
- check kettle is on!

**The thermostat:**

- temperature is 15 degrees C
- setting is 16 degrees
- switch on boiler
- temperature still 15 degrees
- maintain boiler on
- etc.

Next time you solve a problem, whether an electrical item at home, or a complex issue in the workplace, pause and think through how you approach the issue. You'll be using simple feedback loops and your knowledge and experience to work through the possibilities until you reach an acceptable solution.

Business planning and reporting is an extension of this process on a large and formal scale. Companies, of course, are large and complex organisations which require teams of people to manage this process. They must also be subdivided into manageable chunks in order to achieve the objective of keeping control. This is done by structuring the plan into small units as follows:

# Structuring the plan

Organisations are sub-divided into groups. This is so obvious and commonplace that we take it for granted, but there are many ways in which an organisation can be structured. Groupings typically are functional, i.e. Sales, Manufacturing, Marketing, Finance, etc. There can also be regional groups or other structures based on product lines, or customer type, or any combination of these groupings.

Many organisations contain hierarchies within them. You might have US and European regional organisations, within both of which there is a Manufacturing division. Inside the Manufacturing Division you might see Finance or Human Resource staffs. These can often have 'split' reporting lines – both to the operational management (in this case manufacturing) and to the central functional areas.

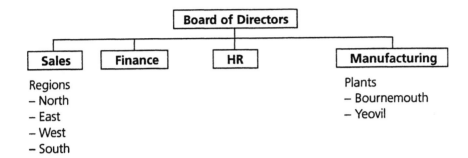

Processing of orders for sales could be done in either the Sales or Finance organisations and you would expect the manufacturing facilities to have their own support staffs, such as finance and HR on site.

Organisations are sub-divided in this way in order to allow unit managers to take responsibility for their own operation. In this way a salesperson would have a target for sales of each product perhaps per week. The regional sales manager for the Northern region would more likely have targets for his or her whole region set by month.

The Director of Sales would be responsible not only for total sales figures, but for total advertising spend, and would be responsible for the sales budget covering salesstaff's salaries, annual sales conferences, and total sales overhead.

It is in this way that the operating as well as financial plans are built up for the year as a whole. Mini financial plans are developed for each of the departments or activities which, when consolidated, create a plan for the company as a whole.

Plans can be developed in either a top-down or bottom-up fashion; again, typically, the process will include a combination of these processes with the first detailed plans being developed bottom up.

## Making budgets effective

In some organisations budgets are regarded as 'the enemy' rather than as an essential business tool. For budgets to be fully effective, managers at all levels need to understand and agree with them. For a performance measurement system to be fully effective, managers should:

- agree budget targets and believe they can be achieved
- receive budgets in a form relevant to their work – such as number of units produced or delivered
- be trained to understand the need for budgets and how they are used overall.

## Do budgets motivate?

Research has shown that setting defined goals, such as budgets, improves performance as compared with a climate in which no goals are set. When called upon to review and agree the targets of subordinates, consider not just the apparent current situation but also past performance where possible.

- If past performance has been substantially better than budget, then this may indicate 'home run' performance but will probably also mean that targets were set in order that they be beaten. Consider a substantial increase in budget difficulty to maintain and further improve performance.
- If past performance has been in line with budget ensure that budgets are adjusted carefully to reflect changes in conditions.
- If past performance has been well below budget, full investigation is required. Targets may well need to be revised downwards to prevent motivation levels falling, particularly where the budget has not been met due to external factors.

These principles emphasise the need to set targets as high as possible without causing a negative reaction. Budgets which are always met are an unhealthy sign and suggest that performance could be improved.

Consider the use of a 'stretch' target as well as a budget where you believe that the budget may be a little 'soft'. Where the culture is one of budgets being exceeded 'or else' then a less formal target of budget plus 5 per cent determining who out of the sales force is invited on the annual conference will serve as an incentive to push that bit harder!

Let's look again at the elements of the overall budgeting system in a company:

1. Budgets imply a plan. The planning process varies between organisations. All levels of the organisation should be familiar with the aims of at least their own area. Issues of confidentiality, such as potential rationalisation of one division

discussed at board level and incorporated into the plan, may preclude full openness.

**2** Parameters and assumptions about the size of the market, major production or product changes, expected sales growth, exchange rates and so on should be set early and disseminated to form the base of the plan.

**3** This allows the budgeting process to begin. The first budget in most companies is the sales budget. This will reflect the economic forecasts of the market and the effects of competition.

**4** Following this drawing up of an initial sales budget, all other budgets can be developed consistent with the sales volumes. Manufacturing production targets, stock levels, advertising, engineering and support and so on.

**5** Once the budgets are shaping up, a cash flow budget is needed to assess affordability. This will ensure that the budget, when finalised, is consistent with the broad financial parameters and does not, for example, assume unrealistic borrowing requirements.

**6** An effective budgeting system demands good communications up, down and across the organisation. Junior managers submit their budgets upwards, and at each level of seniority a manager will reconcile these with one another. This will produce anomalies, so the manager will have to go back to his or her staff who submitted the budgets to negotiate changes. This bargaining process helps to ensure that all managers understand and agree their budgets, and appreciate the reasons for necessary changes. Budgets may move up and down the organisation several times before they can all be co-ordinated.

**7** In a large company, 'the budget' will be comprised of literally thousands of targets and objectives for each measured item: people, sales, prices, manufacturing cost, etc. Put together, all this is a massive and extremely detailed exercise. In order to look at the figures overall, they must be reconciled to ensure consistency and then consolidated to form the top-level budget.

It is the top-level budget that senior management will then review. If, for instance, they feel that the return on investment (ROI) is not high enough, they will look for ways to increase it, and the budgeting process must start again, in search of ways to cut costs, increase efficiency, or increase revenues.

The budgeting process is always iterative: detailed plans being developed, consolidated to a total, reviewed by senior management, modified, re-consolidated and so on.

The first rule of planning states that the first plan is never right, so very often the Sales Director might simply choose to add say 10 per cent to each region's targets, this being 'top-down'.

At the risk of straying away from finance and into the arena of organisational behaviour, let's just discuss the first rule of planning above. A 'sketch' of the process operating in real life follows. When developing a business plan organisations normally request detailed plans from each area.

- On the ground each salesperson is thinking: 'Well this year I've worked pretty hard and sold 100 units, but things are tough and next year I'll struggle to sell 100, so I'll forecast sales of only 95. That way if I sell 100 I'll be a hero and might be in line for the area manager's job.'

- The Sales Director, whose sales force will sell about 1000 this year receives a return from the field totalling only 900. She sends hate mail to each of the regional managers instructing them to sell at least 950 in the year or it's 'overhead saving time'. Meanwhile she tells the FD that things are so tough that in order to sell 950 he'll need a big increase in his advertising and sales force budgets.

- With Manufacturing telling the FD they need lots of new equipment to remain competitive, and Engineering explaining why they need more resources next year for new product development, it's not hard to see why the FD has a pretty tough time trying to put a sensible plan together. He either runs round putting pressure on the departments to produce more results with less resources or he gets absolutely slaughtered when the Board sees the plan containing the above contingencies, which will result in profits well below the Board's expectation.

Equally, if you're a salesperson who's felt badly treated by an arbitrary increase in your sales targets, now you know why!

Enough of what really happens, and on with some more theory. As well as top-down and bottom-up there are broadly two ways of assigning financial targets to departments. These are:

- cost centre, and
- profit centre.

With a cost centre the manager is responsible for controlling the costs of his or her area. With a profit centre the manager is charged with controlling the profits for his area or activity: that's tough to remember!

# Cost centres

A cost centre is simply the smallest group for which costs are collected separately. A cost centre may be a department of twenty salespeople or it may be a single individual. The trend, with increased and more sophisticated computer systems, is for more and smaller cost centres. This author believes that it will not be long before many individuals are treated as cost centres in their own right. Powerful systems can consolidate these cost centres into departmental totals, with flexible 'look-up tables' quickly handling the effects of organisational changes.

Each cost centre is the unit for which management accounts are produced for comparison with the budget, and is controlled by a supervisor or manager.

All costs for the section are charged to that cost centre and classified by type of costs. When consolidated into larger reports, it is possible to determine that, for example, the sales overhead exceeds budget because of higher than expected airfares in three out of the twenty or so cost centres. Referring back to the feedback loop, the Sales Director could then determine whether there was corresponding higher sales because of these costs or whether his or her salesmen had started flying first class.

Developing a cost centre budget is a simple matter of collecting together all of the costs for the section for which you are responsible. These will include:

- salary costs including employers' NI, pensions and insurance
- travel and entertainment, floorspace/office costs, IT and communications.

If you are called on to develop such a budget, ask for the standard cost report for the department for the last available period and develop it from there.

> **!** To work from the last full year report to avoid forgetting any annual payments which may not be correctly accrued, and don't forget that any new equipment will need to be depreciated.

The example above brings us to the main drawback of cost centres when used as a management tool in isolation. A sales manager is given a cost centre to manage of, say, £300,000 for the year. Assuming that his sales targets were proceeding in line with expectations, he might forego the opportunity of a trip to the United States because it would exceed his overhead budget, even if it could have resulted in a substantial and profitable order for the company.

For this reason, it would be argued, the sales manager should be given a target based not on sales and overhead costs but on profits generated for the company. Budgets and targets can indeed be structured in this way – they are referred to as profit centres.

# Profit centres

The theory behind profit centres is wonderful. Make every departmental manager responsible for the profit for his or her activity. Advocates claim that this requires all managers to feel the 'cold wind of competition'. Of course they're absolutely right, and the move to profit centres is also in line with management thinking on empowerment.

Let's take our sales manager above again. If he were measured on profits instead of costs he might use a small improvement versus his sales targets to 'fund' the trip to the US in the hope of catching that big order. He would not have to worry about overrunning the travel budget but could focus on the big picture and on winning more business.

With support services it becomes more tricky. The IT manager is only supplying services within the organisation. It is possible, though, to allow internal competition by exposing the IT manager to competition. Many external organisations provide IT support to varying levels of response times, and the internal service could be allowed to compete with outside providers.

This does carry with it the administrative burden of 'doing business with ourselves', but in a profit centre environment the ability of any activities to 'de-source' another internal service provider is a useful way of ensuring that in-house support services regard the user areas as customers and not as a burden. The authors have participated in such an exercise with excellent results.

In theory, then, the practice of measuring each manager's performance on a broad measure of profitability rather than on the narrower measures of cost and, say, sales volumes or even revenues should be welcomed as an advantage, and indeed has been adopted by many companies.

In this way managers can trade-off increased cost levels against greater increases in other performance to the overall benefit of the company. They may also feel greater empowerment with increased operating flexibility in such an environment.

Why then do many companies retain a cost centre based set up? The answer is that in practice a profit centre based system is substantially more complex and can also generate other problems which are discussed below.

## Profit centres – the difficulties

Difficulties with the use of profit centres instead of cost centres fall into two main areas:

- conceptual
- administrative.

Conceptually, the problems are manifold, and are probably best explored by use of an example consistent with our sales manager above.

## Example

We need to develop a control mechanism to measure the profit earned for the business by each sales manager in a given period and then to compare that with a target. The problem comes in measuring the level of profit correctly in order that the objectives of the organisation are achieved.

Our example of a profit report for a sales manager might look as follows:

**Profit centre return for Sales Manager – Fred**

| | |
|---|---|
| Number of units sold | 1000 |
| Profit per unit | £750 |
| Total gross profit | £750,000 |
| Fred's departmental overhead | £(250,000) |
| Fred's department net profit | £500,000 |

This looks fine, and if Fred's objective profit is only £450,000 then Fred's a hero. Looking deeper though:

- What profit are we using up in the profit per unit line?

- Is this amount of £750 the budget profit or the actual profit?

- Is Fred responsible for price setting? If he can't control price levels then we'd expect him to be measured using a budget unit profit, in which case he'll be keen to give away maximum discount in order to secure the sales.

- If he is responsible for price setting, then we'd correspondingly expect the measure to be on an actual profit basis. In which case, what happens when the market prices start to trend upwards unexpectedly? Does Fred get all the credit for market factors outside his control?

- The other side of unit profit from the price per unit is the manufactured cost, which is certainly outside Fred's control. What happens when the costs per unit go up or down versus budget?

Most profit centre systems base unit profit on either budget or recent current cost levels. If Fred's unit profit is based on budget levels let's look at what happens when:

- costs fall – profit margins increase for the company but Fred is working on 'old' data. He may lose sales to competition who also have lower costs which have been passed on to sales staff. He is undercut in the market place.

- costs rise – Fred's competition may also face cost increases. Fred can either undercut the competition, or take a price increase and comfortably exceed budget profits with no real sales increase. If Fred DOESN'T increase prices he may, in a low margin business, find himself selling at a loss at the end of the year.

If the costs used to determine Fred's profits are based on actual data, what happens to poor old Fred when he finds that he's made all his sales targets but the manufacturing area had cost overruns which caused him to miss his target (and hence his bonus!).

---

The product cost to be used is also difficult to establish. For decision making we should use the variable and/or marginal cost on which to base the pricing and discounting decisions. In isolation this might lead to under-recovery of the organisation's fixed cost base. For a more detailed discussion of costing and pricing refer to Chapter 5. For a discussion of transfer pricing see below (and also Chapter 9).

> **!** The above is not meant to decry profit centre based systems, rather to point out some of the difficulties with such techniques which must be agreed before the system can operate with full effectiveness.

Equally, if you are a manager who is measured on a profit centre basis, you should ask yourself whether you understand the measurement tools on which it is based. In such a situation ensure that you understand all of the variances to your objectives *including* any 'internal' charges.

Having explained some of the conceptual difficulties with profit centre systems, the administrative difficulties inherent in managing this level of complexity should be plain to see. In practice a sophisticated management information system (MIS) is essential to manage properly a quality measurement system of this kind. In addition it is essential that *all* users of the system understand its operation, and this should include the customers of the information, including non-financial managers and the senior management team.

## Budgeting with spreadsheets

The advent of computer spreadsheets, at least in the smaller organisation, has made budgeting a lot simpler. Changes can be made easily, and the effect of changes is rapidly calculated by the computer. This enables managers to review many more possible scenarios by simply adjusting parameters on their spreadsheets.

 **Examples**

- What if material costs increase by 5 per cent in May?
- What if that big order is paid 90 days after delivery instead of the agreed 30 days?
- What if the mailshot produces a 1.5 per cent response rate instead of the budgeted 0.5 per cent?

# Measuring performance

If you use comparisons between actual and budgeted performance to beat your managers over the head, you will inevitably find that they will be less co-operative about budgeting in the future. The point of looking at performance is to find ways of improving it where targets are not being met. When there are highly complex budgets being used, it is sometimes possible to find clues to the problem by analysing the figures in detail, but normally the managers who drew up the budget are in the best position to discover what is going wrong.

## Measuring performance in service companies

Service businesses have overtaken manufacturing in their importance in the economy, and need non-financial performance measures as well as financial ones. Let's look at some of the characteristics of service businesses.

### Examples

- It is hard to identify what the customer is buying; for example, do customers go to a restaurant simply for the food, or are they also buying the atmosphere and location?

- Unlike products, services can't be stored. A table which is empty for two hours in a restaurant has lost those two hours for ever – they cannot be stored and sold later.

- The quality of service can vary. If a waiter has an off day, for instance, the service will not be as good as normal.

Companies use a combination of the following methods to measure such intangibles.

### Examples

- Finding measurable substitutes for intangibles. For example, a supermarket might measure the average waiting time in a checkout queue as a partial test for customer satisfaction.

- Testing the quality of service by using 'mystery shoppers' who report back to the management.

- Using customer surveys and analysing their comments and complaints.

# The performance of divisions

Multinationals that operate a large number of businesses providing a wide range of products and services all over the world have particular problems with control. The head office often cannot deal with the mass of complexity, and must devolve some of the responsibility for control onto the people who work in the various businesses. This can be done by organising the company into divisions which are each given a great deal of autonomy.

Clearly, if a division is given too much autonomy, its managers may develop goals that are not in line with the company's policy as a whole, so there has to be a system for monitoring each division's performance while providing incentives to managers to perform at their best.

Divisions can be delineated in several ways, but the most common is to have a separate division for each major product or group of products. There may also be a centralised division which deals with research and development, industrial relations, and head office administration that serves the rest of the company.

The other main type of structure for large companies is the 'functional' organisation, which divides the main activities into different sections – Marketing, Production, Purchasing, and so on. This is generally a far more centralised company structure, with all the major decisions being taken by a small group of individuals at the centre.

Divisional organisations, by contrast, are run almost as separate enterprises, with the divisional management having a clear responsibility for the overall profitability, pricing, production, sales and costing in their own divisions.

Let's look now at the advantages and disadvantages of splitting a company into divisions:

## Advantages

Making each division a profit centre can be a very effective way to motivate senior managers in the divisions. It should speed up the decision-making process, and allow decisions to be made by people who are 'on the ground' and should be more familiar with their products and localities. It is also believed to free up the time of top managers of the company for strategic planning.

## *Disadvantages*

Too much freedom can cause problems, though. Divisional managers may start to compete with one another in destructive ways, such as taking actions which increase their own profits but make those of other divisions suffer. The divisional structure may also be more expensive to run than a centralised one because of the duplication of activities, such as a separate accounts department for each division.

 Companies that have several separate businesses are the most suited for divisional organisation. When you want to evaluate how a division has performed, you want to know two different things:

- how the division is performing in relation to its competitors
- how the management of the division is performing.

As we will see in a moment, this requires several separate measures containing different information.

 **Example**

Let's look at a sample profit statement from a division:

> **XYZ plc Aerospace division**
>
> **Sales to outside customers**
> Transfers to other divisions
>
> **Total sales revenue**
> *Less* variable costs:
>
> **Controllable contribution**
> *Less* non-controllable fixed costs
>
> **Divisional contribution**
> *Less* allocated corporate expenses

The controllable contribution is the total sales of the division less the costs that the divisional managers actually control. This would include overheads such as heating and lighting and fixed labour costs. Over the medium term, a divisional manager can increase or reduce such costs by changing the scale of operations, so they are regarded as 'controllable' by the manager.

You can assess a divisional manager's performance by looking at the controllable costs, since the figure gives an indication of how well he or she is using the division's resources. To assess fairly, you would also have to look at the division's market position generally; if, for instance, the division's competitors were all going bust, a high 'controllable costs' figure might actually result from outstanding performance of the division in tough market conditions.

It can be hard to decide on what items to count as 'controllable costs'. Let's look at some examples.

## Examples

- A division that is free to purchase any service or goods externally is clearly responsible for those costs.

- A division that is obliged to obtain some goods and services from within the company may be able to control how much it uses, but has to accept the 'price' at which these items are charged. Here it may be appropriate to say that 'excess' use of such services is a controllable cost.

- A division may be obliged to obtain some services from within the company without being able to control either the quantity or the price – for instance, the head office may charge a fixed proportion of the company's overall industrial relations costs to each division. In this case, these expenses are not controllable by the division at all.

NOTE: the controllable costs measure is used to assess the divisional manager's performance, not that of the division itself as a business.

## Profit centre – transfer pricing – sub-optimisation

Another common method of managing profit centre targets is through the use of transfer pricing. Under this method, the Manufacturing Division 'sells' product to the Sales Division. This form of internal transfer pricing can also be used when profit centre management is being used, with a similar problem called 'sub-optimisation'.

| Variable cost | 100 | | Profit Sales Division | | | | Profit Manufacturing Division | | | Total Company Profit |
|---|---|---|---|---|---|---|---|---|---|---|
| Divisional Transfer price | | 100 | 125 | 150 | | 100 | 125 | 150 | |
| Price to company | Sales volume | | | | | | | | |
| 150 | 1500 | 75,000 | 37,500 | 0 | | 0 | 37,500 | 75,000 | 75,000 |
| 160 | 1400 | 84,000 | 49,000 | 14,000 | | 0 | 35,000 | 70,000 | 84,000 |
| 170 | 1100 | 77,000 | 49,500 | 22,000 | | 0 | 27,500 | 55,000 | 77,000 |
| 180 | 1000 | 80,000 | 55,000 | 30,000 | | 0 | 25,000 | 50,000 | 80,000 |
| 190 | 800 | 72,000 | 52,000 | 32,000 | | 0 | 20,000 | 40,000 | 72,000 |
| 200 | 600 | 60,000 | 45,000 | 30,000 | | 0 | 15,000 | 30,000 | 60,000 |

Figure 4.2   Transfer pricing

## Example

Let us look at a numerical example to demonstrate the issue more clearly. The first three columns of Figure 4.2 show the price at which the company can sell the product, and the volume which it can sell. Note that the costs are all variable costs (refer to Chapter 5 for more information on costing), fixed or overhead costs are ignored. It is clear that the company would maximise profits by selling 1400 units at £160 each. The planning volume is set at 1400 units.

Now let's consider the Manufacturing Division. They need to set a price which gives them an incentive to maximise volumes and covers their fixed costs. Let's further assume that Manufacturing have a fixed cost base of £30,000. They will need to set the transfer price at at least £125 and probably closer to £150 to give them a good profit level. Again let's assume that the final agreement is to set a price of £125 per unit as a transfer price between the divisions.

Manufacturing now have a profit objective of £35,000 profit at the planning volume of 1400 units less fixed costs of £30,000 equals £5000.

The profit target for Sales is then set at (£160 – £125) × 1400 = £49,000 (less any overhead). The Sales Division management, however, are now in a position to increase prices to £180 at a cost of 400 units of sales. If they do so their profits will rise to (£180 – £125) × 1000 = £55,000.

This would optimise profits for the Sales Division but at the expense of the Manufacturing Division and the company as a whole.

---

This difficulty will always be present where decisions are based on transfer prices and not on true corporate cost. This problem is referred to as **sub-optimisation**.

What's the answer? Well, you could set prices centrally, but then you take away from the Sales Department the ability to manage revenue and you are in effect measuring the Sales Department performance on their sales and overhead performances, which of course is where we started.

## The divisional contribution and ROI

To assess how well a division is doing as a business, you must use a different measure, since controllable costs will not normally include such non-controllable costs as depreciation and a contribution to running the head office.

Subtract the 'non-controllable' costs from the controllable contribution to get the 'divisional contribution'. This gives you an idea of how much profit the division is actually making for the company.

Most companies use another measure to assess the performance of divisions as well: the ROI (*introduced on page 35*). The ROI gives you the percentage return the division is making on the total amount of capital invested in the division. If you only looked at the divisional contribution figure, you would not know if one division was using far more assets than the others to generate similar figures – the ROI solves this difficulty.

Some companies also use the ROI to assess the performance of managers, but there are problems.

### Example

Suppose that two divisions of equal size are considering making investments of equal amounts of cash. Division A can get a higher return on its investment than can Division B, but because Division A's current ROI is higher than both the estimated return on the new investment *and* Division B's current ROI, it decides not to proceed:

|  | Current ROI | Investment cost | Estimated Return on Investment |
|---|---|---|---|
| Division A | 20% | 10 m | 15% |
| Division B | 5% | 10 m | 10% |

Division A's managers may reject the project in order to prevent their overall ROI dropping, while Division B's managers are likely to approve the investment in order to increase their overall ROI. A top level manager, however, might think that both projects should proceed, since collectively they will improve the whole company's ROI.

Suppose that a division has an asset to sell, such as a building, which currently produces a return lower than the division's overall ROI. It will be tempting to sell the asset, since the division's ROI will automatically increase, even though the asset might be a sound investment which is worth keeping.

# Residual income

One way of motivating divisional managers to work in the company's overall interests is to measure their performance using 'residual income'. This is found by subtracting a charge for the capital used in the division from its controllable contribution.

### Example

Suppose the managers of Divisions A and B in the previous example are assessed on the residual income, and are considering the same two investment projects:

|  | Div A | Div B |
| --- | --- | --- |
| Estimated controllable contribution from new investment | 1.5 m | 1 m |
| Capital charge | 10% | 10% |
| Estimated residual income | 0.5 m | 0 |

This indicates that Division A's overall residual income would increase, while Division B's would stay the same. Thus, Division B's managers would not invest merely to improve their apparent performance, as they might if they were assessed by ROI. The amount of capital charge can be varied according to the risk of the investment (the higher the risk, the higher the charge).

Where divisional managers do not have control over investment divisions, however, ROI is a good performance measure.

# CHAPTER FIVE

# Costing

- Introduction
- Cost – some definitions
- Traditional (absorption) costing
- Standard costing
- Activity based costing
- Sales versus inventory
- Accounting for throughput
- Costing – some general thoughts

## Introduction

In this chapter we will discuss costing in the sense of looking at how the cost structure of the business as a whole relates to the production cost of the individual units which the company manufactures. If the company manufactures bowling balls, you will need to know not just the cost of an average ball but also the cost of each bowling ball in the range.

The main uses for this sort of unit cost information are:

- **Planning** – the development of plans and budgets for the organisation will include sales targets by product and unit profits. This means that you need to know the cost per unit of each item for current and future products.

- **Control** – during the manufacturing process, the cost per unit is an essential control parameter. Should, say, raw material usage increase, then product profits will be reduced requiring feedback control action to correct the change.

- **Analysis** – both sales mix and potential future product lines require cost information. For example, you can only review a potential sales promotion which will generate incremental sales if you have reliable cost information.

- **Pricing** – when you analyse pricing you need to know the unit cost data for each marketable item or 'extra' in the range.

# Cost – some definitions

 **Example**

Let's take a very simple example to discuss some of the basic costing terms. We'll assume a very simple factory which produces a single product: a bowling ball. All the output goes to Big Joe's Bowling Halls, so there are no sales expenses.

After the first year, with sales of 100,000 bowling balls, the management accounts are as follows:

| | |
|---|---|
| *Sales* 100,000 balls at £20 per ball | £2,000,000 |
| *Costs* | |
| – administration department | £(250,000) |
| – materials | (800,000) |
| – factory labour | (500,000) |
| – factory heating, lighting, etc. | (150,000) |
| *Total costs* | £(1,700,000) |
| *Total profits* | £300,000 |

So far so good; we're at least making a profit! Let's take a closer look at some figures.

The return on sales, or margin, is £300,000 on £2,000,000, or 15 per cent, which is pretty good.

The profit made per ball is £300,000/100,000 or £3. Another way to calculate this is to divide the unit profit by the price of each ball (£20): you get the same result, i.e. a sales margin of 15 per cent again.

**Q** So what happens when the sales increase by 10,000 balls to 110,000 balls?

**A** You might think that a 10 per cent increase in sales volume would result in a 10 per cent increase in profitability, giving 1,100,000 × £3 = £330,000, but this is *not* the case.

Let's go back to that cost structure again. Administration will be able to cope with producing an extra 10,000 balls without requiring an extra clerk. The factory won't need to be run any warmer, or lit any brighter to produce the extra product. In fact you could consider these costs to be *fixed* in nature almost regardless of the number of balls produced. You might expect them to be called **fixed costs** and you'd be right!

Of course more materials will certainly be needed to produce more balls, and it is very likely that more factory labour will be needed to produce more. These costs change with the level of production and are known as **variable costs**.

So let's recast the accounts above to reflect the classification into fixed and variable costs.

| | |
|---|---|
| *Sales* 100,000 balls at £20 per ball | £2,000,000 |
| *Costs – fixed* | |
| – administration department | £(250,000) |
| – factory heating, lighting, etc. | (150,000) |
| *Total fixed costs* | £(400,000) |
| *Costs – variable* | |
| – materials | (800,000) |
| – factory labour | (500,000) |
| *Total variable costs* | £(1,300,000) |
| *Total costs* | £(1,700,000) |
| *Total profits* | £300,000 |

So we can say that the variable cost of the bowling ball is £1,300,000, or £13 per ball. The gross profit per ball, *before overheads*, is £7. Following on from this the cost of producing an extra 10,000 balls should be £130,000.

The cost structure of the organisation could be said to be (Volume × £13) *plus* £400,000 or more generally:

(Variable cost × volume) *plus* fixed cost

while total profit is:

Profit = (unit profit × volume) *minus* fixed cost

or in this case:

Profit = (£7 × 100,000) *minus* £400,000 = £300,000

and an extra 10,000 units gives:

Profit = (£7 × 110,000) *minus* £400,000 = £370,000

which is quite a long way from the £330,000 above.

Given that we have a formula for assessing profit from volume we can graph this data, as in Figure 5.1. We can now develop forecast profits at any given volume level. We can also check the level at which profits become zero. This is known as the **break-even**. We know that:

Profit = (unit profit × volume) *minus* fixed cost

so when profits are zero at the break-even point,

Profit = (unit profit × volume) *minus* fixed cost = 0˙
Unit profit × volume = fixed cost

Or, in other words, at the break-even, profits (unit profit x volume) are only enough to recover the fixed cost. You can express this as:

Break-even volume = $\dfrac{\text{Fixed cost}}{\text{Unit profit}}$

In our example this is:

Break-even volume = $\dfrac{£400,000}{£7}$

or 57,143 units, as we see in Figure 5.1.

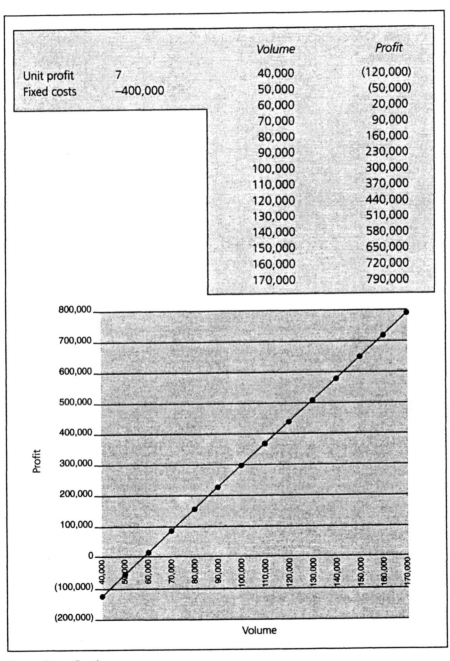

|  |  | Volume | Profit |
|---|---|---|---|
| Unit profit | 7 | 40,000 | (120,000) |
| Fixed costs | −400,000 | 50,000 | (50,000) |
|  |  | 60,000 | 20,000 |
|  |  | 70,000 | 90,000 |
|  |  | 80,000 | 160,000 |
|  |  | 90,000 | 230,000 |
|  |  | 100,000 | 300,000 |
|  |  | 110,000 | 370,000 |
|  |  | 120,000 | 440,000 |
|  |  | 130,000 | 510,000 |
|  |  | 140,000 | 580,000 |
|  |  | 150,000 | 650,000 |
|  |  | 160,000 | 720,000 |
|  |  | 170,000 | 790,000 |

Figure 5.1    Costing

We can now see how the cost structure can be broken down into those costs which vary with production levels, *variable costs*, and those which are fixed irrespective of production levels, *fixed costs*.

Classification of costs into these categories allows us to forecast profits easily at any volume level we choose, and also to calculate the level at which we would cease to earn profits, the *break-even* level.

> Try to obtain the cost structure for your organisation's products. What is the split between fixed and variable? Can you calculate the break-even?

# Traditional (absorption) costing

In the example above we assumed that factory labour was all directly involved in the production of the finished product. Thus any increase in production volumes was assumed to require a proportional increase in factory labour.

This type of labour is referred to as **direct labour**. In practice we will also have people who perform other tasks, such as foremen, maintenance teams, stock control, etc., whose costs will be more fixed in nature. This is known as **indirect labour**. By breaking down production costs in this way, we achieve a still more accurate picture of the cost structure of the business.

### Example

Back to the bowling balls: suppose that only £200,000 worth of the factory labour was actually assembling the product and the remainder are foremen, electricians and other indirect people.

We could recast the data as follows:

| | |
|---|---|
| *Sales* 100,000 balls at £20 per ball | £2,000,000 |
| *Costs – fixed* | |
| – administration department | £(250,000) |
| – factory heating, lighting, etc. | (150,000) |
| *Total fixed costs* | £(400,000) |

| | |
|---|---:|
| *Costs – Production – indirect* | |
| *– factory labour* | £(300,000) |
| *Costs – Production* | |
| *– materials* | (800,000) |
| *– direct factory labour* | (200,000) |
| *Total direct variable costs* | £(1,000,000) |
| *Total production costs* | £(1,300,000) |
| *Total costs* | £(1,700,000) |
| *Total profits* | £300,000 |

We could say that the gross profitability of the bowling ball is now:

$$£10 \ (£20 – £1,000,000/100,000).$$

This ignores, however, the indirect production costs required to maintain the factory.

So what does a bowling ball really cost us to make and who cares anyway? We need to know this for planning purposes and also for control purposes. It is mainly for control purposes that the traditional absorption costing process has developed. This is built around the concept of a **standard cost** for the product.

Remember that this simple example assumes that only one product is being made in this factory. Suppose that the factory also makes golf balls. In this instance it would be important to know the relative profitability of the products being made. We would therefore have to allocate the indirect costs of the factory, such as indirect labour, to the products actually being made by the direct labour workers.

The way this is done using traditional costing methods is to use the direct labour hours required to produce each product as an allocation base for all other indirect expenses. This is known as **absorption costing**. Direct costs are attributed to each product, including the hours required to produce it. Indirect costs are absorbed by the different products being assembled in proportion to the number of direct labour hours used.

# Standard costing

A standard cost is the cost of a product under a set of standard conditions, normally budget or plan conditions, and forms the basis from which feedback control can take place via variance analysis. Under absorption costing costs which are indirect or fixed are expressed as a cost per direct labour hour.

 **Example**

A standard cost for the bowling ball would be as follows:

| Direct costs | | |
|---|---|---|
| – material A | 3.0 kg @ £2/kg | 6.00 |
| – material B | 2.0 kg @ £1/kg | 2.00 |
| – direct labour | 30 minutes @ £4/hour | 2.00 |
| Total direct costs | | 10.00 |

The total standard hours for the projected production run is:

100,000 balls × 30 minutes per ball = 50,000 hours.

Indirect cost absorption will, therefore, be

| Indirect labour | £300,000/50,000 = | £6.00 per hour |
|---|---|---|
| Fixed costs | £400,000/50,000 = | 8.00 per hour |

The standard cost for the ball therefore becomes:

| Direct costs | | |
|---|---|---|
| – material A | 3.0 kg @ £2/kg | £6.00 |
| – material B | 2.0 kg @ £1/kg | 2.00 |
| – direct labour | 30 minutes @ £4/hour | 2.00 |
| Total direct costs | | £10.00 |
| Overhead recovery | | |
| – indirect labour | 30 minutes @ £6.00 per hour | £3.00 |
| – fixed costs | 30 minutes @ £8.00 per hour | 4.00 |
| Total standard cost | | £17.00 |

| | |
|---|---|
| *Standard revenue* | £20.00 |
| *Standard unit profit* | £3.00 |
| *Projected sales volume* | 100,000 |
| *Projected profits* | £300,000 |

See Figure 5.2 for the detailed workings.

---

Given the projected profits previously shown of £300,000, you are probably wondering why it is necessary to apply such detailed analysis at this stage. The main object of the exercise is to acquire a tool in order to allocate indirect overheads in a multi-product environment. In a more complex environment the standard cost of the product would then be used as a benchmark against which to compare actual costs as they became known. The total standard cost of £17 is also known as the fully accounted cost.

In Chapter 4 we looked at the control cycle. Here's a reminder:

**1** Collect the data (which may be actual or forecast – production volumes or profits).

**2** Compare with objectives.

**3** Understand reasons for any variances.

**4** Take actions as required to correct adverse variance or capitalise on favourable ones.

**5** Collect data on outcomes.

Now in this case the analysis on point 2, 'compare with objectives' takes the form of a structured variance analysis.

| STANDARD COSTS | Volume | Price per unit | Unit factor | Total | Total hours | Cost per hour | Standard cost allocation Standard hours | Standard cost |
|---|---|---|---|---|---|---|---|---|
| Sales | 100,000 | 20 | 1 | 2,000,000 | | | | |
| Costs – fixed | | | | | | | | |
| – administration | | | | (250,000) | | (5.0) | | (2.5) |
| – factory heating, lighting, etc. | | | | (150,000) | | (3.0) | | (1.5) |
| | | | | (400,000) | | (8.0) | | |
| Costs of production | | | | | | | | |
| – indirect labour costs | | –6 | 0.50 | (300,000) | | (6.0) | | (3.0) |
| – direct labour costs | | –4 | 0.50 | (200,000) | 50,000 | (4.0) | 0.50 | (2.0) |
| – material A | | –2 | 3 | (600,000) | | | (6.0) | (6.0) |
| – material B | | –1 | 2 | (200,000) | | | (2.0) | (2.0) |
| Total direct costs | | | | (1,000,000) | | | | |
| Total production costs | | | | (1,300,000) | | | | (17.0) |
| Total costs | | | | (1,700,000) | | | | (1,700,000) |
| Gross profit | | | 35% | 700,000 | | | | |
| Net profit | | | 15% | 300,000 | | | | |

Figure 5.2   Costing example

# Direct labour variance

## Example

Suppose that the actual direct labour cost of our ball was reported as £3.00 compared with the standard cost of £2.00. This, if left uncorrected, would give rise to an adverse profit movement of £100,000 which we would need to attempt to correct.

First we need to understand the reason for the increase in labour cost. Given that the standard cost is £4 per hour times 30 minutes it is clear that the overrun in actual cost could be due to two factors:

- the price – or labour rate

- usage or efficiency

Further investigation shows that the actual cost of £3 is comprised of a rate of £4.50 per hour and a time of 40 minutes.

The adverse variance of £1.00 can be subdivided as follows:

**Price variance formula:**

Actual hours worked × (actual rate – standard rate )

(40/60 hours) × (£4.50 – £4.00) = 33 p

**Efficiency variance formula:**

Standard rate per hour × (actual hours – standard hours)

£4.00 × (40/60 – 30/60) = 67 p

So our labour variance would be as follows:

| | |
|---|---|
| Standard direct labour cost | £2.00 |
| – labour price variance | (0.33) |
| – labour efficiency variance | (0.67) |
| Actual direct labour cost | £3.00 |

By the same methods, other variances can be produced to explain all of the possible differences between actual and standard costs. These are then reported to the appropriate management teams for corrective actions.

A hierarchy of variances would look something like this:

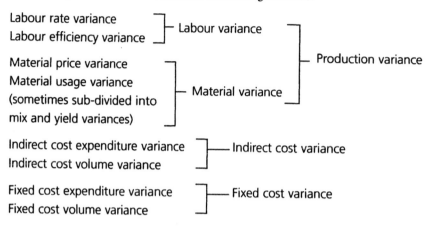

## Traditional costing – the pitfalls

The use of the traditional absorption costing methods described above is widespread throughout large manufacturing organisations, and has been for decades. More sophisticated users recognise the limitation of using fully accounted costs for decision making and focus their analysis on the fixed and variable cost structure.

There has recently been substantial criticism of the use of this costing method within industry. In an age of increasing automation, just how useful or relevant is it to use direct labour as an allocation basis for other indirect costs? Probably the most influential of the critics was Professor Robert Kaplan, who in his book *Relevance Lost* (1987), put  forward a thorough case for the replacement of traditional direct labour based costing systems.

## Activity based costing

Most prominent of the potential replacement systems of traditional costing is known as ABC, 'Activity Based Costing'. The main intellectual basis behind ABC is to establish the key activities and cost drivers in a business, and to develop the costing system from this analysis.

## Example

A commonly used example might be a manufacturer and distributor of products to various outlets. In manufacturing their own products they would use a direct labour absorption system. This shows the fully accounted cost of each product by allocating on the basis of standard direct labour hours. Further analysis might indicate that the cost of packing items for transport was a significant part of the total cost, particularly for the smaller order.

Traditionally a function such as packing would be accounted for as indirect support and simply allocated on the direct hours.

The standard costing system would, therefore, show that the cost per unit was the same for a small order as it was for shipping a much larger order. This 'information' would be a distortion of the true costs to the business of servicing the order, since large orders would generally be cheaper to ship, per unit.

Understanding the cost drivers within the packaging section gives us a greater insight into the cost of servicing each particular customer. It could well suggest a change to the pricing structure to charge more for smaller orders with corresponding larger discounts where required for larger orders. In this way, an ABC based system could well yield much more useful information than a traditional system.

This is simply another way of stating that the business must be fully understood and that the costing system must reflect the true cost structure of the business.

## Example

Here's another further example. A tool shop has a piece of equipment taking two hours to machine a complex piece. Each item attracts a substantial overhead cost as a result of the direct hours used. A simpler piece might require only 30 minutes machining and would attract much less overhead.

Further analysis might show that the more complex piece is run off in substantial numbers while the simpler piece is done in smaller batches resulting in increased downtime from the frequent tool changes.

Again, this would not be correctly reflected in the traditional costing system. What would be needed is an analysis into the cost drivers of the business. In this case ABC would focus not only on the direct hours required but also take into account the size of the batch and the time lost through tool changes to gain a much more accurate picture of the true cost to the business of producing each product.

The study of cost structures required to implement ABC may well reveal insights into the business which create opportunities to change processes and generate cost savings.

How do you know the true cost of your product? Do a little research into what the various products in your company cost, and then ask some awkward questions:

- Does this cost include any overhead absorption?
- Does this cost include an allocation of indirect production costs?
- If so – how are these costs allocated?
- When was the last time the allocation system was reviewed?
- If the costs are true variable costs are they up to date?
- Would the variable cost hold for increases in production?
- What volume range would the cost hold true for?
- Where are the bottlenecks?
- How are the costs of changeovers in production accounted for?
- How is product complexity reflected in the reported costs?

In the bowling ball factory example above we calculated the variable cost of the bowling ball and then assumed that an additional 10 per cent can be produced by simply buying more materials and recruiting additional people.

To use the correct terminology, we have assumed that the current variable cost is equal to the **marginal cost** of additional production. This is the sort of assumption that we frequently make in business, and fortunately it is often true, particularly when considering small changes to current volumes.

In some instances, though, and for larger volume changes, the marginal cost will often be substantially different to the existing average variable cost.

- It could be lower due to efficiencies in batch production or the procurement of raw materials.

- It could be substantially higher if there is a requirement for additional resources to break a production bottleneck of some kind.

It is important to understand that the reported variable cost should reflect – subject to the issues discussed above – the average variable cost of existing production. For many purposes, such as pricing the bulk of the sales volume and general financial planning, this will be adequate. When considering, for example, the profitability of increasing sales volumes, by, say, expanding into a new market, we would need to establish the marginal cost of the incremental production, which would require an understanding of the production process and the identification of bottlenecks and any further economies. The cost of the additional production could well be very different from the existing average cost.

The final point to make when discussing this traditional costing is the **stepped fixed cost**. This is the attempt to quantify changes in 'fixed' cost as a result of large changes in volumes. Understanding the way in which indirect and fixed costs may change with production levels is on the way to understanding the differences between average variable and true marginal costs. An example of the stepped fixed cost might be the requirement for an extra despatch clerk when sales volume exceeds a certain number of shipments per month. Note that this would be correlated not just to sales volumes but also to the size of the average shipments.

## Sales versus inventory

All things being equal, we'd usually rather have cash in the bank than inventory cluttering up our shelves. After all, it doesn't earn interest, it costs money to store, and when you turn your back there's a product change and the stuff's obsolete. So your financial system should, if anything, penalise the building up of inventories unless there is an immediate customer on hand.

Good old absorption costing gets it wrong again. In this system the more direct labour hours that are worked, the more overhead is absorbed. Plant managers try to optimise their financial performance by producing as much as they can for stock. There is no question of whether the product leaves stock for a customer: to the plant manager, who is concerned only with his or her performance, the priority is to keep on building product. In the absorption cost system, the larger the batches and the lower the number of changeovers the better.

This sort of production-led philosophy is now considered to be very much old-school in a world moving towards the need to be customer focused. As the need grows to focus the company towards the consumer rather than the production facility, so the financial community must respond by developing costing systems and analysis tools which reflect the change in orientation.

To find out more, you should read the classic management text, *The Goal*, by Elihayu M. Goldratt and Jeff Cox. This is a highly readable indictment of the standard costing system, and the behavioural anomalies that they can generate. This lucid book points the way to many major issues which plague traditional costing methods, including the effect of building inventories and the handling of production bottlenecks. It also discusses the Theory of Constraints (TOC) in a very clear fashion, which is beyond the scope of this book.

In *The Goal*, the hero is guided to identify production bottlenecks, and to manage the production schedules around them, ensuring that they are run flat out, while production ahead of the bottlenecks is kept at a level to ensure a steady flow to the bottleneck. These areas 'in front' of the bottlenecks may then stand idle for periods when not required. This, of course, contrasted sharply with the previous practice of attempting to run the plant flat out at all times to maximise the conventional measures of cost performance described above.

In this way, the overall performance was maximised at the expense of short-term financial measures generated by a somewhat outmoded conventional costing system.

What was needed at the hero's plant was a more sophisticated measure of manufacturing plant performance; one that measured useful production rather than production at all costs. What was needed was a way of accounting for throughput.

## Accounting for throughput

Eminent among the new costing systems is 'throughput accounting', a new system aimed at addressing the problems inherent in standard costing systems, and providing more relevant cost and performance information to management.

> Throughput accounting is essentially the measurement of total plant performance through the identification of the plant's bottlenecks and the ranking of products by their contribution per unit of bottleneck resource.

Throughput accounting is not, however, a product costing system but rather an alternative measure of plant productivity and would therefore be used in association with a product costing system such as ABC above.

# Costing – some general thoughts

The development and criticism of costing systems generally is currently the subject of some debate. It is clearly essential to have some measure of:

■ the *total* cost of the manufacturing facility to allow for good planning of business profitability and to manage growth and financing properly.

■ the unit cost to allow analysis of marketing and pricing strategies.

To a large extent problems have arisen, and therefore costing systems have been criticised, because of two basic problems:

■ one system and one set of output data has been used to address the two requirements above.

■ users of the cost data have often not understood the cost system used to collect the data, and have therefore misapplied the data which has been produced.

■ the producers of the data have not guided the users of the data with the requisite skill, again resulting in the data being misapplied.

Readers should bear in mind that any costing system is a model of the business and of its manufacturing process. It will contain many assumptions and produce several sets of 'costs'. In order to use the data effectively, it is important to understand the underlying model and its assumptions. When you are called upon to use cost data do ensure that you understand the data that you are using; don't be afraid to challenge the cost data that you are provided with.

## General guidelines

■ When using costs to make decisions check that you understand the cost structure properly.

■ Check which costs are truly variable and those which are truly fixed; understand any stepped fixed costs and the volume parameters for which they are valid.

■ Check the capacity and the cost of breaking any bottlenecks and then check that the marginal cost of extra units really is equal to the variable cost that you have been given.

# CHAPTER SIX

# Pricing

- Introduction

- Competitive position

- Product revisions

- Return on sales

- The 'Special Value Programme' (SVP)

- General points on pricing

## Introduction

In this chapter we will look at some of the considerations that make up the pricing decision. Pricing is the establishment of the prices of a company's product offerings in a given market. Pricing structures vary greatly by market and by industry. It is an area which can logically fit into either financial or marketing departments within a company's organisational structure.

> **!** Pricing requires a good knowledge of financial analysis techniques as well as a thorough knowledge of the market place including the relative strengths of the companies' products.

As with many business disciplines there can rarely be said to be a 'right' answer when it comes to setting prices; it is easy to give the blame for a poor sales performance to a price that was set too high, while when a product sells strongly it is easy to think of how much better the profits might have been had the price been that little bit higher.

By pricing, in this context, we are discussing published price lists including normal volume discounts. We are not referring to deals done with individual customers that by their nature tend to be one-offs.

There are several areas where pricing analysis might be required:

- **Competitive position** – Pricing a product is very rarely done in isolation: with the exception of new and unique product 'breakthroughs' most products have competitors which are either similar or in some way substitutional to our own.

- **Product revisions** – A product change is to be launched into the market and the price position must be reviewed to support the launch.

- **Special promotions** – The 'limited period, three for the price of two' type of offer.

To examine pricing in detail, we will take an example from the motor vehicle industry. Each of the tools described could easily be applied, with a little modification perhaps, to other industries.

In pricing, you look at real value differences between similar products, such as a car with or without a sunroof. These differences are not the same as those which are simply created by good marketing in industries where the same products are sold under different brand names and are artificially differentiated by advertising.

This points up a major difference between pricing and marketing as disciplines. While marketing is concerned with focusing on any differentiation in product performance and promoting the favourable differences, when we are pricing we must put this aside. To be objective about the pricing decision we must gather as much information as we can on our product and how it compares with the competition and then attempt to assign value to the differences that objectively reflect the value that a customer might place on the feature.

> How is the pricing done in your organisation? Pick up some typical analysis from your company and compare it with the tools we describe as we review them. You might find that the tools which at first do not seem to be applicable can be modified to suit your products and markets.

# Competitive position

Pricing starts with a review of the competitive position of our prices – how our company's product is priced versus the competition.

 **Example**

As an example we'll suppose that we make Car M, which is similar to our competitors' products, Car V and Car R.

| | Actual price | | Equipment | Adjusted price | |
| | amount | per cent | difference | amount | per cent |
|---|---|---|---|---|---|
| Car M | 13,500 | | | | |
| Car V | 13,485 | 15 | 0.1% | 350 | -335 | -2.4% |
| Car R | 13,895 | -395 | -2.9% | -500 | 105 | 0.8% |

| Equipment differences | Car M | Car V | Car R |
|---|---|---|---|
| Sunroof | 250 | 250 | 250 |
| CD player | 350 | | 350 |
| Leather trim | | | 500 |
| Total equipment value | 600 | 250 | 1,100 |
| Equipment value vs Car M | | 350 | -500 |

Figure 6.1    Pricing

The first piece of pricing analysis is to compare the retail prices. In this piece of analysis, we have shown the absolute retail prices in the first column. In the second column are the differences in prices, in £ and percentage terms. Thus we can see that Car M is £15 or 0.1 per cent over the facing Car V.

Notice that we are using **retail** prices. But what happens when customers go to buy one of your shiny new cars from a dealer? They may have a car to trade in, and in any case they are going to haggle. This means that the dealer uses some of his or her margin to clinch the sale, which in turn means that, for this analysis to be accurate, we would have to know that dealer margins were the same for every product.

Alternatively, we could conduct the analysis at wholesale prices. We need to have some idea as to how any additional bonuses paid to dealers might be affecting the actual dealer sales price to the customer. In any case, we need to be aware that the retail price may not always reflect the true trading conditions in the market.

In this case competitor's Car R is £395 or 2.9 per cent above our Car M.

Let's now move to the shaded column in Figure 6.1 which reflects the equipment differences which are listed below. Here we can see that Car M has a CD player not fitted to Car V. Our Car M can be said to have a £350 equipment advantage. If we were to set a price of Car M equal to Car V after adjusting for equipment the price would be

| | |
|---|---|
| Car V price | £13,485 |
| Equipment difference | £350 |
| Nominal Car M price | £13,835 |
| Actual Car M price | £13,500 |
| Variance | -£335 |
| | -2.4% |

Against the notional price of Car V adjusted for equipment differences, Car M can be said to be £335 or 2.4 per cent under-priced. The table in Figure 6.1 is a simplification of the pricing position of the product and is designed for presentation to management.

We can go further by setting strategies for pricing which could then be used as measurements or benchmarks for the performance of Sales and Marketing departments. If our strategy was to be equal to competing Car V after adjusting for equipment differences then we would say that we were under-performing our pricing target by £335 per car.

In reality prices will not move continually, but rather be changed several times a year. In the case of the motor industry in the UK, prices typically change in the new year and then again at the 'model year', around September. In these circumstances it is difficult  to make small detail changes to respond to competitive reaction, and other strategies are needed (*see SVPs on page 114*).

Another important question is how to set the value of the equipment differences. Where there is a published price list for such added features, such as the list of the optional extras in the motor industry, we could use these values. These prices may well be higher than the value placed on them by the average consumer though. In the example above we might know that only 40 per cent of customers would pay £350 for a CD player, and only 15 per cent would pay £500 for a leather trim.

We could, of course, modify the equipment values by applying a factor to the option prices but, as in the costing arena, we should accept that we are creating a model and ensure that the users of the model understand the assumptions which have been used.

# Product revisions

When considering a revision to a product, whether an all-new product launch or a general update to the looks of the product to keep it fresh in the market, we need to consider the impact on the prices of the product.

This will need to be done and updated at all stages of the new product planning from the first conceptual discussions of the all-new product through to the actual launch of the product.

### Example

Let's consider the implications of launching an all-new product to replace our Car M; we'll call it the Belluno.

| | |
|---|---|
| Car M retail price | £13,500 |
| Revenue to company (assume 66%) (before dealer commissions, taxes, etc.) | £8910 |
| Manufactured cost of vehicle | £(6000) |
| Unit profit | £2910 |

The retail price has been converted into revenue to the company by deducting the dealer's margin, distribution costs and all taxes. The manufactured cost of the vehicle is the variable cost of producing the car (see Chapter 5) and, therefore, excludes any recovery of fixed or development costs.

Now let us consider the upcoming Belluno model. For the sake of this simplistic model, we will assume that it is a slight facelift of the Car M design with comparable performance, and equipment levels, but with a new navigation system built into the dashboard.

To minimise the cost and price increase effect on the new model, marketing have decided to de-standardise the CD player. With the change in feature, the cost of the Belluno is £100 more than that of Car M. Let's say that the cost of development was £3 million, while additional investment for tooling to allow high volume production was £2 million.

We might consider these pricing options:

- **No increase in prices.** To introduce a facelift with an exciting new 'talk-about' feature with no price increase would only be done if the underlying product was ageing badly and the sales were flagging. Financially this would be undesirable and only acceptable if you believe that the alternative is an unavoidable drop in volume.

- **Recover the increase in cost.** Again, an undesirable strategy financially, with no prospect of additional profits to recover the investment and development costs.

---

# Return on sales

The trouble with both of the above strategies is that they would also reduce the key return on sales ratio (*see Chapter 2*). You should really only consider this when there is a substantial requirement to increase sales or to maintain them against a more hostile market environment.

In the longer term, and across a portfolio of products, you need to maintain or improve the return on sales figure to ensure the ongoing attractiveness of the business. Other things being equal, the return on sales figure is a big picture view of the percentage profitability of the average of all the individual products, less the total overhead.

To ensure that we maintain total return on sales we should ensure therefore that we maintain or improve unit percentage profitability, while keeping a tight check on overhead.

## Example

Going back to our example,

- this gives rise to another pricing strategy which is to maintain the existing unit margin on the new product; this would therefore increase company revenue by £100/(1 − 0.327) = £149, an increase in retail price of £225

- a final strategy might be to increase the prices by the increase in product value added, or £600 − 350 = £250.

Figure 6.2 shows the profitability impact of the various strategies, together with the price positioning of the vehicle assuming that unit margins are maintained.

You might favour the 'margin maintenance' assumption whereby product value is slightly improved (by £25, the difference between price increase and equipment value) added to the fresh new look of the car which often gives a sales impetus; while profits are improved, with unit profitability increasing by £38.50 after amortisation of the investment required.

> Again it is worth stressing that there is no right answer when tackling pricing. The purpose of this chapter is simply to try to highlight some of the financial considerations behind a complex and important decision.

It is also worth noting that within the motor industry there are many people from different departments and organisations who input into the pricing decision, with proposals being developed and presented to committees of the most senior management. The example above will hopefully give some insight into this complex decision process.

In reality there is consideration given to:

- each option price
- every engine surcharge versus key opposition
- each price differential for five doors instead of three, estate versus saloon, and this company versus that competitor.

| Model change | | Actual price amount | per cent | Equipment difference | Adjusted price amount | per cent |
|---|---|---|---|---|---|---|
| Belluno | 13,725 | | | | | |
| Car M | 13,500 | 225 | 1.6% | 250 | -25 | -0.2% |
| Car V | 13,485 | 240 | 1.7% | 600 | -360 | -2.5% |
| Car R | 13,895 | -170 | -1.2% | -250 | 80 | 0.6% |

| Equipment differences | Belluno | Car M | Car V | Car R |
|---|---|---|---|---|
| Sunroof | 250 | 250 | 250 | 250 |
| CD player | | 350 | | 350 |
| Leather trim | | | | 500 |
| In-car navigation | 600 | | | |
| Total equipment value | 850 | 600 | 250 | 1,100 |
| Equipment value vs Belluno | | 250 | 600 | -250 |

| | | Retail Revenue | Cost | Profit | Per cent |
|---|---|---|---|---|---|
| Car M | 0.66 | 13,500 8910 | -6000 | 2910 | 32.7% |
| Belluno | 0.66 | 13,725 9059 | -6100 | 2959 | 32.7% |

**Launch and development costs**

| | |
|---|---|
| Volume | 100,000 |
| Additional investments | −2,000,000 |
| Development costs | −3,000,000 |
| Additional variable cost | −100 |

| Profit impact | Pricing strategy | zero | cost recovery | maintain margin | equipment value |
|---|---|---|---|---|---|
| Additional revenue | | 0 | 100 | 149 | 165 |
| Additional unit variable costs | | (100) | (100) | (100) | (100) |
| Change to unit profit | | (100) | 0 | 49 | 65 |
| times volume | | 100,000 | 100,000 | 100,000 | 100,000 |
| Change to total unit profit | | (10m) | 0 | 4.85m | 6.5m |
| Additional investment | | (2m) | (2m) | (2m) | (2m) |
| Additional development | | (3m) | (3m) | (3m) | (3m) |
| Total additional cost | | (5m) | (5m) | (5m) | (5m) |
| written off over five years | 5 | (1m) | (1m) | (1m) | (1m) |
| Total annual profit change | | (11m) | (1m) | 3.85m | 5.5m |
| Total profit change per car | | (110) | (10) | 38.50 | 55 |

Figure 6.2   Pricing(2)

# The 'Special Value Programme' (SVP)

Within many industries it is sometimes necessary to market 'specials' based on the regular product but offering something a little extra in the way of enhanced value. This may be done to:

- support sales that may be flagging due to economic factors, or general market slackness

- maintain product visibility in the market

- counter competitor actions such as their own value programme

- as a 'spoiler' to attract attention to your product ahead of or simultaneously with a competitor's new product launch

- maintain product sales during the final phase of a product cycle, sometimes called the 'runout'.

The financial review of these SVPs will take a fairly standard form irrespective of the industry, but again we'll look at the motor industry here, which uses SVPs extensively. You'll see them advertised all the time: special editions often with unique metallic paint colours to add interest with one or two added standardised features, such as sunroofs, radio-cassettes or power toys such as electric windows.

Many other industries also play the game: the recent Dark and White Mars bar or orange Kit-Kat; the 8-pack of beer complete with free glass this week; all are examples of the special product.

## Example

The analysis sheet is laid out in Figure 6.3 for the Car M SVP. The example assumes the addition of metallic paint together with larger wheels and tyres with a total value of £500 for a price addition of only £250. Typically when looking at a special value product we might want to choose those product additions with the highest perceived value at the lowest cost. In this case metallic paint is normally added with its high visual benefit at what is often only a small increase in manufactured cost.

The analysis is then structured into two sections. First we look at what happens if the SVP is *not* successful in generating incremental sales volume. In this case you still sell all of the specials but only to people who would have bought the standard car anyway.

Next we have to calculate the lost profit on the option of fitting metallic paint to the standard car at the rate which could have been expected. Add this to the cost of promoting the special and you have the cost of the special assuming that no extra sales of the range are made. This is called the **cost at constant volume**.

Here we predict that, of those who buy specials instead of regular models, 70 per cent would have bought the LX whilst 30 per cent would have bought the GLX. We can calculate the average unit from which the special has drawn by calculating the mixed average from these percentages. (*For more on calculating averages, see Appendix B.*)

The average unit from which the special draws its purchasers has a unit profit of £3,057, £132 better than the special. Lost option profit is simply the loss of the profit from the 20 per cent of LX/GLX buyers who would have paid extra for metallic paint had they bought regular models, calculated at the full option price for the option.

Combining these two elements of lost profit in the final box, at the special build volume of 10,000 units, gives us the loss at constant volume of £1,653,000.

We then need to calculate the effect of the incremental sales generated by the SVP. To do this we assume that 20 per cent of the specials sell to people who would have bought, say, the competitors' Car V or Car R. The unit profit of these incremental sales is calculated at the average substituted unit and *not* at the special unit profit because we have already assumed the loss effect of 100 per cent substitution.

This gives a net expected profit of the program of £4,161,600. We can also calculate a profit/cost ratio of 2.13. (Simply £4161/£1953).

---

This ratio can be used to compare specials or even to establish a hurdle which all programmes must achieve. Senior management could for instance stipulate that all specials must achieve a profit:cost ratio of at least 2 with maximum assumed incrementality of 25 per cent. This would keep pressure on the developers of the programmes to maximise prices and returns.

## Special Value Program

| | | Actual price | | Equipment difference | Adjusted price | |
|---|---|---|---|---|---|---|
| | | amount | per cent | | amount | per cent |
| Car M 'Sport' | 13,750 | | | | | |
| Car M | 13,500 | 250 | 1.8% | 500 | −250 | −1.8% |
| Car V | 13,485 | 265 | 1.9% | 850 | −585 | −4.0% |
| Car R | 13,895 | −145 | −1.1% | 0 | −145 | −1.1% |

| Equipment differences | Car M 'Sport' | Car M | Car V | Car R |
|---|---|---|---|---|
| Sunroof | 250 | 250 | 250 | 250 |
| CD player | 350 | 350 | | 350 |
| Leather trim | | | | 500 |
| Larger wheels and tyres | 250 | | | |
| Metallic paint | 250 | | | |
| Total equipment value | 1100 | 600 | 250 | 1100 |
| Equipment value vs 'Sport' | | 500 | 850 | 0 |

### Effect of model substitution

| | | Retail | Revenue | Cost | Profit | Per cent |
|---|---|---|---|---|---|---|
| Special | 0.66 | 13,750 | 9075 | −6150 | 2925 | 32.2% |
| Standard LX | 0.66 | 13,500 | 8910 | −6000 | 2910 | 32.7% |
| Standard GLX | 0.66 | 14,850 | 9801 | −6400 | 3401 | 34.7% |

| Substitution at constant volume | Mix effect | Revenue | Cost | Profit | Per cent |
|---|---|---|---|---|---|
| – from LX | 70.0% | 8910 | –6000 | 2910 | 32.7% |
| – from GLX | 30.0% | 9801 | –6400 | 3401 | 34.7% |
| Average substituted unit | 100.0% | 9177 | –6120 | 3057 | 33.3% |
| Special | | 9075 | –6150 | 2925 | 32.2% |
| Special better /(worse) than substituted unit | | –102 | –30 | –132 | 0 |

| Lost option profit | | Retail | Revenue | Cost | Profit | Per cent |
|---|---|---|---|---|---|---|
| Metallic paint | 0.66 | 250 | 165 | –50 | 115 | 69.7% |
| Option take | 20.0% | | | | | |
| Average unit lost profit | | | | | –23 | |

| Profit impact | | per unit | Total effect |
|---|---|---|---|
| Volume | | | 10,000 |
| Effect of substitution | | –132 | (1,323,000) |
| Lost option profit | | –23 | (230,000) |
| Advertising costs | | | (400,000) |
| Total effect at constant volume | | | (1,953,000) |
| Effect of incremental volume | | | |
| – number of specials which are incremental | 20.0% | | |
| – profit of incrementality | | 3057 | 6,114,600 |
| Total profit effect at projected volume | | | 4,161,600 |
| Profit:Cost ratio | | | 2.13 |

Figure 6.3   Pricing(3)

# General points on pricing

Many of the financial disciplines require business judgement to be applied to develop assumptions about future outcomes which are then used to determine the appropriate course of action. When considering a project we must establish projected future costs and benefits.

For many decisions it is possible to validate the accuracy of our assumptions after the event to compare the predicted with the actual outcome. This can aid the assessment of subsequent projects.

With pricing decisions, we are using analysis in the world of the market place and attempting to assess the reaction of the consumer to new product and pricing actions. After the event we can be none the wiser as to whether our pricing actions were correct. To this extent pricing is almost an art as opposed to a science.

Nonetheless it is important to establish a framework through which such decisions can be reviewed and made. The tools described in this chapter can be applied in many industries and should enable a more objective view of the market place when making what are ultimately only calculated guesses.

# CHAPTER SEVEN

# Project analysis

- What is project analysis?

- The basic tools

- Payback

- Internal Rate of Return (IRR) and Discounted Cash Flow (DFC)

- Some more advanced considerations

- WACC – the Weighted Average Cost of Capital

- Cashflows in perpetuity

## What is project analysis?

Previous chapters have discussed the reporting required by companies of past and immediately expected financial results. We have also looked at the costing and pricing of the company's output. These are all primarily techniques which focus on the past or current activities of the organisation.

Many times in business, though, we are required to make substantial investments of cash in projects which are expected to benefit the company far into the future. This requires tools which enable us to assess the attractiveness of future benefits against known immediate costs.

**Q** What techniques are used when analysing the future?

**A** There are a variety of tools in the area referred to as Project Analysis which are explained below.

 **Examples**

Let's look at some of the decisions which would require the application of these tools. Should we:

- purchase new equipment or not? A new truck or computer system, perhaps.

- undertake a new venture or not? Pursue the opportunity to develop and market a new product

- buy-in components or invest in the capacity to produce them ourselves? This is the classic make/buy decision.

- acquire another company? Will the future profits stream justify the cost of acquisition?

These are all decisions which involve spending substantial sums of money *now* for benefits *later*.

There are broadly two sets of criteria which can be used to make a judgement on the attractiveness or otherwise of the decisions described above:

- financial analysis of the known facts and figures at one's disposal. An objective view of returns, which can be measured against risks to develop a go/no go recommendation

- a subjective analysis of the industry and environment using the organisation strategic plans, the mission of the company, etc. and the 'gut-feel' of its management.

In practice, most decisions are made by applying a combination of the two methods above.

The objective analysis is referred to as **investment** or **project analysis**, although the decision-making process which will include subjective factors is often given this name as a total process.

Thinking of your own organisation and its decision making, can you identify how it is done?

If you're a production manager who's just tried to buy a new fork-lift, you'll probably be thinking that 'Finance' squeeze you for information, half of which is nonsense, and put the numbers in a great big machine which produces the result.

If you're a marketing executive who's just spent mega-bucks on a huge mail-shot, you may be wondering if any of this applies to you.

But whatever your role, the same tools will be applicable, and these are described in this chapter.

These tools enable you to take a mechanistic view of the decision you have to make. You will be forced to evaluate the costs of implementing the decision, as well as the benefits which accrue. These will not always be clear, and will sometimes be subjective, but you should always attempt to evaluate them.

- If the costs are not known with certainty, why not?

- If the future benefits are uncertain, on what do they depend?

- What can be done to increase the certainty of these variables?

The senior decision-makers in industry understand these financial tools, apply them when they can, are aware of the limitations of the tools, and then make the decision based on a combination of factors which include financial, strategic and other considerations.

At lower management levels, the production manager will often want 'the best for his men', the marketing manager 'maximum visibility', while the finance department are concentrating on achieving this/next month's budget.

This sort of 'natural conflict', when properly structured, can achieve a good balance, with projects approved only when each affected department is happy that the project is of overall benefit and is affordable.

# The basic tools

The tools which I describe here will form the objective measurement for any project decision. They all attempt to evaluate the worth of the project and can be used in broadly two ways:

- Shall we pursue the project? This is the classic go/no go decision.

- Which project should we pursue out of a number of alternatives? This is typically called ranking, and is most often used when we have a number of viable projects but a limit on resources that prevents us from pursuing all of them. Resources here normally means cash, but can mean people, production capacity, equipment and so on.

All of these tools can be used to measure projects against other projects, or against an internal benchmark to determine the go/no go decision. They are equally valid in either application.

- Payback is the simplest of the tools, comparing simple money amounts to determine how quickly a project 'pays for itself'.

- Internal Rate of Return (IRR) and Discounted Cash Flow (DCF) also consider the fact that money now is intrinsically more valuable than money tomorrow.

Both have their uses. All these tools assume certain (i.e. risk free) outcomes; we'll discuss risk management later on.

Now let's look at payback, the simplest of the tools.

# Payback

The payback method is the simplest form of investment measure. When we've looked at the more sophisticated tools, you'll be left wondering why such a simple measure should continue to be discussed in such weighty financial tomes or indeed be in use in industry. Even so, there are some compelling reasons for its inclusion.

- It's easy to understand, easy to apply, and easy to explain to your boss who didn't buy this book. Apply it in meetings after two minutes' analysis to impress your colleagues, use it to discount quickly those ideas which don't warrant further study.

- It works in real life because it normally correlates pretty closely to the more sophisticated forms of analysis and, as it's so easy to understand, many large companies rely on payback and payback alone in making project decisions.

- It helps cash flow because no matter how good a return a project makes *in the long term*, if a company is struggling with short-term cash flow, payback can be equally important.

## So what is payback?

 **Examples**

You are planning to spend £10,000 on a new fork-lift to save £500 per month on maintenance bills.

Savings come to £10,000 after 20 months.

Payback is 20 months.

That marketing mailshot costs £50,000, and the marketing director thinks you'll shift an extra 10,000 units per month at 50 pence profit per unit.

Extra profit equals £5,000 per month,

Payback is 10 months.

---

**Payback is the length of time taken to recover the initial investment.**

- The shorter the payback period, the better the project.

- The better and quicker the returns, the shorter the payback.

So which of the above examples would you go ahead with?

- Consider how certain are the outcomes. Can the factory manager really demonstrate that he can make these maintenance savings?

- Can the marketing director justify her prediction for extra sales? Was she right last time?

As a rough guideline, payback periods might be considered as follows

| | |
|---|---|
| Two years or less – | *very attractive* |
| Three or four years – | *quite attractive* |
| Four years and over – | *less attractive* |

The above would hold true for smaller, day-to-day decisions. Major infrastructure projects might still be attractive with longer payback periods, and require the more sophisticated tools, which follow.

# Internal Rate of Return (IRR) and Discounted Cash Flow (DCF)

Let's establish a couple of important definitions.

- **Internal Rate of Return is the effective return generated for the organisation on the original investment made in the project.**
- **Discounted Cash Flow is the net money value of the project to the organisation after adjusting for the time value of money.**

Both of these techniques work on the same principle, one that is inherently known to any businessman, housewife, prime minister or schoolchild, namely: *money now beats money tomorrow.*

**Q**   By how much is money now better than money tomorrow?
**A**   The interest rate, or discount rate.

 **Example**

---

We have £100 now which we can spend or invest in a bank. If we invest, we can do so at 10 per cent :

| Value now | £100 |
| Value in 1 year | £100 + £100 × 10% = £110 |

So we can see that £100 *now* is worth £110 in a year's time, and in two years' time the value is

$$£110 + £110 × 10\% = £121$$

---

 Note: we've gained a 'spare' £1 here. This has come from 'compounding' the interest, i.e. in year 2 we're earning interest not only on the original £100, but also on the interest in year 1.

The formula, therefore for interest earned is:

$$A_n = A_0 \times (1 + i)^n$$

$A$    is the amount or value

$A_0$   is the amount at time 0, or now

$A_n$   is the amount at end of year $n$

$i$    is the interest rate

$n$   is the number of years invested

There aren't many formulas in this book. If you're engaging in project analysis, you must learn and understand this one fully.

From above, the principal ($A_0$) is £100, and the interest rate $i$ is 10 per cent, so after two years

$$A_n = A_0 \times (1 + i)^n$$
$$\text{or } A_2 = £100 \times (1.1)^2 = £121$$

The formula works. Try it out on some of your own projects to become familiar with the concept.

Now we will look at the same principle in reverse.

> **!** Note: the interest rate is raised to the power of the number of periods, and not simply multiplied by the number of periods.

The same £100 invested for two years does not generate £100 $\times$ 1.1 $\times$ 2 years, which would be simple interest. Let's look at some simple factors:

|       | two years |          | four years |          |
|-------|-----------|----------|------------|----------|
|       | simple    | compound | simple     | compound |
| 10%   | 1.2       | 1.21     | 1.4        | 1.41     |
| 20%   | 1.4       | 1.44     | 1.8        | 2.36     |
| 30%   | 1.6       | 1.69     | 2.2        | 2.61     |

Just check that you agree with these factors.

Tables giving the relevant factors for the usual combination of discount rate and period are generally available. (*We've included one in Appendix D for your reference.*)

Looking at the factors you can see that for shorter periods and lower rates the use of simple interest can offer an approximation. With longer periods, and higher rates, compounding has a more dramatic effect on the calculation of present value.

125

**Q** What is the present value of £121 in two years' time assuming a discount rate of 10 per cent?

**A** £100.

The formula:

$$A_0 = A_n/(1+i)^n$$
$$\text{or } A_0 = £121/(1.1)^2 = £100$$

No apologies if you think I'm labouring this equation because this is the key to understanding DCF and IRR. If you've understood the above sums, you've understood all the theory necessary to understand project analysis. Now we can start to apply the technique to judging projects.

**Q** Does the above include any allowance for risk?

**A** No.

We're equating £100 now with the certainty of the investment maturing. We can consider that we have perfect information, that the bank in which we can invest is perfectly sound.

We'll consider the effect of risky outcomes later, but for now remember that the equation which lets us compare the value of money is based on **no risk**. This is a surprisingly common misunderstanding.

## Example

Invest £1 million now to increase capacity to produce additional units. Equipment has a useful life of five years. In each of the five years, the effect on profits is as follows:

| | |
|---|---|
| Revenue per unit | £10 |
| Variable costs of production per unit | (6) |
| Net profit added per unit | £4 |
| Increased capacity | 100,000 units |
| Total increased net profit | £400,000 |
| Additional sales promotion costs | £(50,000) |
| Additional distribution costs | (50,000) |
| Net additional profits per year | £300,000 |

We can now arrange this by calendar year:

|  | Cash flows |
|---|---|
| Year 0 | £(1,000,000) |
| Year 1 | 300,000 |
| Year 2 | 300,000 |
| Year 3 | 300,000 |
| Year 4 | 300,000 |
| Year 5 | 300,000 |

Now add the factors, assuming a discount rate of 10 per cent. You can look up the factors in published tables, but to work out the factors use the formula on page 125. For example, if the value is 1 after one year, the factor is $1/(1 + 0.1) = 0.9091$.

|  | Cash flows | Factor |
|---|---|---|
| Year 0 | £(1,000,000) | 1 |
| Year 1 | 300,000 | .9091 |
| Year 2 | 300,000 | .8264 |
| Year 3 | 300,000 | .7513 |
| Year 4 | 300,000 | .6830 |
| Year 5 | 300,000 | .6209 |

The Net Present Values are:

|  | Cash flows | Factor | NPV |
|---|---|---|---|
| Year 0 | £(1,000,000) | 1 | £(1,000,000) |
| Year 1 | 300,000 | .9091 | 272,727 |
| Year 2 | 300,000 | .8264 | 247,934 |
| Year 3 | 300,000 | .7513 | 225,394 |
| Year 4 | 300,000 | .6830 | 204,904 |
| Year 5 | 300,000 | .6209 | 186,276 |

The cumulative Net Present Value, therefore, is £137,235. Assuming that the cost of finance to the organisation is 10 per cent, then, the project would increase the organisation's Net Present Value and would be undertaken.

Note that this example completely ignores:

■ Risk, commercial risk, such as the inability to sell the extra capacity.

■ Taxation (*see Chapter 9*).

■ Inflation.

As a next step, ask to see the investment appraisal model used by your finance organisation. It will be much more complicated than the above example but the principle will be the same. If you have time, ask to be guided through the model. Any model is a simplification. Now that you understand the basics of generating return information, look instead at some of the commercial assumptions being made.

■ Are the assumptions correct?

■ Are they too prudent, or too aggressive?

■ Where are the provisions or contingencies? They're in there somewhere; if you can't see them, keep looking.

■ Are the contingencies appropriate?

If you have several versions of the analysis:

■ Check the payback for the projects.

■ Does the return correlate to the payback? If yes, make a note of the correlation for your business area. If not, why not?

Is the model right? (Lots aren't!)

## IRR versus DCF

The above has looked at the method of comparing the 'present value' of money received in the future. When discounted at 10 per cent, we could see that the above project had positive value.

Let's consider the project at 20 per cent discount rate. The net present values are:

| | Cash flows | Factor | NPV |
|---|---|---|---|
| Year 0 | £(1,000,000) | 1 | £(1,000,000) |
| Year 1 | 300,000 | .8333 | 250,000 |
| Year 2 | 300,000 | .6944 | 208,333 |
| Year 3 | 300,000 | .5787 | 173,611 |
| Year 4 | 300,000 | .4823 | 144,676 |
| Year 5 | 300,000 | .4019 | 120,563 |
| Total Net Present Value | | | £(102,817) |

The NPV is now negative, meaning that if the organisation has a cost of funds of 20 per cent it would not choose to pursue the project.

If the NPV is positive at 10 per cent discount rate, and negative at 20 per cent discount rate, then there must be a discount rate between 10 per cent and 20 per cent at which the NPV is zero. What does this discount rate signify?

The rate at which the Net Present Value would be zero is in this case 15 per cent or 15.24 per cent to the pedantic. Assuming the cost of funds is 15 per cent, the organisation would be indifferent to the project. But this rate is also the rate of return generated to the organisation, by pursuing this project, and this is called the Internal Rate of Return or IRR.

## Working out the Internal Rate of Return with a computer spreadsheet

To calculate IRR using the computer spreadsheet Excel simply input the figures above in a column, use Function Wizard or type IRR(A1:A6), and Excel will return 15.24 per cent.

## Pitfalls to watch out for with IRR

**1  Positive and negative cash flows**

If a project offers positive cash flows followed by negative cashflows, the NPV rises as the discount rate is increased. You should accept such projects if their IRR is LESS than the cost of finance, the opposite of the normal rule.

**2** **Strange answers**

If the cash flow changes from positive to negative several times, you can get odd results – either two IRR figures for the same project or none at all.

**3** **Mutually exclusive projects**

Where the organisation has to choose between two projects which are mutually exclusive, IRR must be used with care. This is explored more fully later. (*See project comparison on page 132.*)

## Average return on book value

This is a rule-of-thumb measure that some companies use. It is calculated by dividing the average book value of the investment by the average forecast net profits (after tax and depreciation). The result can be compared with the overall figure for the company, or with the average return in the industry.

 **Example**

Suppose you are assessing Project Z, which will require your company to invest £20,000 at the outset. You depreciate this figure in equal amounts of £5000 over the four years:

**Project Z**

|  | Year | | | |
|---|---|---|---|---|
|  | 1 | 2 | 3 | 4 |
| Income (000) | 20 | 15 | 10 | 10 |
| Cost | 6 | 5 | 5 | 4 |
| Cash flow | 14 | 10 | 5 | 6 |
| Depreciation | 5 | 5 | 5 | 5 |
| Net income | 9 | 5 | 0 | 1 |

Project Z's average net income is £3750 a year. Its average return on book value is:

average annual income/average annual investment
$$= 3.75/5 = 0.75$$

Suppose you had a Project X with identical figures for depreciation, average income and average profit as Project Z, but where more of the income was actually received in later years. You would get the same figure for average book return, even though Project X would be worth less because of the longer time you would have to wait for your income.

Another drawback to this measure is that it does not take the true cash flow of the project into account.

## Some more advanced considerations

This section has outlined the tools necessary to evaluate the financial worth of *any* project in *any* organisation. We can calculate:

**a)** payback – length of time to recover original investment

   and, using Discounted Cash Flow techniques,

**b)** the NPV (Net Present Value) of a project at the organisation's discount rate, and

**c)** the IRR (Internal Rate of Return) of a given project.

Let's now explore the uses of these techniques, which fall into broadly two categories:

- the go/no-go decision
- comparison of projects.

### Go/no-go decisions

These are simple decisions of whether to proceed with a given project or not. The project returns are calculated, and these are compared to a benchmark or hurdle rate. Projects which beat the hurdle rate would normally proceed, those which do not would normally be dismissed. I say normally here because of the potential impact of strategic, non-financial factors on the decision making.

**Examples**

Examples of hurdles are:

**a)** Payback – 4 years – projects are only undertaken if they payback in four years or earlier.

**b)** IRR of 20 per cent or higher – projects have to generate a return of 20 per cent or more to be undertaken.

- Do you know the hurdle rates used by your organisation?
- How are they set?
- How often are they revised? (See WACC on page 134.)

## Project comparison

Again, once we have analysed the project returns, etc. we can use these measures to compare projects. This is necessary where we have to choose between two options, for instance two depot locations or fit-out levels, or between two products, only one of which can be launched.

We could suppose that the project with the quickest payback, or the highest IRR must be the better project, but would this be correct?

### Example

Simplifying finance is fun, but we have to be a little careful comparing projects, so let's use an example.

|  | Project A | Project B |
|---|---|---|
| Year 0 | £(1,000,000) | £(250,000) |
| Year 1 | 300,000 | 150,000 |
| Year 2 | 300,000 | 100,000 |
| Year 3 | 300,000 | 100,000 |
| Year 4 | 500,000 | 50,000 |
| Year 5 | 500,000 | 0 |
|  |  |  |
| Payback | 3+ years | 2 years |
| IRR | 23% | 26.5% |

So which project should be pursued?

Project B is the smaller, quick payback project, that ceases to generate a return after four years. Project A, however, earns substantially higher returns in the fourth and fifth years.

Comparing them to a hurdle rate of, say, 15 per cent, both would be pursued, but these are mutually exclusive projects. Before we pick project B on the grounds of a higher return or quicker payback, let's look at the NPVs.

|              |          | Project A       | Project B      |
| ------------ | -------- | --------------- | -------------- |
| Year 0       |          | £(1,000,000)    | £(250,000)     |
| Year 1       |          | 300,000         | 150,000        |
| Year 2       |          | 300,000         | 100,000        |
| Year 3       |          | 300,000         | 100,000        |
| Year 4       |          | 500,000         | 50,000         |
| Year 5       |          | 500,000         | 0              |
| Payback      |          | 3+ years        | 2 years        |
| IRR          |          | 23%             | 26.5%          |
| NPV          | at 15%   | £219,430        | £50,390        |

Project A has a substantially higher Net Present Value, and should be chosen above project B.

I hear cries of protest from my audience. How can it be that I've chosen a project with an IRR of 23 per cent above one with an IRR of 26.5 per cent? Are these accountants completely mad? Well yes actually, but let's run through a slightly different logic path. Let us assume that we 'choose' project B with its IRR at 26.5 per cent.

Now let's calculate the effect of choosing project A *instead* of project B, as follows:

|              | Project A       | Project B      | A versus B     |
| ------------ | --------------- | -------------- | -------------- |
| Year 0       | £(1,000,000)    | £(250,000)     | £(750,000)     |
| Year 1       | 300,000         | 150,000        | 150,000        |
| Year 2       | 300,000         | 100,000        | 200,000        |
| Year 3       | 300,000         | 100,000        | 200,000        |
| Year 4       | 500,000         | 50,000         | 450,000        |
| Year 5       | 500,000         | 0              | 450,000        |
| Payback      | 3+ years        | 2 years        | 4+ years       |
| IRR          | 23%             | 26.5%          | 22.3%          |
| NPV at 15%   | £219,430        | £50,390        | £169,040       |

So having 'selected' project B, the effect of choosing project A instead of project B has an IRR of 22.3 per cent, and an NPV of £169,040. Only the payback period is poor at 4+ years.

> The point of this example is to point towards the danger of using IRR alone as a measure when comparing mutually exclusive projects. In these instances, use NPV to paint the full picture.

As the management of the company, you may choose project B, the smaller investment, if there are problems with funding, or a desire to maximise profits in the short rather than longer term.

Armed with the full portfolio of these tools, these decisions can be made in a rigorous and logical fashion.

# WACC – the Weighted Average Cost of Capital

Having discussed hurdle rates for projects to support go/no-go decisions, we will need to establish what the most appropriate rate is for the organisation, and the answer of course is that 'it depends'.

Organisations need to understand their own cost of borrowing capital before they establish hurdle rates for projects. The most simplistic way of establishing the cost of borrowing is by looking at the marginal cost of borrowing: the cost of borrowing the next pound. If the bank facility is at (say) LIBOR plus 1 point, then this is the cost of borrowing.

But the organisation cannot borrow indefinitely at this rate, and this borrowing is only available due to the existence of shareholders' funds which form the 'risk-capital' of the business.

The most appropriate rate to use, therefore, is the average of the cost of equity and the cost of debt. This is known as the Weighted Average Cost of Capital, or WACC.

## Example

For an organisation funded 60/40 debt to equity, this is calculated as follows:

| | | |
|---|---|---|
| Debt financing at 10% p.a. | 60% | 6% |
| Equity financing at 20% p.a. | 40% | 8% |
| Total/Average | 100% | 14% |

For this organisation then, funded 60/40 debt to equity, the Weighted Average Cost of Capital is 14 per cent.

## Example

Suppose that your company has an excellent credit rating, and you know that you can borrow 95 per cent of the cost of an investment project. Calculating the WACC at the same rates as before:

Debt financing at 10% p.a.    ✕    95% = 9.5%

Equity financing at 20% p.a.   ✕    5% = 1.0%

WACC = 9.5 + 1.0 = 10.5%

---

This figure is gratifyingly low, but it is erroneous because overall your company is only financed 60 per cent by debt. Thus, if you borrow 95 per cent of the cost of the project, you will in part be borrowing against the value of the existing assets. In addition, by increasing the gearing of the project you are increasing its risk, so the shareholders will expect a commensurately higher rate of return. Thus, when you apply WACC to projects, make sure that they resemble the whole company in terms of their debt to equity ratio and general risk. The WACC can be used as a hurdle rate but two other issues often prevail:

■ The desire for a 'buffer' or contingency to allow for unquantifiable risk could lead senior management to add a couple of points to the hurdle rate

■ In many organisations, there are more potential projects than the organisation can afford to finance at any one time. This problem is known as capital rationing. The easiest way to ease the pressure on investment projects in such an organisation is to increase the hurdle rate, to a level at which the amount of project finance being approved matches the financing available. This is particularly the case in small high growth companies.

> Obtain the hurdle rate for your organisation and understand the logic behind the level. Is your company capital rationed?
> Check the section on balance sheet ratios too.

## Capital rationing

**Example**

Suppose your company has a capital ration of £200 million and it can invest in Government bonds at 10 per cent. It is considering the following four projects:

| Project | Cash flow | | | | NPV (10%) benefit/cost ratio |
|---------|-----------|--|--|--|------------------------------|
| | | Year | | | |
| | | 1 | 2 | 3 | |
| 1 | −200 | 600 | 300 | 420 | 3.1 |
| 2 | −100 | 100 | 400 | 320 | 4.2 |
| 3 | −100 | 100 | 300 | 240 | 3.4 |

You can either invest in project 1 or in both projects 2 and 3. The two latter projects have a combined NPV higher than that of project 1, but if you were choosing your projects solely by the size of their individual NPVs you would choose project 1. By calculating the benefit/cost ratios, you see that projects 2 and 3 are also more profitable than project 1.

Very large companies arguably have no real capital ration; they are able to obtain very large sums if they wish. Nevertheless, they may use capital rationing as a way of keeping control on their divisions. By setting an amount of capital available to a division, the head office puts the burden of deciding which projects are the most rewarding on the division itself, which encourages it to pick its projects carefully.

If a company really does have severe capital constraints it may be forced to pass up projects with attractive NPVs.

# Cashflows in perpetuity

Often a project will give rise to benefits which continue indefinitely into the future: the development of an all-new product line, for instance, or an ongoing reduction in cost levels given a new piece of machinery.

In order to calculate the value of these flows into infinity, all you have to do is add up all the amounts as follows.

## Example

To take an example using a discount rate of 20 per cent, the value is as follows:

$$PV = \frac{1}{1.2} + \frac{1}{1.2^2} + \frac{1}{1.2^2} + \frac{1}{1.2^4}$$

etc. into infinity.

Fortunately some maths whiz has proved that this can be abbreviated to

$$PV = \frac{1}{0.2}$$

This means that with a cost of capital at 20 per cent, £100 from now to infinity is worth £100/0.2 or £500.

## Example

Now, you're in a meeting discussing a project with an approximate investment of £1 million, for a machine with a useful life of ten years. The hurdle rate in your organisation is 20 per cent. Benefits are straight line, i.e. the same in each year. They often are assumed to be even if they're not.

So the PV of the benefits for ten years is as follows:

Value to inifinity *minus* Value to infinity discounted ten years

$$\text{or } PV = \text{Annual benefits} \quad \times \quad \left( \frac{1}{0.2} \left( 1 - \frac{1}{1.2^{10}} \right) \right)$$

$$\text{or } 5(1 - 0.16)$$

or about 4.2 times the annual benefits.

So going into the meeting you know that the £1 million investment must make annual savings of about £1 million/4.2 or about £240,000 to make the hurdle rate. Sure, this is only a rough guide, I've ignored tax and things, but you have a ready reckoner which can be applied.

Those investment models you obtained from finance. Compare the results to the ready reckoner above. Develop a 'feel' for how they vary. For similar investments, you should be able to develop a good idea for the savings or additional profits required to justify any expenditure, which will prove useful as a rough guide in the future. Developing this sort of gut feel is not magic: it's simply a matter of understanding these sorts of relationships, and how they work in your business area.

# CHAPTER EIGHT

# Organisational control

- Introduction
- Internal control
- Fraud – a general profile
- Organisational control – whose responsibility?

## Introduction

This chapter will look at the ways in which an organisation is controlled. Control of an organisation is in practice an ongoing and continuous process. As managers you are engaged in the control of your parts of the organisation on a daily basis. Each time you authorise an action or activity you are either

- pursuing a goal on behalf of the organisation which is within your own authority or which has been agreed as part of the organisation's larger plan, or
- taking action to correct a deviation from the agreed plan.

Control, as can be seen from Figure 8.1, is the continuous monitoring of results against targets and the correction of deviation from those targets. This control action is known as the **feedback loop**. Action to correct or reverse a trend is known as **negative feedback,** while action to reinforce a trend is described as **positive feedback**.

Control in the manner of this cycle is done at all levels. The foreman will control his own area in this manner, monitoring output against his own daily targets, while the

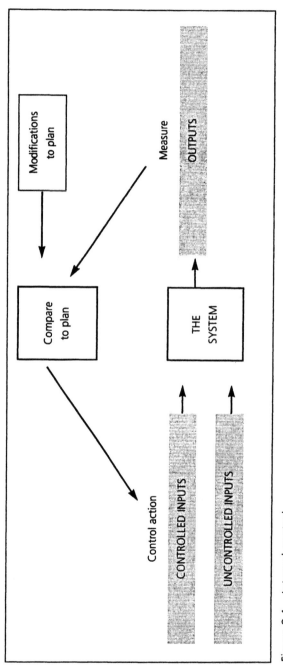

Figure 8.1    Internal control

plant manager will monitor the output of the entire factory against her own objectives. This type of feedback is known as higher level or double loop feedback.

Output measures can be specific measures of physical output such as units of production, or financial results such as cost or profit measures.

Systems can be described as 'open' or 'closed'. An open system is one which is open to the environment or outside world. In practice the vast majority of systems are open but the degree of openness varies. Typically the lower the level of feedback loop in the organisation the less open the system is to external influences.

The chairman of the organisation will be 'controlling' a system in which many factors are completely beyond his or her control; these are the uncontrolled inputs of the diagram. These might include changes in market environment, exchange rates, and changes in the legislative environment (*see also 'Strategic risk' in Chapter 12*). His or her potential actions are confined to that which he or she can control.

Control is effected against a plan, which may be modified at any time to reflect the uncontrolled environmental inputs. If raw material prices change substantially, the plan would be updated to ensure that results were monitored properly against latest available targets.

Feedback control as used in all organisations to some extent is an essential means of control. This can be combined with the more forward looking feed-forward control technique.

Feed-forward control is the continual projection forward of key targets updated to latest available information to anticipate potential problems before they occur. An example here might be the continual updating of cash planning to monitor the projected cash balances expected in the next periods. These would be compared with the financing facilities available to anticipate potential liquidity problems.

The production and use of management accounts forecasting performance for the balance of the year is an example of feed-forward control with which you may be familiar (*see also Chapter 4*).

# Internal control

Feedback and feed-forward methods are essential for maintaining control of the performance of the organisation as it continues to operate. We must also consider the potential effects of malpractice by employees or management. This is the potential for damage to the organisation when an employee takes an action that is not in line with the organisation's goals. Such actions might be stupid, ignorant or dishonest. It is not enough in these instances to use feedback controls to identify that cash is substantially below plan only to discover that the reason is that the accounts clerk has the cash in a suitcase and is on the way to Brazil.

Other types of fraud might include over-claiming of expenses, which would be difficult to spot if allowed to occur because of the relatively small amounts lost over a prolonged timescale.

To protect themselves against such actions all organisations larger than one-man band must adopt internal control procedures to prevent such actions from happening at all, rather than attempting to correct them after the event. You will take most of these procedures for granted; they include:

- **Expense claims** – a form is completed by the employee who signs to confirm that all of the claim represents expenses properly incurred whilst pursuing company business. The claim is then reviewed by the next management level as a check before being processed. This is a simple example of the most basic and common form of internal control: double signatory.

- **Purchasing** – an employee wishing to procure an item on behalf of the company must complete a requisition form explaining the requirement together with other details. This is normally subject to a second signature by the employee's manager before being sent to the purchasing department. Purchasing are responsible for ensuring that the correct form of procurement is adhered to. This will normally require at least two or three quotes from competing suppliers before the business is placed. This is to avoid the possibility of collusion between an employee and an outside company. Without procurement controls an employee could favour one outside supplier who could charge the company a premium for the goods or services and pass some of this back to the employee.

Other elements of an internal control system will include:

- **Authority limits** – the authority of a manager should be established with a monetary limit. The board may, for instance, delegate the authority to purchase items of up to £250,000 to two directors, who in turn may delegate to a set of managers the authority to make purchases of up to £100,000. Secretaries will often have authority to purchase stationery items up to £100 in value from designated suppliers.

- **Cash limits** – autonomous areas of the company may operate their own banking facilities. These would have pre-set cash limits on them to prevent cheques over a certain size from leaving the account and the ability of central staffs to 'sweep' any balances over a pre-set limit into the main accounts.

These authority limits will typically be maintained by the department responsible for maintaining internal control, normally the finance department. They will issue rules and guidelines including the procedures for claiming expenses and making purchases and the limits for each employee or management level.

A final element of internal control, often overlooked, is on a more strategic level. Often the more difficult type of fraud or wrongdoing to spot is that which occurs over a prolonged period. The surest way to prevent this is to ensure a healthy rotation of those personnel who are responsible for areas where there is a risk of loss. In your company how long has the financial controller been *in situ*? Does he or she take holidays? Has he or she turned down a job move recently? Does he or she drive a Porsche? OK, the majority of such people will be as honest as ... but why take the risk?

> As a manager you are a part of your company's internal control system. Think back to the last expenses claim you signed for one of your employees.
>
> - Did it include a newspaper? Should it have?
> - What tips did it include?
> - If the employee went abroad what exchange rate did he or she use?
> - What class of travel did he or she use?
>
> Do you have a copy of your company's rules on these items?

The selection of such items as tips and newspapers may seem trivial but some very large companies have some very strict rules on these items. Some don't allow the reclaiming on expenses of publications, including newspapers, believing that the employee should pay for such items as he or she normally would if he or she were working from the office.

Since in some large organisations the penalty for the first offence of the wrong completion or approval of expense claims can be dismissal, the message is simple: ignore 'custom and practice' – check the rules and stick to them. If the rules need changing then work to change them, but don't ignore them.

# Fraud – a general profile

In a survey of a sample of *The Times* Top 1000 companies in 1994 ('Fraud – the Unmanaged Risk') drawn up by Ernst & Young, it was reported that on half of all occasions the main fraudster was an employee of the company, and in nearly three-quarters of cases there was employee collusion. This is one of the main reasons why strict internal controls are so important, despite the hostility that many employees have towards them.

Apart from the waste of management time, the discovery and investigation of a fraud adversely affects company culture and trust between staff; much more so, it is argued, than the burden of internal controls.

Most fraud is preventable; in some industries, the opportunity for fraud is very great, and can have very damaging effects on profits. Insurance and retailing are two of the worst affected, insurance because of the large sums passing through a small number of individuals' control, and retailing because of the large number of sales staff handling cash in proximity to a profusion of small value items. By contrast, the paper and printing industries suffer very little fraud since there are few opportunities to steal.

As a manager, it is worthwhile developing some understanding of how temptation arises, what assets are most vulnerable, and what kind of controls are effective. Let's first consider two typical fraud cases, one by a low level employee and another by a senior manager. While both are petty in nature, they both cost their companies substantial sums because they went undetected for many years.

## Example: A factory floor fraud

In routine checks a dairy discovered that van-loads of goods were being stolen on a regular basis, and following an investigation, found the employee responsible. To the company's consternation, he confessed to further thefts involving the loss of hundreds of pounds worth of goods per week from the factory floor which had been going on for over ten years. The source of the problem was that each member of staff was allowed one free carton of milk a day. The thief had begun his career relatively innocently, taking an extra carton of milk home to his family each day. He explained that there were no checks, and that soon the practice had become widespread amongst his workmates, with many individuals taking home a generous variety of dairy products each evening.

He had always told his wife that the goods were bought at a discount from his employer, and when she asked him to provide more goods 'at cost' to her friends he couldn't bring himself to admit that he was stealing them. Instead, he began to supply his friends and neighbours in increasing quantities, enjoying his new-found status as a person of importance. As demand grew, he resorted to stealing van-loads of goods, at which point even this company's lamentable stock control system showed up the problem.

---

Clearly, the company's internal controls were very poor indeed; simple supervision of the free milk system would have prevented the theft going as far as it did, but the story illustrates another point – that the thief had relatively innocent motives at first, and it was only because the system was lax that the thefts began. Managers sometimes make the mistake of thinking that as long as none of their staff are obviously criminal there will be no problems, but temptation can get the better of most people, so internal controls are largely about reducing the opportunities for wrongdoing.

## Example: A management fraud

This principle of using internal controls should apply to all employees of a company, including senior managers.

The manager of a branch of a large construction company was discovered to be using company materials in the building of his own house. Further investigation revealed that, in company with the branch's buyer and bookkeeper, he had not only stolen large quantities of building materials over the years, but had also diverted company labour to his own extra-curricular building projects and persuaded suppliers to collude with him in invoicing his own company for materials, plant and labour which he used or sold elsewhere. As the senior manager in the branch, the thief was able to construct locked cabins within the branch's warehouses where many of the stolen goods were kept. Despite regular audits and stock checks, this was not discovered until a local gossip reported the rumour to the management.

---

The abuse of positions of authority is more common than you may think, and demonstrates the need for another principle in internal control systems: 'divide and rule'. Ideally no individual within a company should have control over the whole process of any transaction, and people working closely together should not jointly have such control. (*In Appendix A on page 257 there is a detailed checklist of the main financial controls a company should have.*)

## Organisational control – whose responsibility?

In most organisations, as explained above, the responsibility for maintaining internal control rests with the finance department.

In law, though, the responsibility sits squarely with the directors of the company. It is their responsibility to ensure that the affairs of the company are managed in a proper and responsible manner.

## Responsibilities of directors

Directors have many responsibilities under law encompassing the good conduct of the operations of the company. This section will briefly look at the main responsibilities of directors.

> If you are a director of a company and are not aware of your legal position, you are strongly advised to take legal advice. At the very least obtain a copy of the Coopers & Lybrand book Being a Director published by Gee. This is an excellent summary of the rights and responsibilities which go with the appointment to a company directorship.

Incidentally, if you have the title of director, e.g. Regional Director of Sales, but are told not to worry because you're not actually on the board, you still need to take advice as the title may mean that you are considered to be a director by the law.

Essentially as a director you are responsible to your company, which in essence means the shareholders. These duties can be summarised as follows:

- **Fiduciary duty** – the requirement to act in the bona-fide interest of the company. This includes avoiding personal interest and conflict of interest. Should a director find him or herself in a conflict of interest situation the conflict must be declared to the board.

- **Duty of care** – this is the duty to exercise due care and reasonable skill in the position of director. It should be noted that due care will be considered on an individual basis. Thus a qualified accountant who is a director will be expected to demonstrate these skills in his or her actions. If he or she worked in, say, the biotech field he or she would not be expected to show technical knowledge of the field.

- **Authority** – directors must act within their authority as defined in the company's memorandum and articles.

## Financial responsibilities

Companies must comply with various requirements; these include the maintenance of accounting records, the preparation of annual accounts and other reports and their delivery to Companies House, and the disclosure of accounts to shareholders at the necessary meetings. The directors also have a responsibility to ensure that they have the necessary information to discharge their duty to manage the company's business.

Although in practice most companies delegate this task to the Finance Director, it is important to note that the responsibility remains with the directors, and each is potentially liable for any breach of the law in this area.

There is a further issue which relates to a company which experiences difficulty in trading, i.e. one that is at risk of ceasing to be able to pay its bills as they fall due. A company which is at risk and continues to trade may be guilty of wrongful or fraudulent trading. In a liquidation where the assets of the company are not sufficient to pay all of the creditors, and wrongful trading has taken place, the directors may be ordered personally to contribute to the company's assets. Where fraudulent trading has occurred there may also be criminal penalties.

## The role of Non-executive Directors (NEDS)

One of the key recommendations of the Cadbury Report was that NEDs should play an increasing role in corporate governance. The main purpose of this is to raise the standards of companies' accountability to their stakeholders, who include shareholders, employees and the public at large. Since NEDs are, by definition, outside directors who are not employed full-time by the company, they represent an independent force that can serve to ensure that companies are actually accountable.

In the future, you can expect to see a continued increase in the number of NEDs leading, or participating in, teams and committees responsible for monitoring internal controls, remuneration, performance and internal audits. The Cadbury Report, and corporate governance more generally, is discussed in more detail in Chapter 2.

## Management performance audits

As we have seen, there is no point in having systems if you don't check that they are working properly. This applies whether you are working in a listed company or in a non-profit organisation. The best way to conduct these checks is by having a management audit – also known as a performance audit or a value for money audit – which is designed to help managers do their work better by identifying problem areas and how they can be improved.

Although management audits can take many forms, most will have the following features:

■ A detailed analysis of the company's performance indicators, including financial statistics, and a comparison with the results of previous periods and the performance of competitors. This analysis should highlight areas which need attention.

■ A review of the systems used to set targets, implement company policies and monitor performance. The purpose of this is to make these systems operate as efficiently as possible.

■ A detailed exploration of the effectiveness of internal controls.

- An overall assessment of efficiency and effectiveness, with particular emphasis on questioning why systems and services are organised in the way that they are, whether alternatives have been investigated and how their performance is measured.

- A report of the results.

Management audits can be carried out by internal committees, often headed by a NED, management consultants or external auditors.

## Internal audits

As was mentioned in Chapter 2, the Cadbury Report recommends that companies use Internal Audit Departments (IADs), controlled by an audit committee with non-executive directors among its members, to monitor the control systems. About 60 per cent of large companies have an IAD, but their size varies greatly. A further 20 per cent intend to establish one shortly. Some companies outsource some part of their internal audit function, in particular information technology systems where a company lacks in-house expertise. An alternative is partnering, which is where a department works together with an external supplier who can provide additional skills and resources to supplement the in-house resource. Some companies see this as a more flexible arrangement than outsourcing.

*(For a detailed list of the types of financial controls used by companies, see Appendix A.)*

# CHAPTER NINE

# Corporate taxation

- Tax – a strategy

- The main taxes on companies

- Capital allowances

- The taxation of multinationals

- Double taxation treaties

- Transfer pricing

- Using offshore centres and tax havens

- Holding companies in Holland

- Company structure

- Summary

*'But in this world nothing can be said to be certain,
except death and taxes.'*

This chapter will consider the basic workings of corporate taxation. Corporate bodies are taxed on their income after deductions in fundamentally the same way as individuals. You are doubtless all too familiar with the dreaded tax return which you must complete annually. Corporate taxation too works on the basis of completing a return to establish liability for tax. With the current move the Inland Revenue is making towards self-assessment, personal taxation becomes more like corporate taxation.

A company is responsible for declaring to the Inland Revenue (IR) the amount of taxable profit made in the year, and for paying that amount of tax over to the revenue within the statutory deadline.

**Advance Corporation Tax (ACT)** is that corporation tax paid over on payment of a dividend which is then reclaimed from the main corporation tax bill.

**Value Added Tax (VAT)** is the tax paid on inputs, whether goods or services, and charged to customers on behalf of the exchequer on the outputs of the company.

# Tax – a strategy

To a business, tax should be considered to be a cost, much like any other. As such it can be managed. Good management of this cost item will reduce the cost to the business, while poor management will lead to the burden of additional taxes.

Equally, in the same way that different businesses have differing attitudes to personnel cost, so different businesses will have different attitudes to the management of the tax charge. Within the same industry, one business may be renowned for treating staff well with good salaries and conditions, while another may put up with high turnover and rely on low wages and tight centralised operational control to achieve the same aims.

So different businesses will have differing attitudes to the management of the tax charge. The largest companies will employ high quality legal and tax advisors to ensure that their very substantial tax charge is managed by full time professionals. Medium sized companies should spend time and external resources to ensure that the basic structure of the organisation is right and that there is a tax review of the most important decisions before they are made. Smaller companies, particularly those with only domestic (UK based) business have less scope for tax planning, but will still benefit from professional external tax advice probably twice yearly.

## The difference between tax avoidance and tax evasion

**Tax avoidance** is the legitimate structuring of a business, transaction or activity in such a way that tax is minimised within the rules of the tax regime(s) in which the company or person is operating. The use of a Dutch holding company (*see page 176*) is an excellent example of this practice.

**Tax evasion** is cheating. It is the manipulation of records or events, including non-disclosure, in order to evade tax charges. One of the most common of these is the 'cash' transaction which evades VAT. Penalties, particularly for evasion of VAT, are severe and include imprisonment.

The complexity of tax legislation, combined with the fact that much of it is redrafted for the annual spring budget, means that there are often grey areas and loopholes which can spring up. Companies will have their own views on the exploitation of these areas, which are beyond the scope of this book.

The right of companies and individuals to avoid (not evade) tax is well-established; in a famous tax case of 1929, Lord Clyde said that a person does nothing wrong by arranging his or her affairs to take advantage of the rules, so long as they are not broken.

## The Ramsay doctrine

The Ramsay doctrine is a set of principles which the courts use when dealing with tax avoidance cases. It sets out the rule that when a person or company makes arrangements to reduce tax, no artificial steps can be taken. 'Artificial steps' don't mean fraudulent steps – which would be tax evasion – but that the primary motive overall is to avoid tax. Companies can avoid falling foul of the doctrine if they arrange the steps so that either they are not under the company's control the whole time, or so that a third party receives partial benefit from them during part of the sequence. It is these principles that tax advisers apply when designing complicated tax plans for a company.

Within the realms of avoidance there are different degrees of 'playing the game'. Tax, after all, is a complicated field, full of minor revisions and fundamental annual updates (the budget) and lots of highly paid experts. There is a significant difference between making a commercial decision based on a number of factors, one of which is taxation, and the deliberate searching out and use of tax loopholes.

### Example

As an example, a multinational company might establish a manufacturing facility as the branch office of a Bermudan registered company. This could well meet all the legal requirements including demonstrating that the company is actually managed in Bermuda. The multinational must, however, accept that there is an on-cost in maintaining this structure, in managing the additional administration. The saving in ongoing taxation must yield a good return on the additional fixed cost, and can be evaluated in the same way as any other project.

The searching out of loopholes is another matter. Given the drafting process of the legislation there sometimes arise opportunities where tax can be legally avoided by exploiting some specific wording in the acts. In these instances the management of the company must weigh up the benefits of pursuing the loophole against the unquantifiable down-side of making the tax man livid.

For the non-financial manager then, tax can be left to the experts, in-house in the larger company, and bought in for the medium and smaller companies. The message of this chapter, though, is that when planning a large new project you should ensure that tax advice is taken early in the process, as seemingly small details can lead to significant differences in future tax liabilities.

# The main taxes on companies

Let's look at the different taxes that a company must face.

## Value Added Tax

VAT is the tax paid on inputs, whether goods or services, bought into the company, and charged on goods or services as invoiced to customers on behalf of the exchequer.

 **Example**

A simple example is probably the easiest way of describing the process. Let us assume that in a given quarter a company has the following transactions.

The amounts are first shown excluding VAT.

**Amounts**

| | excluding VAT |
|---|---|
| Sales (outputs) | £100,000 |
| Purchases (inputs) | |
| – Materials | £60,000 |
| – Labour | 25,000 |
| Total inputs | £85,000 |
| Gross profit | £15,000 |

The invoice from the company for the sales will be

| | |
|---|---|
| Goods supplied | £100,000 |
| plus VAT at 17.5% | 17,500 |
| Total payable | £117,500 |

The company will therefore collect from the purchaser £117,500 for the sales of £100,000 above. Equally the materials purchased would have come from the supplier as follows:

| | |
|---|---|
| Materials supplied | £60,000 |
| plus VAT at 17.5% | 10,500 |
| Total now due | £70,500 |

Let's look at the profit schedule again:

| | Amounts excluding VAT | VAT | Amounts including VAT |
|---|---|---|---|
| Sales (outputs) | £100,000 | £17,500 | £117,500 |
| Purchases (inputs) | | | |
| – Materials | £(60,000) | £(10,500) | £(70,500) |
| – Labour | (25,000) | | (25,000) |
| Total inputs | £(85,000) | £(10,500) | £(95,500) |
| Gross profit | £15,000 | £7,000 | £22,000 |
| Due to Customs and Excise | | | £(7,000) |
| Profit after VAT settlement | | | £15,000 |

We can see that the company has charged VAT on its outputs of £17,500, which it receives from its customer. Equally it has paid VAT of £10,500 on its inputs.

At the end of the VAT accounting session, normally quarterly, the net amounts collected in VAT on behalf of the revenue must be declared and paid over. In this case the net collection was the difference between the £17,500 collected and the £10,500 paid, or £7000. The company is no worse off than if the transaction had been done excluding VAT – the exchequer collects the amount of VAT on the difference between outputs and inputs – simply put the value added by the company. The eventual VAT burden, therefore, is borne by the final consumer of the goods.

There are various oddities in terms of VAT registration: exempt firms do not have to charge VAT on services, these include banks and companies that are not registered for VAT. Firms with a turnover under the threshold (currently £46,000) may choose whether or not to register.

## Example

A VAT avoidance case recently reported concerned a hairdressing salon. Normally a salon would employ hairdressers and charge the customers. The salon would have a turnover in excess of the £46,000 limit, have to register for VAT and charge VAT to its customers. The salon in question structured itself as a hairdressing *facility* only. Self-employed hairdressers each paid the salon owner for the usage of a chair. Since each hairdresser was below the VAT threshold none of them was required to register for VAT.

## *VAT and the European Union*

The different member states of the EU apply different VAT rates and have different rules, but there are moves towards simplifying procedures for companies trading across several member states. A 1995 survey carried out by KPMG tax advisers, 'VAT and the Single Market', reported that, overall, companies found that the increased administrative burden of dealing with VAT in more than one country was an inconvenience, rather than a discouragement from doing business.

## Example

Companies involved in 'sales chains' felt that the rules were unfair. Sales chains are where, say, there are four different companies, call them Companies A, B, C and D, in four different countries who are trading with each other.

As shown in Figure 9.1, Company A sells to Company B, which in turn sells to Company C, which in turn sells to Company D, but the goods are sent direct from Company A to Company D. A surprisingly large amount of trade is done in this way – about half of large companies in the survey said they did this. The trouble is that some of the companies in a sales chain find that they have to register for VAT in more than one country, which increases the administrative burden and can affect cash flow

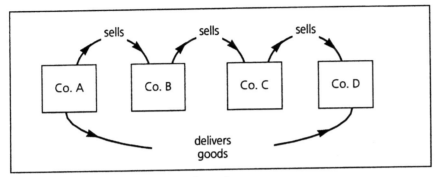

Figure 9.1    VAT and movement of goods

adversely. Since 1992, there has been a simplification of the rules which usually allows Company B to avoid registering for VAT in Company A and C's respective countries; only one company in a chain can avoid multiple VAT registration, however long the chain.

---

This means that most large companies find that they have to register for VAT not only in the UK, but in other EU countries as well, notably France and Germany.

The rules put companies involved in 'distance selling' at a disadvantage. If an EU company sells products to customers in another EU country it must charge local VAT and register in that country. Companies based outside the EU are not required to charge local VAT, and can thus keep their prices lower.

## Corporation tax

Corporation tax (CT) is now administered under the 'pay and file' system, so called because the tax payment to the revenue is now due *before* the actual tax return is due. The timing is as follows:

- 9 months after the company's financial year is closed the company must pay to the revenue its estimated liability for CT

- 12 months after the company's financial year the company must submit its corporation tax return.

Once the final assessment of taxes due is agreed with the Revenue any underpaid taxes are due together with interest from the original due date. Amounts overpaid are returned with interest. There are also penalties for late filing and late payment; these become severe if the tax or return is substantially overdue. Neither fines nor penalty interest are allowable as an expense for CT.

## Calculating corporation tax

The amount of corporation tax disclosed in the company's profit and loss account is not often the tax rate times the profits before tax. The reason for this is that the taxable profits are not the same as the profits declared in the profit and loss account. There are two different 'profits', primarily because there are a number of adjustments which are made.

Let's discuss the major adjustments:

- **Provisions** – general provisions against potential future losses are *not* normally allowable for tax. Although specific accruals for known future expenses are normally allowable against profit the IR generally work on a cash basis. Unlike accounting prudence where a loss is recognised when reasonably foreseeable (*see Chapter 3*) the IR will only give tax relief against a loss when it has actually been made

- **Depreciation** – the accounting convention of depreciating assets and charging this against the profit and loss account is not recognised by the IR. Instead 'capital allowances' are claimable against such new fixed assets. The timing of the claiming of these capital allowances can be varied to suit tax planning.

- **Accounting treatment** – an item that might be allowable as an expense for tax purposes could be treated as an asset in the published accounts. An example could be building related, but note that the tax rules here are complex.

- **Non-allowable expenses** – a number of expenses may have hit profits but not be allowable for tax – these would certainly include some entertainment expenses.

We have just looked at the reasons for differences in a UK context; things become really tricky when we look at overseas tax (*see later in this chapter*).

# Advance corporation tax

As well as the corporation tax above, we must address the issue of ACT, or Advance Corporation Tax, which becomes payable when a dividend is paid.

> Any dividend paid out incurs a charge of ACT which is an advance payment on the total corporation tax payable.

## Example

A company which pays a dividend of £800,000 must also pay ACT of £200,000. The shareholder receives his or her dividend with a corresponding tax credit equal to the ACT which has been paid. This simply means that the payment of a dividend by a UK company can accelerate the payment of taxes due.

The difficulty with ACT arises in a company with significant foreign income. Such a company could find that it is required to pay more ACT than is due under mainstream corporation tax (MCT). An example will illustrate the point.

## Example

|  | Income before taxation | Taxation charge | Income after taxation |
|---|---|---|---|
| UK profits | £100,000 | £(33,000) | £67,000 |
| Foreign profits | 300,000 | (99,000) | 201,000 |
| Total profits | £400,000 | (132,000) | £268,000 |

All well and good, the tax payable in the UK will be as follows:

| Profits earned | £400,000 |
|---|---|
| Tax due at 33% | (132,000) |
| *less* tax already paid* | 99,000 |
| UK Corporation tax payable | £(33,000) |

This relief for foreign taxes paid is normally contained in the various double taxation treaties signed by most industrialised countries.

---

* The foreign tax relief will be capped at the UK tax rate of 33 per cent; thus if foreign taxes had actually been paid at 40 per cent or £120,000, relief would have been capped at 33 per cent or £99,000.

The problem comes when a dividend is declared. Let us assume that a dividend is declared of £200,000. ACT will be payable at 25 per cent of the net dividend or £50,000. This is in excess of the mainstream corporation tax which would be payable of only £33,000 leading to excess ACT of £17,000.

Excess ACT is non-refundable and can only be carried forward (or carried back in some cases) until subsequently offset against MCT.

## Capital allowances

The principal variance between the profits declared in the annual accounts and those used for calculating the tax charge is that of the use of capital allowances instead of depreciation.

> When calculating accounted profits, the amount by which fixed assets are 'used up' is reflected in the depreciation charge. Within reasonable limits, companies are free to adopt depreciation policies which vary depending on the industry and the type of asset being depreciated.

For taxation purposes there is no recognition of depreciation. Instead, an allowance is available based on the original cost of the asset. This is the **writing down allowance**, WDA, normally referred to as the **capital allowance**.

The amount of WDAs which can be claimed can be quite variable, and is set in the annual budget. In the 1970s WDAs were increased to up to 100 per cent in the first year to encourage investment by companies.

Currently the WDA is at 25 per cent, on a declining balance basis. Thus an asset purchased for £100,000 would be allowed a writing down allowance of £25,000 in year one, £18,750 in year 2, etc. On disposal, the loss or gain for taxation is measured versus the original cost of the asset less the WDAs allowed on the asset.

## The taxation of multinationals

Companies with subsidiaries in several countries are all technically called multinationals, even if they are relatively small businesses. Multinationals have special problems with taxation because they must deal with more than one tax regime.

In recent years, the revenue authorities in different countries have become increasingly active in attempting to maximise the tax bills of companies operating within their countries, and since no two tax regimes are the same, multinationals often find themselves caught between the conflicting demands of several different tax authorities. This state of affairs has been described as a 'global tax war', where countries are competing to tax the revenues generated by global businesses.

Although the details of the tax negotiations and plans are best left to your finance or specialist tax department, if you work for a multinational you may be affected by them, so it is worthwhile getting a grasp of what the basic problems are.

### Example

Here are a few examples of activities which could be affected by international tax rules:

- Opening an office in a foreign country.

- Starting a joint venture with a foreign company.

- Any costing you do for projects involving receiving or providing goods and services between sister companies (companies in your group) in different countries. For instance if you set the price for a product at a certain level based on the price a sister company will be charging you for components, you may find that the component cost will change because a tax authority decides that the component price is too low.

# Double taxation treaties

A double taxation treaty is an agreement between two states designed to mitigate the effects of tax on people and companies that do business in both countries. If two countries do not have a treaty, income arising in one country may be taxed there under a withholding tax rule (which means that profits are taxed before they leave the country), and then taxed again when it arrives in another country.

Although there is a model international agreement, there is great variation in the details of different treaties. This is because strong trading countries, such as the USA, Germany and the UK, have superior bargaining power and are generally able to force agreements which are favourable to them. Treaties may exempt withholding tax entirely from income going abroad, or they may mitigate it.

In general, no country will collect another country's taxes or enforce another country's tax regulations. For well-established companies that lack the flexibility to switch jurisdictions quickly, international tax planning is done to make the best use of double taxation treaties rather than to avoid them; it is, after all, better to have high profits that are taxed tolerably than to have low profits that are not taxed at all.

## Treaty shopping

For over forty years many high tax countries have tried to take action against companies who indulge in 'treaty shopping', which means incorporating a subsidiary or holding company in another country which has better double taxation treaties than its own. Switzerland, for example, denies the full benefit of its tax treaties to treaty shoppers. The UK tries to limit tax refunds available under treaties to treaty shoppers.

# Transfer pricing

Transfer pricing is often the subject of disputes between companies and revenue authorities; in fact, it is probably the most contentious tax issue facing international companies today. Even when companies are not under common ownership or control, transfers of profit in order to avoid tax can be attacked, and profits on currency speculation are taxable. Since countries are becoming increasingly sensitive to any 'artificial' movements of profits internationally to avoid tax, most now have specific rules to prevent transfer pricing being abused.

Transfer prices are the internal prices which a group of companies use to transfer goods around between themselves. The setting of transfer prices will have no impact on the before-tax profitability of a group of companies since the increase in profitability of the supplying company will be offset equally by the increased procurement cost of the purchasing company.

| | | UK | Foreign | Total average |
|---|---|---|---|---|
| Units sold | | | | 100,000 |
| Wholesale price | | | £5.00 | |
| Wholesale revenue | | | 500,000 | 500,000 |
| Manufacturing costs | per unit | (3) | | |
| | total | (300,000) | | (300,000) |
| Admin/sales costs | | (50,000) | (50,000) | (100,000) |
| Profitability | | | | 100,000 |
| | | | | |
| Transfer prices | 4 | | | |
| National profitability | | | | |
| | | | | |
| Revenue | | 400,000 | 500,000 | |
| Unit costs | | (300,000) | (400,000) | |
| Admin/sales costs | | (50,000) | (50,000) | |
| National profitability | | 50,000 | 50,000 | 100,000 |

Figure 9.2  Transfer pricing (1)

### Example

Let us take an example of a UK company supplying to a foreign company. Figure 9.2 shows the (sterling equivalent) price in the foreign market of the company's product is £5, and sales in the period are 100,000. Manufactured costs are £3 giving unit profits of £2, or £200,000 gross profitability. Each company has administration and sales costs of £50,000, giving net profits before tax of £100,000 for the group. The split of this £100,000 profitability between the companies will of course now depend entirely on the transfer price.

In this instance, setting a transfer price of £4, midway between wholesale and unit cost, would split the profits 50/50, at £50,000 each. But how should transfer prices be set?

## The 'arm's-length' rule

The basic rule, reflected in the vast majority of tax treaties, is that transfer prices should be set according to the 'arm's length' principle. This means that the prices should be those at which the two companies would trade if they were *not* part of the same group; that is, if they were completely independent of each other.

In the UK, the Inland Revenue do not like to lose tax from such transactions when they are not principally made for commercial reasons. Some companies are able to exploit the fact that the title to goods can be transferred without physical delivery.

To decide whether or not particular companies are in fact part of a group, the following rules are applied:

- For transfer pricing rules to apply, the companies must either be under common control, or one must control the other.

- A company that does not own more than 50 per cent of another is not regarded as controlling it.

- Interlocking share ownership can sometimes be used to avoid the rule on control.

Different countries take different approaches to transfer pricing, and double taxation can arise. Appeals are long and involved, and tax authorities may agree to settle a dispute on more favourable terms if the company threatens to appeal under the provisions of a double taxation treaty.

### Example

Returning to our example in Figure 9.2, splitting the profits by means of an arm's length price would not be possible where the companies are trading goods which are in any way unique to the group, and for which there is no reasonable way to develop such arm's length prices. In this case, the company will have to generate reasonable approximations to the arm's length price.

The OECD gave these guidelines to the setting of such transfer prices:

- the **comparable uncontrolled price** – where an identical or very similar product is traded on the open market, this price should be adopted, adjusted as necessary for any variation in the product
- **resale price minus** – this assumes that the purchasing company is really acting as a distributor of the product and will effectively operate on a broadly fixed margin to the national selling price
- the **cost plus** method – this might be employed when comparatively little value is being added in the supplying company prior to final assembly in the purchasing company.

Competitor information, where available, can be particularly useful in the setting of transfer prices.

Two areas which are worth examining when setting transfer prices are:

- **Costing out individual components** – companies are able to use pre-agreed terms and conditions to alter prices to some extent. Setting special prices for delivery, assembly, insurance, management charges and after sales service may be allowable.
- **Interest** – some interest payments may be chargeable to tax under the transfer pricing rules. Loans made between a group are not normally taxable. The Inland Revenue sometimes assesses the transfer of royalty-earning property and licences for tax.

Any of these methods is likely to lead to a range of prices which could reasonably be adopted by a multinational group.

### Example

In the example shown in Figure 9.3, a change in transfer price of 10p will lead to a swing in profitability of £10,000 between the companies. Assuming a corporate tax rate of 50 per cent in the foreign country, the difference between a transfer price of £4.10 and £3.90 would generate a tax saving of £3400. This may sound like peanuts when using this small example, but consider that this small change in transfer prices, by 20p on £4.00 has improved *after-tax profits* by 6 per cent.

As shown above, to equate to this tax saving, operating profits would have to increase by 9 per cent to generate a 6 per cent increase in after-tax profits. Clearly companies must act responsibly and reasonably when setting transfer prices. There will, however, often be a range of prices all of which could reasonably be used, which lead to significantly varying outcomes in terms of taxation.

Tax authorities are well aware of the potential for aggressive manipulation of profits by the use of transfer prices. They have the authority to challenge the level of transfer prices which have been set and they will be particularly alert to large changes in the level of such prices. As always, act reasonably and seek advice.

## Advance pricing agreements (APAs)

International companies face grave problems in anticipating what rulings various tax authorities may give. To assist them, many countries are now willing to make advance pricing agreements (APAs), which have a similar effect to a 'bespoke' double taxation treaty between two tax authorities. APAs give companies more certainty in:

- tax planning
- cash flow planning
- borrowing needs
- dividend policy.

Finalising an APA is a lengthy and costly process, with the risk that the tax authorities do not, in the end, come to an agreement. The main disadvantage, however, as

| | | UK | Foreign | Total/ average |
|---|---|---|---|---|
| Units sold | | | | 100,000 |
| Wholesale price | | | £5.00 | |
| Wholesale revenue | | | 500,000 | 500,000 |
| Manufacturing costs | per unit | (3) | | |
| | total | (300,000) | | (300,000) |
| Admin/sales costs | | (50,000) | (50,000) | (100,000) |
| Profitability | | | | 100,000 |
| | | | | |
| Transfer prices | 4 | | | |
| National profitability | | | | |
| Revenue | | 400,000 | 500,000 | |
| Unit costs | | (300,000) | (400,000) | |
| Admin/sales costs | | (50,000) | (50,000) | |
| National profitability | | 50,000 | 50,000 | 100,000 |
| | | | | |
| Transfer prices | 3.9 | | | |
| National profitability | | | | |
| Revenue | | 390,000 | 500,000 | |
| Unit costs | | (300,000) | (390,000) | |
| Admin/sales cost | | (50,000) | (50,000) | |
| National profitability | | 40,000 | 60,000 | 100,000 |
| Tax rate in country | | 33% | 50% | |
| Tax due | | (13,200) | (30,000) | (43,200) |
| Profits after tax | | 26,800 | 30,000 | 56,800 |
| | | | | |
| Transfer prices | 4.1 | | | |
| National profitability | | | | |
| Revenue | | 410,000 | 500,000 | |
| Unit costs | | (300,000) | (410,000) | |
| Admin/sales costs | | (50,000) | (50,000) | |
| National profitability | | 60,000 | 40,000 | 100,000 |
| Tax rate in country | | 33% | 50% | |
| Tax due | | (19,800) | (20,000) | (39,800) |
| Profits after tax | | 40,200 | 20,000 | 60,200 |

Figure 9.3   Transfer pricing (2)

remarked by the representative of a large US company, is that 'you risk bringing to the attention of the authorities a lot of information which could subsequently be used against you'.

# Using offshore centres and tax havens

Not all low-tax countries like to be called tax havens, and although even professionals use the name, it is not a very precise one. Switzerland, for example, is not a low-tax country, but its sophisticated banking facilities and tradition of conservatism and confidentiality makes it an important feature of the offshore world. Some tax havens specialise in the forming of offshore companies, while others have highly developed banking facilities. Most of them are small countries (quite a few are islands), and look to offshore business as an important part of their economies, but none of them can afford to pull up the drawbridge entirely. Not only are they in strong competition with one another, but also they are dependent in varying degrees on the policies and practices of the dominant trading nations of the world.

Even in the EU, where attempts are being made to harmonise company taxation in member states, there have been no moves to set universal standards for personal taxation because of the enormous legal difficulties. For companies based in the EU, offshore centres which are physically close to the EU and have special tax arrangements with the community offer benefits which are not available at home.

Tax havens have, in some ways, become more respectable; the multinationals use them for in-house pension and insurance schemes, many sound investment funds are based offshore, and international offshore subsidiaries of ultra-respectable banks abound – and all these are active in trading in foreign currencies offshore. Businesses investing in unstable parts of the world will often use tax havens as a base for their operations.

Not all tax havens are independent countries. For instance, Ireland's International Financial Services Centre is a district in the Dublin docklands. How much tax you pay often depends upon where you are doing business. Quite a number of jurisdictions exempt companies doing business abroad from tax, while subjecting domestic businesses to high tax rates. Others, notably Holland, have special rules for international holding companies while possessing double taxation treaties with the developed world which allow multinationals to avoid tax. Modern tax havens have good communications and well-developed banking and legal systems.

UK companies must be very careful about how they use offshore finance centres. The

> Multinationals use offshore companies extensively to mitigate tax, particularly in the areas of employee pensions and insurance, and also by using holding companies in favourable jurisdictions. Smaller companies in high tax areas can do the same, but with relatively greater expense and fewer advantages.

UK has introduced laws on 'controlled foreign companies' (CFCs) to limit their use to avoid tax, as have many other countries. Offshore companies must have a commercial justification. Tax breaks must not be the sole means of maximising investment in a given country.

The CFC legislation states that companies with offshore interests must pass one of three tests:

- The acceptable distribution of income test – some profits have to go back to the UK within a given time period.

- The exempt activities test – a company has to show it has genuine business interests in that country.

- The motive test – a company's main motive must be to do business, not just to avoid tax. Evidence includes the number of people the offshore company employs and the size of its offices.

These laws mean that many 'onshore' companies have given up using zero tax rate havens such as Bermuda and the Cayman Islands in favour of other countries with low rates of tax where it is easier to justify a true commercial interest.

## The European Union and offshore centres

There are a number of states and territories within the EU which have an odd relationship with the EU. Some are associates of the union, others are full members, and others have transitional status; most of them have tax advantages, and can be used as bases from which to trade within the community. The full members are:

- Ireland
- Luxembourg.

## Ireland

Although it is a full member of the EU, Ireland offers a wide range of tax incentives to outside investors; these include a low tax rate on manufacturing and licensing companies. It has two low tax zones: one in Dublin, the International Financial Services Centre, entry to which is now limited and is designed for multinationals and financial institutions, and the Shannon Free Zone which encourages inward investment. A wide range of soft loans are available and it is possible to set up a non-resident company in Ireland which is exempt of tax on overseas earnings.

## The International Financial Services Centre (IFSC)

Dublin's IFSC has emerged as a rival to other offshore centres since it was set up in 1987. Among the major companies with a presence there are:

- Danisco Finance
- Asahi Fire and Marine Insurance of Japan
- Daiwa
- Morgan Grenfell
- IBM
- Porsche
- Coca Cola
- Hitachi
- Seagram.

Many of these companies use the ISFC for captive insurance and corporate treasury activities. Companies setting up in the IFSC are offered:

- 10 per cent corporation tax guaranteed by the EU until 2005. Permitted activities included are banking/asset financing, corporate treasury management, mutual fund management, insurance and ancillary services.
- Exemption from local municipal taxes for 10 years.

- 100 per cent deduction for tax purposes of the capital cost of commercial buildings.

- No withholding taxes on interest and dividends.

- Income arising from active trading in stocks, shares, and other securities by a financial institution will normally be treated as trading income and is not liable to capital gains tax.

## Luxembourg

The tiny principality of Luxembourg is a popular location for holding companies and investment companies which can reinvest profits from foreign countries tax free. Some other member states treat Luxembourg holding companies unfavourably for tax, however, and complex group structures may be necessary to take advantage of Luxembourg's tax breaks.

Luxembourg has economic and currency union with Belgium and is a founder member of the EU. The clearing house and custodial centre for the enormous Eurobond market are in Luxembourg, as are the EU Courts of Justice, the secretariat of the European Parliament, the European Investment Bank, some offices of the European Community Commission and the European Court of Auditors. Traditionally a private banking centre for the savers of France, Belgium and Germany, Luxembourg has expertise in fund management, custody and administration, reinsurance and shipping.

Luxembourg is under constant pressure from Brussels and the other EU member states to ensure high standards of banking regulation. Forthcoming EU tax harmonisation may destroy the country's appeal as an investment centre.

# Territories within or dependent on member states

These include:

- overseas departments of France

- Spanish territories in Africa and the Atlantic

- Madeira and the Azores

- the Isle of Man and the Channel Islands

- Gibraltar.

## French overseas départments

These include Guyana, Martinique, Réunion and Guadeloupe. They are part of the EU through their status as parts of the French republic and are subject to EU directives.

## Spanish territories

There are two Spanish towns in North Africa, Melilla and Ceuta, which are subject to the EU but are not included in the EU customs territory and are excluded from the EU's policies on trade.

## Madeira

Madeira is expanding as an offshore centre, and has created a special free zone which gives tax advantages to companies importing from countries outside the EU.

## The Isle of Man and the Channel Islands

These are possessions of the British Crown but are not part of the United Kingdom. They are not full members of the EU, and are exempted from customs duties and trade levies. The territories are well-established tax havens. Jersey, in the Channel Islands, is generally seen as the best developed; the financial services industry is the biggest contributor to the island's economy. About 70 banks operate on the island, with deposits of more than 54 billion pounds. Jersey wants to attract 'quality' business, and wants to preserve its reputation as a reputable international centre.

Jersey's companies are regulated on similar lines to British ones, but it has introduced the International Business Company (IBC):

- An IBC must be owned by non-residents.

- IBCs pay very low taxes on international profits.

- IBCs can be a company incorporated in Jersey, a foreign company managed and controlled in Jersey or a Jersey branch of a foreign company.

- IBCs cannot have Jersey residents as beneficial owners, but they can have a Jersey intermediate holding company.

- An IBC is fully resident for tax purposes in Jersey. It pays tax on profits in the normal way, but is subject to special rates of tax on any profits derived from international business activities. These include inter-company financial activities, industrial and commercial activities and overseas investment.

■ There is deduction of Jersey tax from payments of interest from an IBC to individuals or companies in other countries.

■ Non-resident directors do not pay tax on their fees. It was initially hoped that IBCs could be used to avoid the Controlled Foreign Companies legislation in the UK (*see page 169*), but the UK raised the rate of tax required to avoid CFC legislation to three-quarters of the UK rate, making it 5 per cent higher than the full Jersey income tax rate. The UK Inland Revenue rarely uses CFC legislation, though, concentrating on attempts to show that the management and control of companies are in the UK.

Any company in Jersey is subject to tax at 20 per cent, unless it elects to apply for exempt status for a particular tax year. Exempt companies must be owned by non-residents and can be managed and controlled in Jersey. They do not pay tax on foreign income or on interest earned in Jersey.

Apart from its agreement with the UK, Jersey has no double taxation treaties. There are no withholding taxes, except for a 20 per cent tax on royalties. Jersey has no inheritance tax or capital gains tax. Residents are taxed on world-wide income at 20 per cent, with the exception of Jersey bank interest, which is paid gross.

Jersey's importance as a centre for offshore investment derives from its reputation for a well-managed economy, its unchanging tax rates and its sympathetic authorities. There are over 300 investment funds (such as pension funds) on the island, managing a total of around £16 billion. The island has 'designated territory' status in the UK which means that its institutions can sell certain funds in the UK.

## Gibraltar

Gibraltar is a dependency of the UK, but is exempt from EU regulations on customs and VAT. Gibraltar offers a number of tax advantages to companies and individuals, but is not much used by multinationals.

# Territories close to the EU

These include:

- Liechtenstein
- Malta
- Cyprus.

## *Liechtenstein*

Liechtenstein, the tiny principality between Austria and Switzerland, is well known for its banking secrecy which some say is tighter than Switzerland's, and also for its ability to shun publicity. Even after the enormous criticism resulting from the Maxwell pension fund fraud (*see page 48*), it has remained silent. Liechtenstein's attractions as a haven are based on its favourable tax structures and its flexible attitude towards company and trust formation, in particular holding companies. The country levies virtually no tax on non-resident companies. It is estimated that there are some 40,000 holding companies in the principality, some 10,000 more than the number of inhabitants.

Liechtenstein is one of the few countries whose confidentiality laws are entirely credible. Complete anonymity is on offer. Features of the rules include:

- companies can be formed within five days
- bearer shares are allowed
- minimal information is required to be filed with the Public Register
- shareholders need not reveal their identities in the Public Register.

Liechtenstein has two company types which may be unfamiliar:

- **Stiftung** – these are 'foundations' which are legal entities in their own right, unlike a trust, but in other respects operate in a similar way to trusts.
- **Anstalt** – these are 'establishments' which are legal entities without shares, but are similar to a company; they are often used as holding companies.

Holding companies are free of tax if their daughter companies are outside Liechtenstein.

## Malta

In 1970 Malta became an associate of the EU and has applied for full membership. It has joined the customs union. Shipping is big business on Malta, and the 1973 Merchant Shipping Act offers great tax benefits to non-resident owners and charterers. It is not necessary for owners or ships to visit Malta in order to register. More than 11 million tons of shipping are currently registered as Maltese.

In 1988 the Malta Freeport Corporation was founded to administer a customs-free zone at a harbour on the south of the island. The principal activities of the freeport are:

- breaking down bulk cargo
- storing containers
- storing and blending mineral oils
- warehousing and industrial facilities.

The corporation can issue certificates stating that Malta is the origin of goods that have been processed within the freeport, and can also certify that transhipped goods have not been processed in Malta. It can also issue licences to companies wishing to operate in the freeport.

Licensed companies, their shareholders and employees (if not domiciled and ordinarily resident on Malta) are exempt from

- import tax on most goods
- income tax
- death duties
- stamp duties
- exchange controls.

Banking services on Malta are limited, but it offers many advantages as a base from which transport and process goods can be offered for sale in the EU.

## Cyprus (Southern)

Cyprus is an associate member of the EU, but is also an important tax haven for individuals and companies. There are now over 100,000 offshore enterprises on the island, and 22 foreign banks.

Offshore enterprises are not allowed to do business on the island, though they may be based there, can transship goods through Cyprus and hold bank accounts on the island in foreign currency.

The main points regarding offshore companies are:

- Tax is currently at 4.5 per cent of profits.

- Offshore branches which are managed from abroad are exempt from tax.

- No capital gains tax is payable.

- There is no withholding tax on dividends.

- There are no exchange controls.

- Shipping activities are exempt from tax.

- Non-residents must obtain exchange control permission before purchasing shares in a company.

- Off-the-shelf companies are not available.

- There is no minimum capital for a company.

- Nominee shareholders are allowed.

# Holding companies in Holland

Holland is an EU member state, and is an important domicile for 'onshore' businesses because of its unusual tax advantages combined with its large network of double taxation treaties. It is not a tax haven, since companies are taxed at between 35 and 40 per cent on profits; this has enabled Holland to make double taxation treaties with most high-tax countries, but these treaties are quite favourable to certain companies.

It is possible to arrange the structure of a company or a group of companies so that income into Holland gets favourable tax treatment, avoids withholding tax in the country from which it comes, and then can be paid out to companies or individuals in other countries which are either tax havens or have a double taxation treaty with Holland. The country's policy towards trade aims at 'neutrality' between taxing local and foreign income. Many multinationals from the USA, Britain and elsewhere have holding companies in Holland to mitigate taxes.

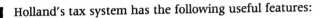

Holland's tax system has the following useful features:

- Advance rulings from the tax authorities. This enables a company to make sure that a particular transaction or kind of transaction will not be taxed unfavourably in Holland before it takes action. In many other countries, including the UK, one is often in the position of not knowing how transactions will be taxed until it is too late to alter arrangements. The advance ruling is also a guarantee that the tax authorities will not change their minds, as they do elsewhere.

- No withholding tax on royalty payments; many groups have a Dutch licensing company and an offshore company based in a tax haven to take advantage of this. Royalties are paid into the Dutch company, subject to a reduced or even nil rate of withholding tax under double taxation treaties, and do not suffer Dutch withholding tax when they are paid out to the offshore company.

- No withholding tax on interest payments – this works in a similar way to royalty payments.

- Companies with a branch in Holland may get exemption from tax on genuine profits made by the branch.

- The 'participation exemption' – this rule enables many companies to avoid Dutch tax on the dividends they receive.

## Advance rulings from the Dutch tax authorities

Advance rulings can be obtained for all kinds of knotty problems, including questions to do with transfer pricing and the 'arm's length' rule. The Inspector of Taxes decides the minimum profit which will be subject to Dutch tax and gives the advance ruling which lasts for three years, and can be extended. The minimum taxable profit will never be less than 10,000 Dutch guilders a year, and claims for other tax relief on this sum will not be allowed.

### Finance companies

A group can create a Dutch subsidiary which borrows money and passes it on to the members of the group, reducing or avoiding income tax on interest payments. Gains made on currency exchange are taxable, though. Finance companies can get advance rulings, and in general pay tax on 0.25 per cent of the average annual borrowings between a group, and as little as 1/32 of average annual borrowings from unrelated lenders.

## Uses of holding companies

Dutch holding companies have many uses. Capital gains tax at home can be deferred indefinitely if it is made by a subsidiary in a country which does not tax capital gains; this is done by keeping the capital gain in the Dutch holding company.

UK companies are often doubly taxed in situations where they have investments in other high tax countries. A Dutch holding company is allowed to average the underlying rates of tax in the different locations of its subsidiaries so that investments in low tax areas can be used to offset unrelieved tax in high tax countries. In addition, Dutch double taxation treaties are often more favourable than those of the UK and other countries, which means that withholding taxes can be lower. Home country tax on dividends can be deferred by using a Dutch holding company, which is helpful to cash flow, especially if a group is expanding overseas. (*See page 179 for an example of how this can work.*)

## Holland – a summary

Holland is an ultra-respectable country whose tax breaks have been used by large businesses for many years. Nevertheless, it does suffer pressure; the US courts have begun to use the idea of tax treaty 'overrides' to disallow some of the Dutch tax advantages, and this has created some uncertainty. If you are doing a lot of business in Europe, though, Holland is hard to beat as a domicile.

1 From your group's published accounts, work out its corporate structure. Where is the holding company, and are there any offshore entities within the group?

2 Try to identify the flows of trade between the different companies, and see if there are any oddities – they may look inefficient, but it may well be that they are there for tax reasons!

3 Discuss your conclusions with a tax specialist in your finance department. Is he or she able to clear up any mysteries, and have you 'read' the structure correctly?

# Company structure

By company structure we mean the ownership pattern of the various legal entities which make up a group of companies. This is particularly important for groups operating internationally. There are many options for such groups and the considerations should be left to experts, but we will outline here the reason for the adoption by many companies of a Dutch holding company for their European operations.

As we have seen, the tax rate for a particular company can be very different from the amount which might be expected from simply taking the declared profits times the nominal rate of tax. Equally the rates of tax in the various European countries vary significantly, and countries outside Europe vary even more.

### Example

Let us take a look at what might happen to a British company with two subsidiaries: one in a low tax country, the other in a high tax country.

|  | Income before taxation | Taxation charge | Income after taxation |
|---|---|---|---|
| UK profits | £100,000 | £(33,000) | £67,000 |
| Foreign profits |  |  |  |
| – low taxed | 100,000 | (20,000) | 80,000 |
| – high taxed | 100,000 | (40,000) | 60,000 |
| Total profits | £300,000 | £(93,000) | £207,000 |

The Revenue will look at this profit stream and regard the foreign incomes as separate from each other. The Revenue will look at the gross amounts of profits made from each source, together with the amounts of tax already paid. The tax already paid will be allowed as a tax credit. We can consider the example again:

|  | High tax area | Low tax area | Average tax charge |
|---|---|---|---|
| Gross profits | £100,000 | £(100,000) | £100,000 |
| Local tax charge | (40,000) | (20,000) | (30,000) |
| – percentage | 40% | 20% | 30% |
| UK notional tax liability |  |  |  |
| – percentage | 33% | 33% | 33% |
| – amount | £(33,000) | £(33,000) | £(33,000) |
| Amount of credit from local taxation | (40,000) | (20,000) |  |
| Credit allowed | £(33,000) | £(20,000) |  |
| UK taxation due | 0 | (13,000) |  |
| Total taxation | £(40,000) | £(33,000) | £(36,500) |
| – percentage | 40% | 33% | 36.5% |

So we can see from this example that the average tax charge on foreign income is

- not the average paid locally of 30 per cent
- not the UK tax rate of 33 per cent
- but an artificially high rate of 36.5 per cent due to the mixing of income from high and low tax areas.

Ever noticed and wondered why many UK and US companies with local subsidiaries will 'group' the subsidiaries under a Dutch holding company?

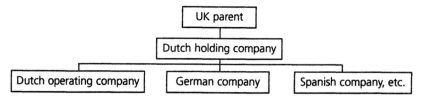

Under this arrangement, the tax credits from the foreign subsidiaries are allowed as relief under Dutch tax law, avoiding the problem experienced under the UK system.

When received in the UK, the dividends are all considered to be from a single source, the Netherlands, and if remitted at an average of 33 per cent will have no further tax due. This would yield a saving of £3500 in the example, equal to 3.5 per cent of gross profits. Tax savings, however, are better than an improvement on gross profits since they are also effectively *after* tax.

## Example

Consider another example:

|  | Before tax management | After tax management |
|---|---|---|
| Gross profits | £105,500 | £100,000 |
| Tax charge |  |  |
| – percentage | 36.5% | 33% |
| – amount | £38,500 | £(33,000) |
| Net profits | £67,000 | £67,000 |

So we can see that in order to equate to the £100,000 after tax, the saving of 3.5 per cent from the tax charge would require an increase in gross profits of 5.5 per cent. When you consider how much management effort would go into increasing gross profits by even 1 per cent, it is clear that the management of the tax charge should also be given due consideration.

The example above is, of course, very simplified; the reality would require careful planning of the dividends from each of the subsidiaries including the timing of such dividends and attention to the year from which the dividend was paid.

The Dutch holding company is but one of the structural ways in which tax can be legitimately managed. The common feature which these structural methods share is that the structure should be put in place at the earliest opportunity. Once a structure is put into place, to change it subsequently, while not impossible, is always more difficult. The message then is clear – get the tax structure right from the start. This will nearly always require expert advice, but the cost of this advice should be considered in the light of the savings and that the fact that payback should be ongoing and can be substantial.

## Foreign business – other considerations

When pursuing business abroad it also pays to consider the requirement for a foreign presence at all. The previous example assumes that a substantial presence is required and that the group has an incorporated presence in the countries in which it trades. This might not be necessary. No foreign tax will be due if the company does business in a foreign territory:

- from the UK, or

- through an independent agent.

In these cases, where the company is not deemed to be operating in the foreign territory, the company should be liable only for UK taxation on the transactions. The rules on what a company can actually do by way of operating can extend to limited life construction projects, but do vary according to territory. Again, advice should be taken, but it is important to remember that it can be perfectly acceptable to trade with other countries without incurring foreign taxation.

> Where a company is required in order to support the business of the group, there are many factors which must be considered including the place and nature of the incorporation. The issue of whether the incorporation will be as a branch or as a separate company will be an important one for the company and subject to many commercial, as well as taxation, considerations.

Given that a company is established in a foreign territory the issue then arises of the companies within an international group trading with one another. Goods which are manufactured in one country and distributed in another must first be sold from one group company to another. This trade requires prices to be established between the companies – these are the transfer prices we discussed earlier.

**SUMMARY**

Multinationals have enormous advantages over smaller companies in the opportunities they have to reduce their tax liabilities. However, their size can count against them, since their massive operations within high tax countries make them sitting targets for changes in tax legislation. The corporate structure of any undertaking abroad can have a huge effect on profitability, so remember to take tax advice as soon as possible in the planning stage.

_____ CHAPTER TEN _____

# Financing

- The balance sheet

- The cash flow cycle

- Forms of financing

- Overdrafts and loans

- Bonds

- Credit terms

- Financing of specific assets

- Equity financing

To understand the need for financing, in this chapter we will first return to the balance sheet, and then review the typical flows of cash within an organisation. The balance sheet was discussed in some detail in Chapter 1, and we are interested here only in the very broadest structure of the company as illustrated by the balance sheet.

# The balance sheet

**Barking Traders Ltd**
**Balance Sheet**
**31st January 1997**

| | |
|---|---:|
| Fixed Assets | £50,000 |
| Current assets | |
| – stocks | £50,000 |
| – debtors | 25,000 |
| – cash | 10,000 |
| Creditors | |
| – amounts falling due within one year | £(60,000) |
| Net current assets | £25,000 |
| Total assets less current liabilities | £75,000 |
| Creditors | |
| – amounts falling due after more than one year | £(50,000) |
| Net assets | £25,000 |
| Shareholders' funds | |
| – called up share capital | £10,000 |
| – share premium account | 5,000 |
| – profit and loss account | 10,000 |
| Shareholders' funds | £25,000 |

We can look at this another way; the total assets of a company are 'financed by' the total liabilities of the company.

| Assets | Liabilities |
| --- | --- |
| *Short term* | *Short term* |
| Stocks | |
| Debtors | Creditors |
| Cash | Overdraft |
| | |
| *Long term* | *Long term* |
| Fixed assets | Long-term loans |
| (buildings, plant) | Shareholders' funds |
| Investments | |

In terms of balance there is nothing to say that a company must 'term match' its financing by matching short-term assets to short-term borrowings *except* that it must maintain liquidity.

To understand this, ask yourself the following questions:

- Given that the assets are financed by the borrowings in the above table, what significance is there to the split between short and long term?

- Does a company have to concern itself with the split?

The answer is yes! In Chapter 2 we discussed the importance of liquidity; meaning that a company must always have enough cash to pay its bills. Although there are exceptions, it is normally reckoned to be good practice to have positive working capital, meaning that net short-term assets exceed net short-term liabilities. Failure to achieve this could lead to the company being unable to pay its bills – which would leave it facing liquidation (or possibly administration).

The reverse situation with the company borrowing long-term funds to finance its short-term requirements is not a problem per se but tends to give less operating flexibility as well as being normally more expensive and is avoided for these reasons.

# The cash flow cycle

Cash is arguably the single most important aspect of managing a business, as well as probably the most difficult. To manage the cash flow of a business is to manage every single aspect of that business. Cash flow management can sensibly only be achieved on a macro-level by:

- assessing and controlling the cyclical nature of the cash flows

- understanding the main flows of cash in and out of the business

- ensuring that the business has sufficient borrowing capacity to meet the lowest dips in the cash flow.

It is for this reason that the vast majority of businesses make use of a banking 'facility'. The facility is an agreement with a bank, in exchange for a fee, that the bank will provide credit as required up to a certain pre-set limit. This is probably the most common form of financing and even cash positive businesses have facilities in place to cover unexpected cash requirements.

Before we discuss borrowing in more detail, we will review the cash flow cycle as shown in Figure 10.1. In operating terms, a factory will require the input of raw materials, labour and other running costs before it can start to produce. To produce and sell the product we must first have the inputs. Fortunately, in terms of cash, we can normally use our material suppliers as our first form of financing by not paying them. Well, not for 30 days or so, anyway. Unfortunately the people actually making the products are not so accommodating and generally prefer a weekly supply of cash. Other costs, e.g. utilities, can also normally be paid on 30-day terms.

In Chapter 5 on costing we saw that normal costing systems 'reward' operating management for the creation of finished stock by absorbing the expenses used in the creation of it. In terms of cash flow, the production of stock is using up cash for no benefit to the business. There may be several processes in the factory each with stock buffers in between them. Think of stock as potential cash which cannot be used to pay the bills or earn interest.

Finished goods then pass out of the factory into the distribution channels to the dealers or final customers. If we use dealers then they will use us as we use our suppliers

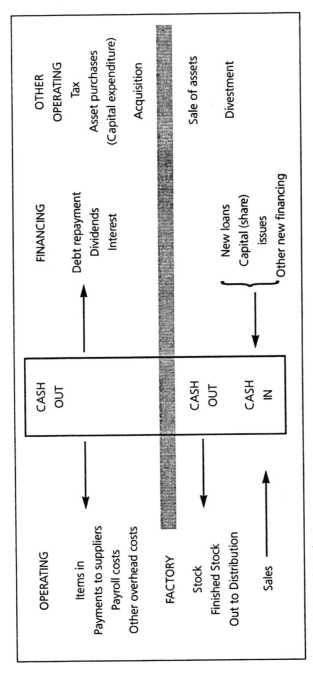

Figure 10.1   Financing

– as financing – and we may have to wait another 30 days before receiving the funds. All this means that we have a substantial lag between incurring the costs required to produce, and actually receiving the funds. See the section on efficiency ratios in Chapter 2 for a discussion.

But what of profits? Profits come at the end of the chain. Only after we have invested in the factory, the labour, the materials, etc., do we finally make the sale which yields our profits. In a *steady state* business, which is making a profit, we would expect to see a corresponding generation of cash as follows:

| | |
|---|---|
| Net profits | £100,000 |
| add back depreciation* | 30,000 |
| Operating cash flow | £130,000 |

There would, of course, be tax and dividends to pay, but even then the cash flow would be positive. If the company is growing, though, sales will be increasing, stocks will increase and the working capital requirement will increase. A company which cannot fund its own working capital growth from trading profits is defined as **overtrading**. This sounds horrible but in fact can be controlled with careful management and sympathetic financiers.

Taking the steady state operating cash cycle and combining it with the other requirements of a business – asset purchases, tax payments and potential acquisitions – starts to build up a picture of a cash-hungry monster.

> The technique of keeping the monster fed with the right amount of cash is known as financing.

# Forms of financing

Financing can be split into debt and equity. Equity financing is the placing of money into the business by the owners of the business. This is the riskiest form of finance. In the event of a deterioration in business prospects the equity holders may not receive a

---

* depreciation is a charge to the profit and loss account which is not a cash item – it is therefore added back to the profit and loss account to determine operating cash flow.

dividend, and in the event of a loss they are the last to benefit from the funds in a winding up. They do, however, remain the owners of the business and are the sole beneficiaries of the business exceeding its expectations.

Gearing was discussed in Chapter 2 where we showed the effects on the return for the owners of an increased level of gearing. There are always equity holders who forget this aspect of equity ownership and who expect to retain part of their funds while the holders of debt, including the banks, share the losses. These people should really stay away from investing in risky projects such as tunnelling under the Channel.

As with much of business, and as outlined in portfolio theory, risk and return are inversely correlated. The Channel Tunnel project was of a high risk nature, and, had the plans succeeded completely, would have made the original equity investors substantial returns. Applying this to financing we can see that investors in the equity of a company accept a greater level of risk and potential return than do the lenders of debt. Debt financing is the lower risk (supposedly!) borrowing of a business which is at a predetermined, fixed rate. Debt must be serviced irrespective of the fortunes of a company, unlike dividends which can be reduced or postponed indefinitely when times become tough for the company.

Debt financing can be further split into broadly three main areas:

- overdrafts and loans
- the manipulation of credit periods (including factoring)
- finance linked to a specific asset.

These are now considered in more detail.

# Overdrafts and loans

Very simply , a company overdraft is identical to a personal overdraft, perhaps somewhat larger, and very often cheaper. It is the simplest most flexible form of financing for companies of all sizes. Very often a company will pay a fee for the arrangement and for the guaranteeing of the overdraft facility. Overdrafts may also be in several currencies to facilitate the management of short term cash flows in a variety of currencies. More than half of all company borrowing in the UK is through overdraft financing.

Some terminology often used when discussing financing of all kinds:

- **Committed, or secured** – the facility is available to the company to use as it wishes and when it wishes, The provider (bank) must give an agreed notice if it wishes to revoke the facility. A commitment fee is normally payable and this is typically around 0.5 per cent of the available credit, or higher, depending on the risk of the borrower.

- **Uncommitted, or unsecured** – this is a borrowing facility which can be withdrawn at no, or very limited, notice. Normally no fees are payable on this kind of facility due to its volatile nature.

- **Interest** is generally expressed as a percentage over the bank's base rate, or over LIBOR. A bank's base rate will typically shadow LIBOR but be much less volatile. This allows for simplified administration for the smaller loans. LIBOR is the London Inter-Bank Offer Rate. This is the amount at which banks borrow from each other in £ sterling in London.

Structured loans, or term loans are again very similar to those available to individual customers. They are for a set term, and at a set rate. Loans can be of fixed or variable interest (*see Chapter 12 Risk and risk management*), and can be in any currency acceptable to the lender. Currency loans will be related to the respective country's interest rate rather than LIBOR. The vast majority of corporate lending in the UK is short term and variable interest in nature.

Both overdrafts and loans will in most cases be provided by the banks. In the case of a divisionalised structure it is typical for the divisions to 'borrow' from the parent company with the parent company arranging group-wide funding through its bankers. In this way the banking community acts as an intermediary between companies (and indeed governments) wishing to borrow money, and those companies, institutions (such as unit trusts and pension funds) and individuals wishing to make deposits.

Many UK companies feel that bankers take a short-term view of them; in one survey, 56 per cent of companies said that their bank's assessment horizon was two years or less. Mainstream banks in the UK have generally steered clear of taking equity ownership positions in companies although this type of funding is common on mainland Europe, where companies are able to obtain much more finance for the medium or long term. Fast growing companies often complain about the lack of credit availability from banks in the UK.

Retail banks should essentially be treated in much the same way as any other provider of services. Although a long-term relationship may be extremely valuable, the company must always ensure that it is receiving good value, and should not be afraid of 'going to tender' at intervals to ensure that the bank is fully competitive.

Companies can now also consider automating as many transactions as possible, using electronic banking where appropriate, in order to minimise charges.

> Another source of friction can be the perceived high charges that banks make for their services. These may be rather variable, and companies should ensure that they are familiar with the charging structure used by their bank. It is also important that a company regularly monitors bank charges.

## Bills of exchange

Bills are used by large businesses who borrow money from banks and financial institutions, issuing a bill in return which promises to repay the money; the rate of interest is usually better than they can get elsewhere. There is one kind of bill of exchange which is familiar to all of us – the cheque – but there are others too. In essence, they are written IOUs promising payment at a future date. Bills of exchange are negotiable, so the recipient can sell them on to someone else who can claim payment on the due date. The issuer of the bill of exchange either promises to pay the bill themselves, noting this on the bill, or addresses it to a bank, who will provide the money.

When a bill is issued it has to be sent to the bank on which the money is to be drawn for 'acceptance', which means that the bank signs the bill and agrees to pay the money on the due date. The law says that anyone signing a bill can be sued if it is not paid, so the safety of a bill of exchange depends upon who has 'accepted' it. For this reason certain banks, called 'accepting houses', specialise in accepting bills, and such bills are generally recognised as secure instruments.

Finance houses, who provide money for hire-purchase and leasing, borrow their funds from banks. Large companies sometimes lend directly to one another, cutting out the banks. The sums involved start at £50,000, and are lent through money brokers. Security is required, usually taking the form of a bank guarantee, and the sums are lent for between three months and five years.

A newer option for larger companies is to use the commercial paper market, in which they exchange promissory notes ('paper') for money. The minimum amount borrowed is £500,000, the paper is owned by the bearer, and they are sold at a discount in the same way as Treasury bills.

## The Euromarkets

For historical reasons large amounts of the major currencies are held outside the jurisdiction of their home country. The prefix 'euro' does not mean that they are all European currencies or that they are held in Europe.

Companies and private individuals are able to hold foreign eurocurrencies on deposit in British banks, each currency earning interest at a rate related to those prevailing in its home country. The relaxation of exchange controls has caused this market to mushroom, and it has become so established that borrowers now include national governments.

# Bonds

The very largest companies are increasingly borrowing directly from the marketplace of investors and not directly from banks. This form of borrowing, known as direct issuing, takes the form of a company issuing its own 'paper', effectively IOUs from the company to the holder. A company can issue debt in the 'euro' markets, directly to the investors, in whatever form it wishes, although the term must clearly be attractive to investors if they are to be successful with the issue.

Announcements frequently appear in the FT after the debt has been issued along the following lines:

 **Example**

---

> This announcement appears as a matter of record only
>
> ### BLOGGS PLC
>
> £100,000,000
>
> 5% bonds 2005
>
> with warrants to subscribe for stock
>
> International Bank of Dorset
> Bank of Middle Wallop
> etc.

This means that Bloggs have issued debt, i.e. borrowed money, to the tune of £100 million. It is not worth issuing this sort of paper unless it is for quite enormous sums of money. The nominal or coupon rate on the debt is 5 per cent and they mature in 2005. To increase the attractiveness of the debt, they come with warrants. This gives the holder of the debt at maturity the option to take a pre-agreed number of shares in the company instead of the cash when the loan matures.

A nominal or coupon rate is the rate of interest compared with the face value of the debt. In this example, a 5 per cent rate of interest would give interest payments of £500 per year per £10,000 of debt at face value. This amount of debt with a face value of '£10,000 worth' will then change hands for differing amounts depending on the changes in interest rates. If interest rates go up the value of the £500 flows becomes less, and the value of the debt would be reduced. The issue was underwritten by the banks whose names appear.

---

Typical issuers of such debt include the banks themselves, and other very large corporates. The motor industry credit companies, who finance large numbers of individuals purchasing cars, are also large scale borrowers in this market.

## The Eurobond market

Despite its name, the market for Eurobonds is truly international; both issuers of the bonds and investors can come from any country, and while most of the banks involved in the market base their Eurobond offices in London, they too are from all over the world. Some seven billion dollars' worth of Eurobonds are traded every day over the telephone across the world. Eurobonds can be denominated in any currency, and are issued outside the country of the borrower (issuer); an important feature is that they are issued in 'bearer form'. This means that whoever is holding the bond owns it, giving a great degree of discretion and anonymity to the investor.

Companies, banks, governments, quasi-governmental bodies and organisations such as the EC (European Community) all issue Eurobonds. Banks are the most active issuers.

Bonds are also bought by banks, insurance companies, pension funds, government organisations and large companies who all invest in Eurobonds, as well as wealthy private investors. Unsurprisingly, most investment is done by financial institutions.

### Interest and the credit rating of Eurobonds

Interest is paid gross, with no withholding tax deducted. Common maturity dates are 5, 7, 10 and 12 years. Like other bonds, most Eurobonds are rated by Moody's and Standard & Poor's, the best quality being rated as 'triple A' (see below). Curiously, corporate bond issuers with household names are often more popular with investors, and can thus offer a lower rate of interest, than obscure companies with higher credit ratings.

### Fixed rate bonds

This is the most common kind of Eurobond, having a final maturity date and paying a fixed rate of interest. As with other kinds of bonds (*see page 194*), if interest rates elsewhere rise above the fixed rate of the bond at some time during its life, the resale value of the bond goes down, and if rates fall, the bond's value will rise.

### Floating rate bonds and other bonds

Floating rate bonds tie the rate of interest to the inter-bank lending rate (LIBOR) or some other short-term interest rate by means of a stated formula.

The Eurobond market is dynamic and innovative, offering a great variety of bonds which are beyond the scope of this book; examples include 'tap stock', 'dual currency bonds' and 'zero coupon bonds'.

The zero coupon bond is essentially a bond which pays no interest during the term. The 'interest' is in the form of a substantial discount to the bond's face value at the time it is issued. Thus, a bond which is worth £10,000 when it matures in five years' time might be sold at issue for £6,000. These bonds are also known as 'deep discount' bonds. They are attractive in some circumstances, since they may be treated as a capital gain for tax purposes rather than as income and be favourably taxed.

## Bond rating systems

The main rating systems for US bonds and Eurobonds are Moody's and Standard & Poor's. They are as follows:

| | Standard & Poor's | Moody's |
|---|---|---|
| Top quality bonds | AAA | Aaa |
| High quality bonds | AA | Aa |
| Good bonds | A | A |
| Medium quality bonds which may be insecure in the long term | BBB | Baa |
| Bonds with only moderate security | BB | Ba |

The following categories are for bonds which are generally considered to be bad investments for small investors:

| | | |
|---|---|---|
| | B | B |

The 'C' categories are for bonds which have sometimes defaulted or are in danger of doing so:

| | | |
|---|---|---|
| | CCC | Caa |
| | CC | Ca |
| | C | C |
| In default | D | – |

As might be expected, the poorer the rating, and consequently the higher the risk, the higher will be the expected return on the bonds. The high risk/high return bonds used in the US, often to finance highly leveraged takeover bids, were known as 'junk bonds'.

## Warrants and convertible bonds

Companies will often issue debt in the form of a package of bonds together with warrants and/or convertible bonds.

Warrants are a kind of option to buy shares at a set price within a certain period of time. (*See Chapter 12 for more on other options*.) Sometimes warrants are linked to a bond and must be traded with it, or they may be detachable, and can be traded separately. If the market price of the company's shares does not reach the exercise price of the warrant, it will expire worthless at the end of the period.

Convertible bonds are exchangeable for shares in the issuing company at a predetermined price. This price may be 'stepped' over time, and investors may be asked to pay a cash sum as well if they convert the bond to shares.

While similar in principle, there are some important differences between convertibles and warrants:

- Warrants tend to be issued in private placements on the stock market, while convertibles tend to be issued publicly. This means that most warrants are sold to financial institutions rather than the general public.

- With a convertible, the bond and the right to exchange it for shares are stuck together – with detachable warrants, the right to buy shares can be separated from the bond.

- If a company wants to pay back its debts, it can simply call in its bonds. It cannot, however, usually buy back its warrants by right, so it cannot be sure when, or if, the warrants will be exercised. Companies sometimes try to extinguish their obligations by reducing the exercise price of warrants for a time, or by increasing the dividend to their ordinary shareholders, which has a negative effect on the value of warrants and will encourage warrant holders to exercise them.

# Credit terms

As discussed above, the normal credit terms of 30 days are a source of finance to the business when making purchases, and a cash drag normally when making sales.

Credit terms can be manipulated to extend this source of finance, but this must be done with care. Reducing the terms extended to dealers may cause them to switch allegiances or result in some loss of competitiveness. Extending payment terms to suppliers might be achievable but is often viewed either as an abuse of a very strong competitive position or as a sign that the company is in some financial distress.

## Factoring (discounting of receivables)

As we have seen, selling goods or services to a customer organisation is effectively the same as granting them credit. This has two aspects to it:

- it absorbs substantial amounts of cash if we always have to wait for our cash for at least 30 days after the goods leave the factory

- we have a credit risk equal to the value of the goods while the amount is outstanding, as the customer might go into liquidation.

In an ideal world we'd receive cash as soon as the sale was agreed. One solution is known as factoring. This is the technique whereby a company can sell its known (or expected) future receipts to a bank (or other finance house) for immediate cash. Factoring is available with or without recourse. This means that either the purchaser keeps the risk of the company going bust before payment or it passes the risk to the bank. If the bank takes the risk, it will expect compensation and this will be in the form of a lower 'purchase price' received from the bank for the receivables.

As with any other form of borrowing, the company will still pay for this facility, with interest rates negotiable in the same way as for term loans or overdrafts. Some banks now offer additional services with factoring, such as the management of the receivables book on behalf of a company. Here's how factoring works:

- The company must have an established trading record and must inform the factor of its large customers' individual trading histories.
- A factor buys the unpaid invoices due to a company as they arise.
- It pays an advance of up to 80 per cent of the value of the invoices, with the balance (less charges) payable after an agreed period.
- The factor may be able to give special advice on credit risks.

The majority of businesses using factors are in manufacturing or distribution; it is an expensive form of finance, and may sometimes be perceived as a sign that the company is in trouble, even when this is not the case. The average turnover of companies using factors and discounters is around £2 million, so it is generally an option for small and medium sized businesses.

Charges for factoring are made in two ways:

- Typical service fees of between 0.5 per cent and 3 per cent of gross annual turnover. A company with a £500,000 turnover could pay a service fee of around £6,000.
- A separate charge, geared to current base rates, for the finance made available against sales often comparable to overdraft rates.

## Invoice discounting

Companies send out their invoices and advise the discounter who then makes an immediate cash payment of up to 80 per cent of the approved invoice value – with the balance due when the customer pays. The client maintains full control over the sales ledger and is responsible for chasing slow payers.

In most cases, a fee is charged to cover the administration of the agreement which is normally between 0.2 and 0.5 per cent of turnover. The principal cost is the finance charge which, like factoring, is linked to established bank base rates and is comparable with overdraft rates.

# Financing of specific assets

The methods above have looked at the raising of cash for general purposes. A prime reason for seeking to raise cash is to fund the procurement of a new asset. Rather than raising general finance to purchase an asset it is often appropriate to look at other ways of acquiring the use of the asset, if not the asset itself. From a non-financial commercial viewpoint, methods other than outright purchase often give valuable extra operating flexibility. We will consider here though, ways to finance the sale when an outright purchase is the alternative logical approach.

## Leasing

Leasing is the method by which a company can pay for the use of an asset over a pre-set period. Instead of using cash, or borrowing money, to purchase an asset outright, a company can enter into a lease agreement.

The lease agreement, which can be for any time period, not exceeding the useful life of the underlying asset, effectively transfers the benefits of ownership to the lessor for the term of the lease. The majority of companies acting as lessors (those who grant a lease) are manufacturing companies and banks.

The main reasons for leasing are:

- If the contract has a clause allowing the lease to be cancelled, the company can pull out of the arrangement if the equipment becomes obsolete, or if it wants to reduce its borrowings. This is a valuable option, but will be reflected in an increased cost of the lease.

- With high-tech or specialised equipment, the lease will often carry a full maintenance guarantee.

- Leasing companies that specialise in certain types of equipment can reduce their administration costs greatly, and do not need to conduct in-depth investigations of a company's finances before they grant a lease. This sometimes makes it cheaper for a company to obtain medium or long-term finance by leasing than by other forms of borrowing.

## Hire purchase

Hire purchase, while similar to leasing in basic structure, allows the added advantage of the 'option to buy' at the end of the hire period. In this way the hirer retains the flexibility of being able to return the asset at the end of the period with the option of retaining it for further use.

# Off-balance sheet financing

This term is often used and applied, and seems to suggest some kind of shady practice. In fact off-balance sheet financing is any kind of financing technique which does not appear on the balance sheet.

## Example

Assume that a fixed asset is required by a company. Let's take the example previously used above as a balance sheet:

**Barking Traders Ltd**
**Balance Sheet**
**31st January 1997**

| | |
|---|---|
| Fixed assets | £50,000 |
| Current assets | |
| – stocks | £50,000 |
| – debtors | 25,000 |
| – cash | 10,000 |
| Creditors | |
| – amounts falling due within one year | £(60,000) |
| Net current assets | £25,000 |

| | |
|---|---|
| Total assets less current liabilities | £75,000 |
| Creditors | |
| – amounts falling due after more than one year | £(50,000) |
| Net assets | £25,000 |
| Shareholders' funds | |
| – called up share capital | £10,000 |
| – share premium account | 5,000 |
| – profit and loss account | 10,000 |
| Shareholders' funds | £25,000 |

Gearing in this case is 66 per cent (*see page 30 for the formula*). If a fixed asset is purchased for £25,000, and an additional loan for £25,000 is taken out over three years, then gearing will increase to 75 per cent, which starts to look precarious. Note that the net assets don't change but the financing structure, or gearing, does.

---

If the asset is obtained on a lease, then it will not show on the balance sheet, and will not impact on the ratios of the company. In effect the company is obtaining the use of assets and corresponding assets without showing them on the balance sheet. This is known as off-balance sheet financing.

## Leasing – the rules

Off-balance sheet financing became a good ruse for potentially over-trading the company without the investors realising this was the case. It is therefore not surprising that the ASB rode over the hill and tightened up the rules.

Without going into the details, the financial standards now differentiate between an operating lease and a finance lease. The use of a finance lease, while still permitted, now requires the full disclosure of the asset and accompanying finance on the balance sheet. The rules for determining that a finance lease exists take account of the total amount of committed payments in relation to the capital value.

To qualify as an operating lease certain of the risks and rewards must remain with the finance company, and the total payments under the lease (including financing costs) must not exceed 90 per cent of the capital value of the asset in question.

# Equity financing

All companies have the ability to sell some of their shares, or to issue new ones, in order to raise money; this is equity financing. Companies which are not listed on the stock market, however, cannot so easily take advantage of this. Essentially, they need to sell their shares to venture capitalists, who regard themselves as being in a high risk business, and who will look for commensurately high returns.

It is the stock market which provides the mechanism for a healthy market in company shares. For this reason, many established companies aspire to stock market flotation once they have grown to an acceptable size. Let's look at the pros and cons of floating a company.

## Company flotation

When a company is first 'brought to the market' it is known as a 'new issue'. The main reasons for a new issue are either to allow the present shareholders to gain the advantage of liquidity for their holding in the company by allowing sale of some or all of the asset, and/or to raise additional cash for the future growth of the business.

The advantages of flotation are gained at some expense. Advisors' and underwriters' fees and the costs of preparing the necessary prospectuses will amount to a substantial sum.

There are three main kinds of new issue:

1. **The offer for sale** This is where shares are offered to anyone, including the general public, who wants to buy them.

2. **The private placing.** This is where shares are sold to a limited number of large financial institutions. Small private investors are excluded except in certain circumstances which are examined below.

3. **The introduction.** This is where there are already many shareholders in the company. Additional money is not sought, and the company's shares simply become officially part of the stock market. This method is often used by foreign companies which are already quoted on another stock exchange. The company's shares must already be widely held in the UK.

The company can choose which kind of issue it is going to offer, whether it wants to sell all or just some of its shares, and can also combine different kinds of issue at once. The 'offer for sale' is the most expensive type of new issue, so many smaller companies prefer a private placing, if they can find institutions to buy their shares.

The rules for a new issue are stringent, and the company must conform to the Stock Exchange's standards for accounting methods, nature of the business, financing methods and so on. These rules are known as the 'Yellow Book'.

## The offer for sale

This is the method used by the big privatisation issues in the UK over the last few years. The government decided to float many of the big industries, state owned since the post-war nationalisation, on the stock market as private sector companies. The size and nature of these issues was unprecedented, and to make sure that the issues worked the government had to try to arrange things so that investors who were new to the stock market would be encouraged to take an interest.

- Investors were sold shares which they paid for in instalments, so they did not have to find all the money for the shares at once. This is called issuing 'partly-paid' shares.

- There was a huge advertising campaign, and several prospectuses were published to make it easier for the less sophisticated investor to understand the process of becoming a shareholder.

- Existing customers of the industry to be privatised were given incentives to invest, such as free shares and priority share applications.

- People were generally given a longer time than usual to consider whether or not to invest, and the time between the closing date for the applications and the commencement of share dealing was extended.

- The share price was set at a level designed to ensure that successful share applicants would see a rise in the value of their investment as soon as market dealing began. This attracted criticism that this was a deliberate undervaluing of the company, which was unfair on those members of the public who did not, or could not, invest. However, when the shares in BP fell following a new issue, the opposite criticism was heard – that it was unfair for the government not to provide an instant profit for the investors!

The principles behind all this are clear enough; the government wanted to widen the number of stock market investors in the UK, and to do this it made efforts to ensure that the new investors' first experiences were happy ones.

When an ordinary company makes a new issue, it publishes a prospectus, giving details of its business. The first thing that investors want to know from the prospectus is what the company intends to spend the new money on. Investors like to see their money being used for new investment and growth rather than being used as an exit route for existing shareholders, so they generally don't like to see more than 5 per cent going to the original shareholders, and another 5 per cent to the employees.

The next thing that investors look at is how much of the money raised is going on fees and expenses associated with the issue; these can be as high as 10 per cent.

The new issue price of the share has to be set by the company. This is done by consulting with banks and other financial institutions who have agreed to 'underwrite' the issue – this means that they have agreed to buy all the shares of the issue that the public do not buy, thus guaranteeing that all the shares in the issue will be taken up. Setting the price can be tricky; it is a fine balance between selling the company too cheaply by choosing a low price, and the risk of the issue 'flopping' by setting the price so high that no one wants to invest. In the case of a flop, the underwriters must take up the shares and sell them off slowly into the market as opportunities arise. Naturally, underwriters hate flops, because the cost can be substantial. Underwriting can be thought of as a form of insurance.

Once the price has been set, the prospectus is published, giving details of the business, its accounts, its future plans and so on. Past dividend yields and the P/E ratio of the offer price are given to help with ratio calculations of whether the share price is good value.

The time from the issue of the prospectus to the closing date for share applications can be suprisingly short, often a matter of days. Once the closing date has passed, all the applications are added up. If the number of shares applied for exceeds the total number of shares to be issued, the offer is said to be 'oversubscribed'. This means that the company has to decide who gets shares, and how many they will get (the 'allocation').

## Tenders

Some new issues set a minimum price at which you can apply for shares, and invite investors to tender a higher figure. Once all the applications are in, the sponsors then decide on the 'strike price', which is the price that everyone will be asked to pay for the shares. If an investor tendered at a price lower than the striking price, he or she doesn't get any shares. Another variety of tender is called 'pay what you bid'; in this case the investor pays the price tendered for the shares if he or she has bid higher than the striking price.

# Offers by subscription

Offers by subscription set a minimum price at which investors can apply for shares, and if there are not enough investors willing to apply, the issue is cancelled, since it is not fully underwritten.

# Private placing

This method is popular with many companies as well as with City institutions. The sponsors place most of the shares with big fund managers, and any other shares tend to go to the favoured clients of a broker. Companies like placings because the costs are lower and the flotation happens with less risk of a flop and more speed. If the money to be raised is between £15 and £30 million, the sponsoring broker must allow at least one other broker to sell shares, and if more than £30 million is being raised, then part of the issue must be offered to the public.

Another advantage to companies is that the debt contract can be specially designed for the company's circumstances. This is especially useful to smaller listed companies, who benefit from the more intimate relationship with the investors than is possible with a public offer.

# Rights issues

When a company whose shares are already listed on the Stock Exchange wants to raise more money, it can do so by a 'rights issue', offering new shares to the existing shareholders. As was discussed above, in case not enough shareholders want to take up their rights, the company will usually arrange for the issue to be underwritten by stockbrokers and banks who promise to buy shares in exchange for a commission.

The problem is that if the rights issue flops, meaning that few shareholders want the new shares, the underwriters are stuck with them and have to dribble them out slowly onto the market; whenever the share price rises, the underwriters will sell more of the shares they are stuck with, and this will bring the price down again.

Shareholders have the choice of whether or not to take up their rights. If they decide not to exercise their rights, they may be able to make a profit by selling the rights themselves. Once dealing begins after the issue, the price will, in theory, be between the old market price and the amount of discount on the issue price, so the effect for the shareholders is that their old shares will come down a little and the new shares will go up.

### Example: Working out rights values

Suppose you own 22 shares in a company with a market value of 300p each, and a rights issue offers you the chance to buy 1 share for every 11 shares you already own at a price of 250p each. You can calculate the ex-rights price as:

2 new shares $\times$ 250p = 500p
500p + (22 old shares $\times$ 300p) = 500p + 6600p = 7100p
7100p/24 shares = 296p per share

Thus, you estimate that by buying the 2 new shares at the discounted offer price, you will see the market price drop from the 300p of the old, 'rights-on' shares to the 296p of the ex-rights price. The value of the two new shares that you bought for 250p each will have gone up, however.

## Clawbacks

Clawbacks are becoming more popular than rights issues; the company issues new shares to one or more institutions, but allows existing shareholders to buy some shares at the issue price, thus 'clawing back' the shares. The big difference for the shareholders is that if they don't exercise their clawback rights, they can't sell them in the market.

## Scrip issues

'Free' scrip issues, also called capitalisation issues or bonus issues, are when a company offers new shares to shareholders in proportion to the number that they already own, but without asking for more money. This is done in order to make the total number of shares in the company larger, so that there are more shares in the market and they can be bought and sold more easily, and also so that the company can transfer some of its reserves into capital on its balance sheet.

The company needs the approval of its shareholders to conduct a scrip issue. The result will be that the company has more capital, though it is not worth more, and there are more shares, but with a lower nominal value to reflect the scrip issue. Generally shareholders like scrip issues, and adjusted share prices often increase at the announcement of one.

## Share splitting

A similar method is 'share splitting', where a company splits each share into several more with lower nominal values that add up in total to the nominal value of the original share. Both these methods are often thought to make shares more attractive because investors don't like to buy shares that have a high market price; it is considered that it somehow 'feels' better to buy 800 shares for a pound each than 20 shares at £40 each.

Some companies have annual scrip issues and increase the amount they distribute in dividends by keeping the dividend rate the same as before. They can also pay 'scrip dividends', which means that they pay the shareholders a dividend on their shares or give free scrip shares. A variation on this is the 'enhanced scrip dividend', which offers scrip shares of a considerably higher value than the alternative of a cash dividend.

## The Alternative Investment Market (AIM)

If a company is too small and/or young to be floated on the 'Official List' of the London Stock Exchange, it can turn to the AIM, which is a new substitute for the now-defunct Unlisted Securities Market (USM).

The types of companies eligible for AIM fall broadly into the following categories:

- Regional firms needing to raise small amounts of capital with local investors.

- Companies already trading under the Stock Exchange's 4.2 Rule, a trading facility which is to end. These are likely to be private or family controlled companies looking for a quotation to raise their profile locally, or to provide more liquidity in the family shares, and who are not particularly looking to raise finance itself.

- Owners of private companies who do not want to sell as many shares as institutional venture capitalists would probably require, but who require small amounts of developmental capital.

- Management buy-outs.

- Growing companies with a short track record that are looking to expand, or increase, product development, and that require a sizeable amount of capital.

To apply for listing on AIM, a company must:

- draw up a company prospectus in accordance with the Companies Act rules

- appoint a qualified advisor to be the 'nominated advisor'

- appoint a qualified stockbroker to be the 'nominated broker'

- complete an application form signed by the directors.

The documents are submitted to the Stock Exchange and, once approval is given, trading in the company's shares can begin.

## General remarks on equity finance

Equity finance by definition depends upon giving up some degree of ownership in the company in return for finance. In recent years, some entrepreneurs, such as Richard Branson and Conrad Black, have actually bought their listed shares back from the public and taken their companies private again, apparently believing that the loss of control and greater regulation of listed companies outweighed their advantages. It is not necessary, however, for owners to lose control of their companies following a flotation; if they retain 51 per cent or more of the voting shares, they will always win the vote at shareholders' meetings, and with large companies with a wide share ownership, a much smaller percentage of shares can effectively give control.

# CHAPTER ELEVEN

# Acquisitions

- Introduction

- Acquisitions – the strategic view

- What makes companies vulnerable to bids?

- Accounting implications

- Accounting policies

- Bids and the stock market

## Introduction

This chapter will look at the financial and accounting implications of acquisitions. Companies will wish to acquire other companies for a host of reasons, some admittedly better than others. Whatever the reason, the acquisition of a company by its new parent requires the new parent to make a number of accounting adjustments. There has been much criticism recently, most particularly in Terry Smith's excellent *Accounting for Growth*, of the methods used in accounting for acquisition. This chapter will discuss the attraction of acquisitions on a strategic level, and then look at the financial aspects which can make the well-planned acquisition look even more attractive when the accounts are filed.

The actual mechanics of the acquisition process vary substantially depending on the scale of the company to be acquired and whether or not it is listed. A small private company can change hands with a simple agreement to sell the shares, and the necessary paperwork in the company's share register. The process for large listed companies is rather complex and invariably will require professional city advisors. This chapter will look at the reasons for acquisitions and take a 'high level' look at the implications on accounting for the new larger parent company.

## Cycles of takeovers

Takeovers seem to come in waves. At the turn of the century there was a flurry of takeovers, then another in the 'Roaring Twenties' and others in the late 1960s and the 1980s. They are associated with bull markets, although one would expect to see takeovers in bear markets too, if the real motive was to pick up a bargain. Since many eager 'predators', as acquisitive companies are called, have come to grief over the years, there is a good deal of adverse criticism that there is something wrong about takeovers, and that they are bad for the economy as a whole. As far as the shareholders are concerned, takeovers can represent an exciting and profitable process.

In 1989, takeover activity for public companies reached a peak of over £26 billion, with the publication 'Acquisitions Monthly' estimating the total, including private companies, to be twice this figure, at some £52 billion. Although acquisition activity declined in the early 1990s we are again seeing a substantial acceleration in takeover activity.

# Acquisitions – the strategic view

Acquisitions are normally made for strategic reasons, or at least justified by a reason other than a purely financial one. You are unlikely to see a company justify its purchase of another company by saying 'it was a bargain'. Even the conglomerate style company will tend to justify the purchase of a company by describing key pieces of a company which it wishes to develop or refocus.

Companies making acquisitions do so for various commercial reasons including that of integration

Integration is of three types:

**1** **Vertical Integration** – this is the process of expanding the existing business up or down the supply chain. A company might choose to purchase a key supplier or one of its major sales outlets in order to eliminate a reliance on an outside party or

to increase competitiveness. Sometimes a new method or product can be made more profitable in this way

**2** **Horizontal Integration** – the purchase of a competing company. This might be to eliminate unwanted competitive forces in the market place or to increase economies of scale. Other examples might include the desire to expand the product range or to acquire other brands. Ford's purchase of Jaguar, for instance, took the company 'up-market' in terms of the brand prestige, allowing the company more of the total market place than it could reach before.

The company may also wish to increase its market share in an attempt to dominate the market, although this may fall foul of antimonopoly legislation (*see page 215*).

**3** **Conglomeration** – this is the amassing of companies in unrelated business into a group. There are several arguments in favour of this which we will look at below.

The acquiring company may have sound business reasons for making the offer, such as the following.

**Economies of scale,** where the combined buying power of the two companies can improve research and development and reduce costs. Horizontal takeovers are very often for reasons of economy of scale, but the same motive is sometimes claimed for conglomerate mergers. This is less convincing, because conglomerates can sometimes create large bureaucracies which can outweigh the benefits of the takeover.

**Improving efficiency.** If the target company is peopled by bad managers who are firmly entrenched, a takeover by a dynamic company who will sack the old regime and increase efficiency is sometimes the only practical way to save the company. The old managers will often attempt to protect their positions by strongly resisting the takeover; this is a primary cause for takeover battles.

**Tax losses and pension funds.** A company may have made substantial tax losses which it cannot use. If it takes over another company, it can benefit by setting off the tax losses against the other company's profits. Some companies hold large pension funds for their employees, which have been known to be an attraction to predators, especially when they contain surpluses over their pension obligations.

**Takeovers.** Taking over a smaller specialist company to market their products better can often be cheaper for a big business than setting up competing products from scratch.

**Key skills**. Companies will also bid for others in order to access key skills which they require but do not possess in house. While merchant banks may do this by 'head-hunting' key people or even whole departments, most industrial companies will tend to buy up a company with the necessary skills.

 **Example**

A good example of this is the proposed purchase of Amstrad by Psion. Psion, makers of hand-held computers, have identified the requirement to integrate into their product offering some kind of communication capability. Amstrad have a number of interests, including retail outlets but also a cellular telephone division. It is the skills-base in the cellular telephone business which makes the company as a whole attractive to Psion.

**Synergy**. This is an argument that 2+2 can be made to equal 5. Often used when companies are in similar markets where research or marketing budgets can be shared or integrated after an acquisition. The acquisition by North West Water, the water utility, of the regional electricity company to form a 'super-utility' was a good example of a management team seeking to combine two companies and create synergy (or savings) by combining the businesses. Instead of two sets of infra-structure, one larger company will be created, which may be more efficient. As these companies share intrinsically a similar customer base, on the simplest level one billing system should be able to manage the process of invoicing more efficiently than before.

# What makes companies vulnerable to bids?

Some companies get a reputation for being likely to attract bids that last for decades without a bid ever actually emerging, so it is difficult to spot winners with certainty. The profile of a likely candidate for a takeover bid is a company with a large amount of assets, a broad shareholder base and a good underlying business. Sometimes they are found in the following situations:

**1** Companies that have been controlled by families for decades, if not for generations, may be amenable to takeover bids; it all turns on whether the major shareholders want to sell, perhaps in order to retire, or whether they are determined to hang on.

**2** Companies that produce a lower return on the capital employed than is normal in their industry can be the target of takeover bids from other more competitive companies in the same industry, the idea being that the acquirer will be able to make the company more profitable than it is at present. The same goes for trading profits – sometimes a famous name is going downhill, and is taken over by a company in the same business who hopes to increase margins through the power of the combined turnover.

**3** Companies in which a possible predator has bought a large number of shares; the share price will rise on this news, but if investors feel that the target company is an attractive one, they may continue to buy now and wait for the bid. Sometimes the stakeholder sells the shares on to another bidder, so other investors play a waiting game. The danger is that the stakeholder may simply drop out, with a consequent fall in the share price back to its original level.

**4** Insider trading. Although it is now illegal in the UK to buy shares because you have inside information, share prices have a curious tendency to rise before any news of the acquisition of a large stake appears. Company employees, their relatives and people in the City who know about the planned bid may buy shares without realising that it is illegal to do so, but even if the insider trading is deliberate, it is very hard to prove.

## The Monopolies and Mergers Commission and other authorities

There are laws to prevent companies buying up their competitors in order to create a monopoly, so there is a chance that a UK takeover bid may be referred to the Monopolies and Mergers Commission. If the bid is referred, a failure can mean a large fall in the price. Although companies take a lot of advice to ensure that their bids will not be referred, some bids do fail. The British Takeover Panel is a City organisation which oversees the takeover process and tries to make sure that everybody plays by the rules. It is not a state-controlled body, and has attracted criticism from outsiders who feel that it does not have enough power to force people to play fair. The European Commission is also becoming increasingly involved with the job of overseeing big European takeovers. The European Commission is expected to try to change the way that takeovers are conducted in the UK in the future.

In the UK, the Panel on Takeovers and Mergers (the Takeover Panel) enforces a Takeover Code on stock market mergers and acquisitions. The guiding principle of the code is that all shareholders should be treated equally during takeovers, so the rules concentrate on ensuring that all the shareholders are properly informed and are able to act before ownership actually changes hands. One of the ways that it does this is by using 'trigger points'.

Trigger points are fixed levels of share holding at which a shareholder must make certain declarations. For example, if a person or company buys more than 3 per cent of a company's shares, it must make a public declaration that it has done so. If the shareholder goes on to build up a stake of 30 per cent in the company, he or she must then make a bid for all the shares unless there is a special exemption.

When a bid for a company emerges, the Office of Fair Trading decides whether or not to refer it to the Monopolies and Mergers Commission. The Commission will investigate a takeover and has the power to veto it if it believes that the merged company represents a monopoly, or near monopoly, in a certain market. These decisions are not always easy to predict, and since the investigation takes several months, a Monopoly Commission referral can mean the collapse of a bid.

In the USA the rules are different. The 'antitrust' laws make it illegal for companies not only to monopolise markets, but also to 'tend' to create a monopoly, use unfair methods of competition or attempt to 'unreasonably' restrain trade. In practice, the bigger the companies, the more likely it is that a takeover bid will provoke anti-trust lawsuits. Such lawsuits have a political dimension; under President Reagan, corporate America was given clear signals that there would be fewer government lawsuits against them, and a greater freedom to seek profits wherever they could be found. The scandals involving Ivan Boesky, an 'arbitrageur' who would buy large stakes in companies in the hope of an impending bid, or sometimes in an attempt to 'greenmail' the shareholders (ultimately the market) into allowing him to sell out at a profit, and Michael Milken, who controlled billions of funds generated by his 'junk bonds', were one result of the greater freedom from regulation.

# Conglomerates

The term conglomerate is used to describe a group of separate companies grouped together which trade separately. The traditional view of the advantage of the conglomerate is that it can spread its risk by investing in widely differing businesses. This view is rather old fashioned now as the more sophisticated investors are considered to be able to spread the investment risk themselves using the market.

'Portfolio theory' is the method used by sophisticated investors to maximise returns while minimising risk by spreading the investment across many companies, and for larger funds across different markets in differing countries and currencies. Of course your grandmother wouldn't call it portfolio theory; she'd say 'don't put all your eggs in one basket'. In less sophisticated times, individual investors might be encouraged to invest in a conglomerate as the risk would have been spread within the company.

The strongest *raison d'être* of the conglomerate now is that of strong management teams adding value to previously under-performing businesses. The 'Hanson-style' conglomerate can add substantial value to the market as a whole if it can identify companies which are under-performing versus their potential as a result of weak or over-costly management. One such strategy which can work effectively is to specialise in acquiring low-technology companies in well-established markets, where returns can be improved by conservative, cost-conscious management.

> Acquisitive conglomerates can thrive by identifying weak companies, acquiring them, and, by the use of better or more appropriate management skills, improving the profitability of the target company.

Critics of this approach (Will Hutton, author of *The State We're In*, being amongst the most eloquent) complain that this leads to an overly short-term management focus. While this may be true, company law makes directors responsible for the interest of the shareholders, on whose behalf they are (at least in theory) managing the company. The owners of a company are clearly served by an increase in the share price.

If the body of shareholders are not convinced that the long-term profits resulting from a company's strategies are sufficient to outweigh the immediate gain from accepting the offer from a hostile bidder, then they are perhaps not best served by arguing about the rules of the game. Companies with efficient management structures, lean production methods, and who have the full support of the body of shareholders for their medium and long-term strategies, have little to fear from a hostile bidder except in very unusual circumstances.

# Accounting implications

The process of acquisition is complicated by a number of aspects:

- Companies within a group (see Chapter 1) are consolidated. This means that instead of showing an investment in a number of shares, the parent company will show the underlying assets which were acquired, i.e. the buildings, assets, stock, etc.

- The accounting policies of the acquired company and its new parent may be different, requiring adjustments to be made to asset values or profits.

- The new parent may wish to undertake restructuring actions which require provisions to be made against them.

## Example

Let's take the company used in earlier chapters as an example of an acquired company.

**Barking Traders Ltd**
**Balance Sheet**
**31st January 1997**

| | |
|---|---|
| Fixed assets | £50,000 |
| Current assets | |
| – stocks | £50,000 |
| – cash | 10,000 |
| Net current assets | £60,000 |
| Net assets | £110,000 |
| Shareholders' funds | |
| – called up share capital | £10,000 |
| – share premium account | 90,000 |
| – profit and loss account | 10,000 |
| Shareholders' funds | £110,000 |

In this example the book value of the assets of Barking Traders is £110,000. Now let's look at the company acquiring Barking Traders Ltd – Raider plc.

**Raider plc**
**Balance Sheet**
**31st January 1997**

| | |
|---|---|
| Fixed assets | £750,000 |
| Current assets | |
| – stocks | £250,000 |
| – cash | 500,000 |
| Net current assets | £750,000 |
| Net assets | £1,500,000 |
| Shareholders' funds | |
| – called up share capital | £750,000 |
| – share premium account | 250,000 |
| – profit and loss account | 500,000 |
| Shareholders' funds | £1,500,000 |

Raider plc acquires Barking Traders on 31 January 1997, immediately after these balance sheets are drawn up. As a plc, Raider will be required to publish balance sheets both for the company itself, and for the consolidated group as a whole. Developing the balance sheet for Raider plc on a company basis is straight-forward. The company has acquired shares in Barking Traders for an amount of cash.

The fixed assets category of Raider is expanded to show the investment in Barking Traders, at the cost to the company of this investment. Assuming a cash consideration only, cash is reduced by the same amount. Whatever the amount paid for the company, the balance sheet looks very much the same, as shown in Figure 11.1.

---

Before we go on to look at the group balance sheet we should consider the valuation of the company. Referring back to Chapter 2 on ratios, we can deduce that the value of a company is more to do with the earnings capability of the company, and such strategic factors as its growth, the sector in which it operates and so on. The net assets of the company may have little to do with the valuation of the company in the market place.

Consider the enormous valuations at which US software companies are being floated. These companies are a collection of very smart people developing very 'sexy'

Internet-related software products which could enjoy explosive sales and profit growth. The market doesn't really care about the amount of assets that is behind the valuation. The extent to which a company valuation is 'justified' by physical assets in the company is known as the asset-backing.

| | Pre-acquisition | |
|---|---|---|
| | Raider plc | Barking Traders |
| Fixed assets | 750,000 | 50,000 |
| Shares in Barking Trading | | |
| Current assets | | |
| – stocks | 250,000 | 50,000 |
| – cash | 500,000 | 10,000 |
| Net current assets | 750,000 | 60,000 |
| Net assets | 1,500,000 | 110,000 |
| Shareholders' funds | | |
| – called up share capital | 750,000 | 10,000 |
| – share premium account | 250,000 | 90,000 |
| – profit and loss account | 500,000 | 10,000 |
| – goodwill written off | | |
| Shareholders' funds | 1,500,000 | 110,000 |
| Purchase price | | |
| Goodwill | | |

Figure 11.1   Acquisitions (1)

So the valuation of a company is not really connected to the 'book-value' of the assets on the balance sheet.

## Example

When Ford acquired Jaguar, the balance sheet of Jaguar showed net assets of approximately £600 million. Since Jaguar was such a respected brand across the world, the company as a whole represented far more than just the physical assets. The company was actually purchased by Ford for some £1,600 million. The premium of £1 billion over the net asset value is known as goodwill.

## Example

Going back to the example, Raider plc will also produce a group balance sheet as shown in Figure 11.2.

| | Raider plc | Pre-acquisition Barking Traders | Group Raider plc |
|---|---|---|---|
| Fixed assets | 750,000 | 50,000 | 800,000 |
| Shares in Barking Trading | | | |
| Current assets | | | |
| – stocks | 250,000 | 50,000 | 300,000 |
| – cash | 500,000 | 10,000 | 400,000 |
| Net current assets | 750,000 | 60,000 | 700,000 |
| Net assets | 1,500,000 | 110,000 | 1,500,000 |
| Shareholders' funds | | | |
| – called up share capital | 750,000 | 10,000 | 750,000 |
| – share premium account | 250,000 | 90,000 | 250,000 |
| – profit and loss account | 500,000 | 10,000 | 500,000 |
| – goodwill written off | | | |
| Shareholders' funds | 1,500,000 | 110,000 | 1,500,000 |
| Purchase price | | | 110,000 |
| Goodwill | | | |

Figure 11.2   Acquisitions (2)

This balance sheet for the group shows the position for the consolidated group now including Barking Traders. Thus the fixed assets in the group are now £800,000, the total for the two companies. Shareholders' funds represent the shareholders in the group. Note that the 'shareholders' funds' in BT have 'disappeared' since they have been bought out. Note also that cash levels are the sum of the two groups less the purchase price.

It is worth working through this simple example before we proceed. Assets are the assets of the total group, less cash used to purchase the new company which left the group. The shareholders of the parent company, Raider, haven't changed because all that's happened is that the company has bought another company. Shareholders' funds are therefore unchanged. What has happened from the point of view of Raider is as follows:

| | Barking Traders | Purchase | Net effect |
|---|---|---|---|
| Fixed assets | £50,000 | | £50,000 |
| Current assets | | | |
| – stocks | £50,000 | | £50,000 |
| – cash | 10,000 | (110,000) | (100,000) |
| Total assets | £110,000 | £(110,000) | £0 |

And everything balances! This is convenient because what has happened is that Raider has paid an amount for the company equal to its asset value. As we have seen above, though, this is highly unlikely. Let us now assume that the company was purchased for £200,000.

We now have a situation where the cash paid out of the group is in excess of the tangible assets received. We have essentially 'bought' the goodwill of the business, representing the brand loyalty, its good name in the market place, the experience of its employees, etc. To try to introduce this into the equation, we have:

| | Barking Traders | Purchase | Net effect |
|---|---|---|---|
| Fixed assets | £50,000 | | £50,000 |
| Intangible assets – goodwill | | £90,000 | £90,000 |
| Current assets | | | |
| – stocks | £50,000 | | £50,000 |
| – cash | 10,000 | (200,000) | (190,000) |
| Total assets | £110,000 | £(110,000) | £0 |

 There are essentially two treatments to this new item under the rules.

■ The intangible can be recognised as an asset. It will then be subject to depreciation which will of course impact profitability in future years.

- The amount can be 'written off' against reserves – effectively this shows as a reduction against total shareholders' funds – there is no impact on forward year profitability.

Astute readers will by now have guessed that the most popular method of treating goodwill is the second.

### Example

In this example the balance sheet will be as shown in Figure 11.3.

| | Raider plc | Pre-acquisition Barking Traders | Company Raider plc | Group Raider plc |
|---|---|---|---|---|
| Fixed assets | 750,000 | 50,000 | 750,000 | 800,000 |
| Shares in Barking Trading | | | 200,000 | |
| Current assets | | | | |
| – stocks | 250,000 | 50,000 | 250,000 | 300,000 |
| – cash | 500,000 | 10,000 | 300,000 | 310,000 |
| Net current assets | 750,000 | 60,000 | 550,000 | 610,000 |
| Net assets | 1,500,000 | 110,000 | 1,500,000 | 1,410,000 |
| Shareholders' funds | | | | |
| – called up share capital | 750,000 | 10,000 | 750,000 | 750,000 |
| – share premium account | 250,000 | 90,000 | 250,000 | 250,000 |
| – profit and loss account | 500,000 | 10,000 | 500,000 | 500,000 |
| – goodwill written off | | | | (90,000) |
| Shareholders' funds | 1,500,000 | 110,000 | 1,500,000 | 1,410,000 |
| Purchase price | | | 200,000 | 200,000 |
| Goodwill | | | | 90,000 |

Figure 11.3    Acquisitions (3)

So the first of the accounting implications comes from the need to produce consolidated accounts. Any excess of the purchase price over the net assets of the company creates a surplus called goodwill, normally written off against shareholders' reserves.

# Accounting policies

Next among the issues facing companies after an acquisition is that accounting policies should be consistent within a group of companies and the newly acquired company may have adopted policies which differ from its new parent. Simple issues such as changing the financial year end of the new group member can be left to your accountants, but you should be aware that commonising policies can have a substantial effect. Differences in the treatment of depreciation, research and development expenditures and reserves can have a material impact on the profits of the company under its new ownership.

### Example

Rover Group in the UK was recently taken over by German giant BMW. In March of 1996, Rover released figures for the year of 1995 showing a profit of some £91 million, up slightly from the previous year. Revised figures issued by BMW, its new parent, admittedly under German accounting rules, showed a loss of £148 million. This change was mostly attributed to higher depreciation costs.

## Provisions

Companies making acquisitions are allowed to make provisions to write down asset values of the acquired companies. Acquisition accounting has been heavily criticised in the past for allowing acquiring companies to provide for future restructuring and even future trading losses.

This practice was described by ASB Chairman Sir David Tweedie as 'The black hole of British accounting'. This loophole has been largely closed with the introduction of FRSs 6 and 7 in late 1994.

Companies may still write down asset values provided that they remain at levels which are 'arm's length'. The lower the asset values that can be made post acquisition, the higher the amount of goodwill charged to reserves, and the greater the flexibility in future profit and loss accounts.

# International accounting

It should be noted that under US GAAP, goodwill created on acquisition is created as an asset on the balance sheet and is then required to be written off *against future profits* over a period not exceeding forty years.

In this way the capital base of the company remains unchanged as a result of the acquisition, and the premium paid for the acquired company must be amortised. In effect, the acquisition and any premium must 'pay for itself'.

# Due diligence

The rather odd-sounding term 'due diligence' is used to describe the audit of a company before purchase. When purchasing a house we find the right property, agree a price 'subject to contract' and then make a number of checks, structural surveys, land register, etc. Only when these checks are satisfactorily completed do we sign the binding contract to purchase the house. Due diligence can be thought of as the checks made after agreeing the basic terms of acquisition but before the final agreement to purchase the company is made.

In this process, a team of people from the acquiring company will check the worth of the company to be purchased. They will make spot audit checks on the company's accounts, both published and internal, and they will report on the other risks inherent in the business, such as term of contracts, reliance on customers or suppliers, inherent risk of the market, etc. Often, items found in the due diligence process may lead to a re-negotiation of the acquisition price, or even to the failure of the acquisition process.

# How much do mergers really cost?

One way of looking at the cost of a merger is to say that it is the amount the bidder pays for the 'goodwill' of the target, over and above its value as a separate company. The trouble is that the current stock market value of the target may not reflect its 'true value'. Often the price of a target company rises on the rumour of an impending takeover bid. Often companies do not pay in cash when they buy a company, but finance the purchase by means of an exchange of shares.

**Example**

Company A wants to buy Company B, and offers Company B 200,000 of its own (A's) shares, which are 10 per cent of the 2 million shares in issue. A's share price is currently £10, so A is offering £2 million worth of shares. Let's suppose that, at the time of this offer, B's stock market value is £1.8 million.

You might say that the difference between the value of the shares offered and the market value of Company B is £200,000 (£2,000,000 –£1,800,000); the 'cost' of the merger. This may not be true, however:

- Company B may not be worth the £1.8 million at which it is currently valued in the stock market.

- Company A may not be worth the £20 million at which it is currently valued in the stock market.

- Company B's shareholders will receive 200,000 shares in Company A if the merger goes through, so they will be getting back some of the gains A will get by merging with B.

Assuming the market values are correct, if Company B's shareholders get $w$ worth of the merged Company AB by accepting the merger, the cost to Company A is:

$$A's \ cost = (w \times value \ of \ merged \ companies)$$
$$- \ the \ pre\text{-}merger \ value \ of \ B$$

Working this out in terms of shares, the value of the merged companies is 2 million shares plus 200,000 shares (note that this is just for the purposes of calculation; no new shares are being issued). The pre-merger value of B is 200,000 of A's shares, so:

$$A's \ cost = (w \times 2,200,000) - 200,000$$
$$w = 200,000/2,200,000$$
$$= 0.09$$

B shareholders' share of the merged Company AB will be 9%.

Let's suppose now that the merger has been a sensible one, and that the merged company will make gains of £500,000.

Value of Company AB = pre-merger market value of A + the pre-merger market value of B + £500,000.

$$Value \ of \ Company \ AB = £20,000,000 + £1,800,000 + £500,000$$
$$= £22,300,000$$

We know that the cost to Company A will be:

($w \times$ value of merged companies) – the pre-merger value of B, and that $w = 0.09$,

so:

$$
\begin{aligned}
\text{A's cost} \ &= \ (0.09 \times 22{,}300{,}000) - 1{,}800{,}000 \\
&= \ 2{,}007{,}000 - 1{,}800{,}000 \\
&= \ \pounds 207{,}000
\end{aligned}
$$

Thus you can see that the cost of the merger to A is £207,000, somewhat more than the apparent cost of £200,000, which we got by subtracting B's pre-merger market value from the pre-merger market value of the shares which A offered.

---

> **!** By paying for a company partly or completely in its own shares, a purchaser is better off if the stock market valuations are wrong than if it paid in cash; this is because the shareholders of B share some of the burden of a drop in value of AB's shares.

# Bids and the stock market

The news that a company is trying to take over a company by buying its shares is almost always good news for the existing shareholders. Often companies compete to take over a target, so its shareholders find themselves the focus of a stream of letters urging them to accept or reject increasingly higher bids for their shares. There then follows the enjoyable task of deciding which bid to accept, and when. Shareholders usually have sixty days in which to decide whether to accept a bid, Once the bid has expired, if the bidding company has succeeded in buying over 90 per cent of the total number of shares in the target company, it can then force the existing shareholders to accept a price for their shares which is lower than the successful bid price. The bids for their shares may offer shares in the acquiring company, or a combination of such shares, fixed interest securities and cash in exchange. These offers may not always represent a profitable exchange. Sometimes a company does not want to be taken over, and decides to fight the bids; it will produce strong arguments for rejecting the offer.

The rules for takeovers say that bids cannot be called 'final' until very near the end of the war, so if shareholders receive a bid that is not described as final they may wait for a better offer. The target company may try to find a 'white knight' investor to counter-bid in the hope that life under the white knight will be better than under the predator. Bidders can improve their offers up to the 46th day of the bid, and the defending company has until the 39th day to produce key financial arguments against the bids. A bidding company doesn't have to own any shares in a company to bid for it, but often it tries to build up a stake in advance of bidding. The UK rules say that shareholdings of over 3 per cent in a company must be declared publicly so that people can have some warning of what may happen.

Once a bidder controls over 50 per cent of the shares, he or she effectively controls the company. Predators sometimes buy up to 15 per cent of a company in a 'dawn raid' on the stock market, after which they may not buy any more shares for a week. They can then build their holdings to 25 per cent before waiting again. Once the shareholding has passed 30 per cent, they must bid for the company. If they can persuade people to sell them 20 per cent more of the company's shares, they can then announce that the bid is 'unconditional as to acceptances', which means that the rest of the shareholders have two weeks in which to make up their minds. If these shareholders refuse the offer, which is unusual, they keep their shares in the company, but it is now under the bidder's control. As mentioned earlier, if bidders manage to get 90 per cent of the shares, they can forcibly buy the remaining 10 per cent.

Once a bidder is in control of the company, it remains to be seen whether the predator has gauged its value correctly; companies engaging in a series of takeovers during a boom, doing their sums on the assumption of ever-increasing values, can be very badly caught out in a crash. Just because an acquiring company is willing to pay a high price does not necessarily mean that its judgement is correct; mergers can and do fail to live up to expectations.

Sometimes existing shareholders prefer to take some of the acquiring company's shares in lieu of cash because there is no capital gains tax to pay when they receive the shares; sometimes they are only given 21 days from the date of the bid in which to decide to choose cash.

Normally after a winning bid the merged company's share price will not move much for some time. However, it sometimes continues to go up. This is an effect of speculation on the hope of improved business results or further acquisitions.

# The 'chain letter' effect

This is when a company with low earnings and high growth conducts a series of takeovers of high earning/low growth companies, financing the offers mainly with its own 'paper' (offering its own shares to shareholders in the target companies). There is nothing wrong about this in principle, but if the acquiring company fools the market into thinking that its rapid growth is for sound business reasons, rather than simply through the acquisitions, it then must continue with the same rate of growth if it is to keep its share price up, and the temptation is to find further acquisitions. In the end there will be no more companies to buy, its growth will slow and its share price will collapse.

**Example**

Suppose that Company A, the acquiring company, has total earnings of £300,000 and 1,000,000 shares, making its earnings per share 30p. Its P/E ratio is, say, 20, so its share price will be 600p.

Now suppose that Company B, the target company, also has earnings of £300,000, 1,000,000 shares and earnings per share of 30p but the lower P/E ratio of 10, making its share price 300p. Company A's market value is thus twice that of Company B's. If Company A can buy Company B by offering half of its own shares, it will then have total earnings of £600,000 and 1,500,000 shares, making the earnings per share 40p. If its share price stays the same, its P/E ratio falls to 15.

If investors think that the increase in earnings per share is 'real' growth, they may invest, pushing up the P/E ratio as the share price rises.

Mergers and acquisitions are a glamorous and lucrative field during times when the stock market is booming, but one hears little about them during less prosperous times. What is clear is that while acquisitions benefit the majority shareholders in the acquiring company, and usually the shareholders of the target company, the actual businesses and management of the companies concerned do not always enjoy the promised improvements.

To see how a classic predator takes advantage of the opportunities for takeovers, we should look at the activities of Sir James Goldsmith, who embarked on a succession of highly lucrative takeovers and takeover attempts during the 1980s.

In 1979 Sir James Goldsmith controlled Cavenham Foods, an international conglomerate in food manufacturing and retailing. Deciding to concentrate on retailing, Goldsmith sold off his manufacturing interests piecemeal, raising £100 million by early 1980.

He began to buy shares in Diamond International, a US wood products conglomerate with sales of $1.2 billion, but which had low profits. Discovering that Diamond owned, since the nineteenth century, 1.6 million acres of land which it was valuing at only £27 million, Goldsmith announced publicly that he planned to make a bid for the company. Meanwhile, Diamond launched a bid for another wood products company, Brooks Scanlon, to be financed by a new issue of Diamond shares.

Goldsmith then offered Diamond shareholders $45 per share on the condition that they rejected the Brooks Scanlon deal, or $40 if it was concluded, and increased his own holding in Diamond to 6 per cent. The stock market price of Diamond's shares was $32.65, but it increased to $38.20 after Goldsmith's announcement.

Goldsmith then tried, and failed, to obtain an injunction to prevent Diamond from holding its AGM. At the AGM, however, the main shareholders in Diamond were divided in their support, so the smaller investors had to be given a vote on whether or not to accept the bid. Diamond made a deal with Goldsmith that they would allow him to increase his stake to 25 per cent on the condition that Goldsmith would not raise it above 40 per cent, and also gave him the right to appoint three directors to the board.

Diamond's shares had gone up to $50 in the market, but on the news of this latest agreement they dropped to $38.25. Goldsmith obtained 21.5 million shares, but the merger with Brook Scanlon went ahead, so he owned only 24 per cent of the merged company; the purchase cost him $105 million.

During the following year a recession hit the wood products industry. Although Diamond was able to maintain its turnover at $1.28 million, its profits were only $41 million, and the share price dropped to $29. The ex-boss of Brooks Scanlon, who now owned 1.6 million Diamond shares, approached Goldsmith, offering to sell the shares at $42 (a premium of $13 per share over the current market price). Goldsmith bought them, increasing his holding in Diamond to about 40 per cent; Diamond's management caved in, and sold Goldsmith a controlling interest in the company. Goldsmith now borrowed the vast sum of $660 million to purchase the rest of Diamond and inject cash into the company. The interest rate was as high as 18 per cent, and Diamond's profits would barely cover a third of the annual interest payments on the loan.

Goldsmith then proceeded to sell off some of Diamond's subsidiaries, paying off, by 1983, all of his debt. This sell-off stimulated adverse criticism of him as an asset-stripper. Goldsmith concentrated on Diamond's vast holdings of forest land, cutting costs and building new saw mills to increase productivity. The stock market went up, and by the summer of 1983 his forests were valued at $723 million, representing a net profit to Goldsmith of around $500 million.

The USA's Reagan administration had taken wide measures to deregulate the economy, and a craze for mergers began, driving up the prices of listed companies. Goldsmith decided to increase his forest holdings from 1.6 million acres to 10 million acres. He found another American wood company, St Regis, which owned 3.2 million acres of forest valued in its accounts at $223 million, considerably less than what they were currently worth. In company with financial backers, Goldsmith acquired 8.6 per cent of St Regis.

This action stimulated other speculators to buy St Regis shares, which rose from around $38 to $40. St Regis agreed that Goldsmith could purchase 25 per cent of its equity for $300 million. Concerned that the management wanted to increase its diversification from wood products, Goldsmith obtained an agreement that any large investments made by St Regis would have to have prior unanimous approval of the board or be put to a shareholder vote.

▶

Bids for the rest of St Regis emerged from various quarters, and a company called Champion International finally took over the company at $52 per share. Goldsmith sold his shareholding to them, netting a profit of $51 million for himself and his backers within a month of the original purchase. Goldsmith's critics now accused him of 'greenmail', the deliberate attempt to manipulate a company's share price by pretending to make a bid in the hope that other bidders will emerge.

Goldsmith, however, was still in the market for forests. In 1984 he bid $50 a share for Continental Group, a conglomerate which happened to own 1.4 million acres of forest, undervalued on its books, and millions of barrels of oil. Realising that the company needed rationalisation, but unwilling to face the hatchet-job necessary, the management of Continental sought other buyers. Goldsmith raised his offer to $58 per share, but a rival bidder offered $58.50. Goldsmith pulled out, selling his shares for $10 million profit plus $25 million in compensation fees.

In December 1984, Goldsmith announced his intention of buying 15 to 20 per cent of Crown Zellerbach, another conglomerate with 2 million acres of cheap forest and large oil holdings; its shares were then at $28. Three months later, he had invested about $80 million to purchase 8.6 per cent of the company's shares, which by then stood at $33.25.

The 'merger mania' of the 1980s was in full swing, and boards everywhere were struggling to make their companies look as unattractive as possible to potential bidders. The method they used most was the 'poison pill', an arrangement to issue new shares at a large discount to existing shareholders in the event of a bid, which has the effect of making a company too expensive for a bidder to buy.

Crown Zellerbach had a 'poison pill' which became effective if someone bought 20 per cent of the company's shares. After an abortive attempt to find another buyer, it approached Goldsmith to offer a deal by which he would acquire no more than 19.5 per cent of the company for the next three years, and Crown would cancel the poison pill. Goldsmith made a counter offer which was rejected; he then proceeded to purchase shares to give him a total of 19.6 per cent of the company, just below the trigger level of the poison pill. Crown were now under pressure – once Goldsmith triggered the poison pill, Crown would become prohibitively expensive to other bidders.

Following bitter litigation, Goldsmith managed to acquire a controlling interest in the company, and it was split into two, the forests and oil going to Goldsmith, and the rest going to a paper company. For $550 million, Goldsmith had acquired assets which were now estimated to be worth about $990 million. With his previous forest holdings, he now owned a total of 4 million acres, which he transferred to his US holding company, GOSL Acquisition Corporation and invested in improving them.

In 1986 Goldsmith tried to take over the Goodyear Corporation, but failed after a public outcry against the bid, accepting a profit of $93 million for himself and his financial backers. He considered making other bids, but eventually decided that the market was overvalued and that there were no more bargains to be had; selling his entire shareholdings in early 1987, Goldsmith pulled off the biggest coup of his whole career. Shortly afterwards the world's stock markets crashed on Black Monday, dropping further than they had for nearly sixty years, and wiping billions off the market value of companies across the globe.

# CHAPTER TWELVE

# Risk and risk management

- Risk analysis

- Environmental/strategic risk

- Financial risk

- The forward contract

- Derivatives

- Financial futures – hedging versus speculation

- Other financial risks

- Longer-term risk

- The risk/reward relationship and the stock market

- The 'equity risk' of a listed company

- Conclusion

## Risk analysis

This chapter will look at the ways of assessing the risk within a commercial organisation. Accountants have a reputation for being careful pessimistic people – a reputation that is richly deserved! In any organisation a balance is required.

The stereotypical image is of the general and sales managers to have a tendency to be gung-ho 'up and at 'em' who find the 'look before you leap' tendency of their accountants somewhat frustrating. This may indeed ring true in many organisations, but the strongest companies will have a good mix of people, and will find the consensus decision with which all are comfortable.

The aim of this chapter is to show the sort of strategic and commercial risks which all financially aware managers should be looking for when assessing a commercial situation. As we've said before, think of your own organisation or company when working through this chapter – think of the risks outlined in this chapter as they might apply to your company.

We need to assess the risk of a company in many circumstances:

- when, as in the previous chapter, conducting due diligence on an acquisition target
- when considering joining a new company
- when deciding whether to invest in a company
- when looking at a potential supplier or trade partner.

Finally this chapter will discuss some of the tools which exist in order to hedge some of the purely financial risks which will be described.

Risk, though, can exist on many levels within an organisation:

- **environmental**
- **strategic**
- **financial.**

# Environmental/strategic risk

There are a number of useful tools which can be applied in assessing the strategic risk of a business. Perhaps the most common of these is SWOT analysis, with which you may be familiar.

| STRENGTHS | WEAKNESSES |
|---|---|
| OPPORTUNITIES | THREATS |

SWOT is a planning tool to assist in the identification of strategic issues, including risks, which impact an organisation.

- Opportunities and threats are those issues which are *external* to the organisation – or environmental.

- Strengths and weaknesses are those areas which are within, or internal to, the company.

It is important that the management of any company have an understanding of their current strategic position when managing the business. In the 1990s it is not melodramatic to say that a company not going forward in terms of its competitive position will be slipping backwards.

## Environmental risk

Looking first at the external factors, all companies operate within an environment. While much of this may be beyond the influence of all but the largest companies, the outside environment should be understood in terms of the potential impact on the company of government policy, fiscal changes, labour laws and practices, exchange rate practices and policy, environmental (i.e. green) laws and practices.

Companies operating in an international market, and most are, need to understand the implications of the environment on their business. Feeling comfortable in a UK business with UK customers? What happens to competitiveness when that foreign competitor manufacturing overseas sees Sterling appreciate in value versus his own cost base – he can sell cheaper – would you still think you're not in an international environment?

What legislation might be on the horizon that could have an impact on your company domestically or overseas? If you have a high proportion of part-time employees, what might the potential pension implications following the recent EC judgements cost you? If you have a large number of low skilled, low paid people, what are the implications of the potential imposition of a minimum wage?

Companies must be aware of the environment in which they operate – constantly evaluating the risks and opportunities that may arise.

## Competitive environment

To examine the competitive environment in which a company operates, one of the most effective tools was developed by Michael Porter, arguably one of the most influential and productive gurus of the 1980s. Porter developed a model describing the 'five competitive forces' as follows:

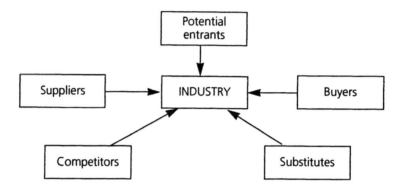

 These five forces need to be explored by addressing:

- The nature of our existing competitors: who is gaining market share; at who's expense? Think of the enormous price warfare between the major broadsheet newspapers.

- How great is the threat from new entrants? What are the barriers to entry? In a service business the barriers to new entrants will be small – in the bulk chemicals or pharmaceutical businesses barriers will include huge investment in research and plants.

- What threats are there from alternatives or substitutes to our product or service? IBM, although dominant in the mainframe market, was hit hard not by anybody doing mainframe computers better but because they could not respond quickly enough when customers shifted towards PCs.

- What is the nature of the relationship with suppliers? Who dictates the trading terms, and holds the power? If you are a small company reliant on the output of a huge concern for your business, what do you do when the large company discontinues the production of the material you require? Can you find an alternative source?

- Conversely, if you find that most of your output is purchased by a single large company who has a number of other companies able to supply it with similar goods, how do you resist its request for a price reduction?

The above can largely be said to be common sense but is often overlooked when looking at companies, to assess them. When assessing a company keep asking yourself 'what if'.

Think of your own company.

- What are the major relationships between buyers and suppliers?

- Are you dominant, dependent or in between?

- Are you a strong player in the market able to influence terms, or an also ran with a low market share having to accept the prevailing price

## Strengths and weaknesses

Going back to the SWOT analysis we noted that the opportunities and threats relate to external factors, while strengths and weaknesses relate to internal factors.

Weaknesses might include a dated product range or a factory with historically high labour content and costs. If the threats include new low cost competition, the combination of the two could be fatal for the company in the medium term unless strong corrective action is taken. Other weaknesses might include a high fixed cost base, or poor market image.

# Financial risk

When we talk of risk we talk of a company being 'exposed' to risk. Clearly the financial implications of the strategic and environmental risks discussed above may be very great. These risks though are normally considered to be managed through the use of long-term strategic plans. Companies running strategic and environmental risks and with no plans to address them tend to go the way of the dodo in Darwin's evolution of species.

Thriving and successful companies will also find themselves with other risks which are considered here as financial risks. There are a variety of tools which have developed to address these risks, and it is well that the non-financial manager is aware of the risks and what can be done to 'hedge' or mitigate against them.

### Example

A company in the UK is manufacturing products which it is trying to sell into the US. The goods will be manufactured in the next eight weeks, and shipped out for delivery in the US in three months' time. Payment will be the normal thirty day terms and we'll therefore expect payment four months from today.

The sales director, reviewing the proposed pricing of the contract, is shown the following figures:

| | |
|---|---|
| Cost to produce | £5.00 |
| Shipping cost including duties | 1.00 |
| Total landed cost | £6.00 |
| Sales mark-up 50% | £3.00 |
| Total sales amount | £9.00 |
| Price quoted to customer | $13.50 |
| (current exchange rate £1 = $1.50) | |

Straightforward stuff: our total cost including shipping and duties is £6 and we normally operate on a mark up to cost of 50 per cent which makes £9. The sales manager then checks his FT for the latest exchange rate and quoted the price in $.

The minute we agree a binding contract on this basis we expose the company to an exchange rate risk.

We won't actually receive the payment until four months after the price is quoted. What will the $ be worth against sterling at this time? Apart from George Soros, who may have picked up this book on his way through Heathrow, the rest of us mortals really don't have a clue, do we?

> As a pure aside, this author has lost track of the number of times intelligent colleagues have said things like 'I'm off to France/the States/Spain later this year – what's going to happen to the currency?' While it's very flattering that they think I might know, my answer is normally 'If I really knew the answer to that question, do you really think I'd still be at work?'

The point of this aside is to illustrate that, despite the attempts by forecasters and commentators to predict the future of exchange rates, we can't. As businesspeople, we must avoid the tendency to think in terms of 'well I think the dollar will strengthen' and instead see the risk. Nick Leeson thought he could beat the market, and he even did for a while.

We have, therefore, established the following:

- normal trading has created an exposure to movements in the £/$ exchange rate

- we can't predict the future movement of the dollar

- what can we do to address this risk?

We could invoice the customer in £ sterling, thus passing the currency risk on to our customer. This may not be acceptable for sales and marketing reasons, but keep it in mind as an option. Some customers may welcome the chance, particularly if you offer them a choice.

Failing this we have to decide whether or not to take a hedging action. In practice we will be looking at the total sales of the company. If we find that 50 per cent of sales are domestic and 50 per cent go to the US, then we have a major exposure which must be addressed. Equally for very large single contracts we would need to consider the options. In practice most companies will simply ignore the effect of smaller one-off contracts.

### Example

So let's consider our example again and assume that half of our sales are to the US. Should we hedge? We need a policy on handling this risk taking into account the following:

- What is the financial implication on the company of not hedging?

- What are our shareholders likely to want/expect?

Addressing the first issue – simply put – can we afford to take the risk of not hedging? In the example we have a fairly large profit margin; the larger the margin of profit the greater would be the currency swing required to turn a profit into a loss. If we have a large exposure to a foreign currency and a low margin such that even a small swing could cause us to lose money on these sales, we may have no reasonable option but to hedge the risk.

---

Bear in mind also that hedging is not free – over time any kind of exposure management programme will cost the organisation money. The banks make money out of selling exposure management products to companies, as you'd expect.

In the long run, and on average, it will be cheaper *not* to buy exposure management products, in the same way that in the long run it is cheaper *not* to buy insurance. Companies must balance insurance needs by weighing the risk against the costs. Medium sized companies will often buy disaster insurance but self-insure smaller risks. Foreign exchange risk and the option to hedge should be viewed in the same manner.

If, therefore, the structure of the business is such that the risk of not hedging is simply to accept a greater volatility of earnings from year to year, we need to ask what our shareholders would expect. If they are aware that a share of earnings is dollar dependent, and that the policy of the company is not to hedge the exposure, they can make their investment decisions on this basis. Large pension funds and the like are generally investing in a portfolio of currencies and will not be concerned by such a strategy. A small privately held company, on the contrary, may want to protect the shareholders from such volatility.

Organisational politics may also play a role here. The division measured purely on one year's sterling returns may well choose to hedge its exposures to eliminate that degree of risk. Directors whose bonuses are at stake may also have a view as to what level of risk is appropriate.

Having decided to hedge the currency risk we now need to view the alternatives. In the current market place there are many possibilities, but for simplicity we'll consider the two most common types of instrument:

- the forward contract
- the option.

# The forward contract

The forward contract is simply a way of swapping the receipt of a known amount of one currency for a fixed amount of another currency at an agreed forward date.

## Example

Taking our example, we are expecting to receive $US in four months' time, and let's assume that we have an order worth $10,000. The forward contract is a simple agreement with a bank to swap our $ into £ in four months' time, at a rate that is agreed now. In fact, because this is relatively common, the FT publishes the 'forward' rates for the major currencies in its 'currencies and money' section.

Alternatively, if we have $ banking facilities, we could borrow the dollars now, and remit them into sterling at the current 'spot' rate. When we receive the dollars from the customer they would pay off the borrowing. This would also eliminate the risk.

|  | $ | £ |
|---|---|---|
| Spot rate          £1 = | 1.5 | |
| Interest rates – for the period | 4% | 6% |
| Amount expected | 10,000 | 6666.666667 |
| Present dollar value | 9615.384615 | |
| Present sterling value | | 6410.25641 |
| Amount received at end of period | | 6794.871795 |
| Equivalent forward rate | | 1.471698113 |

Figure 12.1    Exchange rates (1)

Referring to Figure 12.1, if we trade at the spot (or current) rate of £1 = $1.50, then $10,000 would be worth £6,667. But we would not borrow $10,000 today because, with $ interest rates at 4 per cent, we would then owe more than $10,000 when the customer receipt arrived.

Instead we borrow the amount, which will be equal, including interest, to the $10,000 when it arrives. This is $10,000/1.04 or $9,615. This amount is equal to £6,410 at today's spot rate. If this amount were invested at the sterling interest rate for the period, say 6 per cent, it would yield £6,794 at the end of the period.

So we can say that the expected value of our $10,000 in four months' time would be £6,794, if we eliminated the currency risk by borrowing and investing. This is equal to an exchange rate of £1.472.

So what? Well this will be exactly equal (excluding commissions and things) to the forward rate the bank will quote you. In fact it has to be. If the locked in forward rate deviated from this rate, then it would be possible to borrow, switch currencies, invest for the term, and switch back without risk, while making money. This would be known as *arbitrage*.

You should note, therefore, that the forward rate at which we can hedge a foreign currency risk is derived from the difference in interest rates. It is a purely arithmetical rate which is *in no way a forecast* of future spot exchange rates.

The forward contract, though, does eliminate the risk of exchange rates moving against you before you receive the funds for the contract or delivery.

## Currency options

The forward contract is a powerful tool for eliminating the risk of forward movements. A currency rate, though, to quote our friends in the investment community 'can go down as well as up'.

If sterling weakens in the period, our dollars would be worth more than when we made the sale and, if we had made a forward contract, we would lose out on this additional value – it would go to the bank. What we need is an instrument that protects us against the dollar weakening against the pound, but allows us to keep the benefit of the dollar strengthening.

You guessed it – it's called the currency option. Think of a currency option as an insurance policy. You pay a premium to buy the option (policy), and exercise it only if things move against you (the event you insured against).

### Example

Using the same example as above, we might find an option available that would allow us to sell $ into £ at 1.50 in four months' time.

In Figure 12.2 we can see that, at the spot rate of 1.50, the $10,000 are worth £6,667. Assuming we buy the option with a 'strike rate' of £1 = $1.50, then we would receive £6,167, after deducting the premium of £500, assuming no move in the exchange rate.

If the rate moves against us, we can exercise the option to protect ourselves, receiving the £6,167. If the rate moves favourably, we let the option lapse (like an insurance policy that is not claimed against) and receive the effect of the better exchange rate, less of course the premium. On the graph in Figure 12.2, the effect of the altered outcomes is clear.

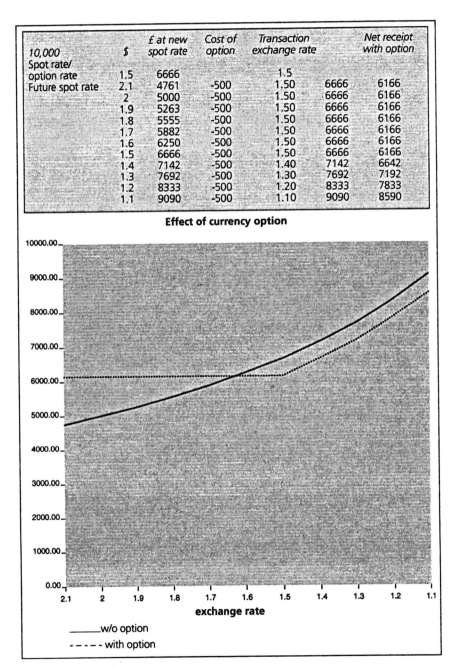

| 10,000 Spot rate/ option rate Future spot rate | $ | £ at new spot rate | Cost of option | Transaction exchange rate | | Net receipt with option |
|---|---|---|---|---|---|---|
| 1.5 | 6666 | | 1.5 | | | |
| 2.1 | 4761 | -500 | 1.50 | 6666 | 6166 |
| 2 | 5000 | -500 | 1.50 | 6666 | 6166 |
| 1.9 | 5263 | -500 | 1.50 | 6666 | 6166 |
| 1.8 | 5555 | -500 | 1.50 | 6666 | 6166 |
| 1.7 | 5882 | -500 | 1.50 | 6666 | 6166 |
| 1.6 | 6250 | -500 | 1.50 | 6666 | 6166 |
| 1.5 | 6666 | -500 | 1.50 | 6666 | 6166 |
| 1.4 | 7142 | -500 | 1.40 | 7142 | 6642 |
| 1.3 | 7692 | -500 | 1.30 | 7692 | 7192 |
| 1.2 | 8333 | -500 | 1.20 | 8333 | 7833 |
| 1.1 | 9090 | -500 | 1.10 | 9090 | 8590 |

**Effect of currency option**

_____ w/o option

- - - - - with option

Figure 12.2    Exchange rates (2)

# Derivatives

Having explained how a currency option can be used to reduce the risk inherent in a business, you may now be expecting a dire warning against the use of derivatives. After all, Barings, the local authorities and Sumitomo all hit trouble through using derivatives. A currency option explained above is a derivative. Essentially these are powerful tools, and like any such tool must be used carefully.

> If you take the view that organisations will open up certain financial risks in the course of trade, then it may be appropriate to use tools such as derivatives to reduce these operational risks. Using these tools to take positions on the market, increasing rather than reducing the organisation's exposure to risk, is speculation, and should not normally be allowed within commercial organisations.

Derivatives are essentially financial instruments that are related to the prices of 'real' things such as shares, bonds and raw materials (commodities). The derivatives markets are systems for the reduction of risk ('hedging') in trade between companies, overlaid with a large number of speculators who hope to make profits from price fluctuations. The markets have a reputation for being highly volatile and dangerous, but this is true only for the speculators; the underlying business of hedging is an important part of the world's economy.

## Commodities

To understand how derivatives have become so important, we should look at commodities. These are the basic raw materials that the world needs in order to function. They include wheat, coffee, oil, sugar, livestock and precious metals such as gold and platinum.

Companies that produce or process commodities find that prices fluctuate according to supply and demand, often in seasonal cycles. For instance, the cash price for wheat is lowest at harvest time, when there is plenty of it about. Precious metals have seasonal cycles too; prices usually increase in the autumn, as jewellers begin to prepare their products for sale at Christmas and need more raw materials.

Commodity prices are unpredictable; all kinds of events can affect prices, including wars, strikes, extremes of weather and the activities of speculators. This has been the case throughout history, and it makes life difficult for producers and users alike, since it is very hard to run a business if you don't know how much you can buy and sell your goods for.

For this reason, 'commodity futures' were invented.

## Commodity futures

Buyers and sellers of commodities can make a contract to deliver a product at some time in the future at an agreed price, thus taking the uncertainty out of their operations. They can agree on the amounts, quality and date of delivery, and both parties will put down deposits to protect each other from one side defaulting on the deal. This is a 'futures contract'.

Futures are a kind of insurance policy against the risks of price volatility; businesses can simultaneously trade in futures and in the cash market. In fact, most futures contracts are cancelled before the delivery period.

This is where the speculators come in. It is argued that speculators are a vital part of the futures market, because they provide it with greatly improved liquidity. Speculators aren't interested in using the commodities themselves; they are gambling on the difference between the price of a futures contract and the actual delivery price.

Thus the commodities businesses, or 'hedgers', and the speculators behave differently in the market. The hedgers are able to offset, roughly, gains or losses in the cash market by an opposite effect in the futures market, and are thus able to run their businesses more steadily. The speculators have to watch the fluctuations of futures contracts every day, and get out on top when they can.

## Buying on margin

Traditionally, when you purchase a futures contract, you only pay a small percentage of its value as a deposit. This is the main attraction for speculators, since it means that you trade futures 'on margin'; in other words, if you buy £200,000 worth of a futures contract, you only have to pay, say, £20,000 as an up-front deposit. If the gamble pays off and the value of the contract goes up to £280,000, you can sell, making a profit of £80,000 on a deposit of £20,000, an increase of 400 per cent rather than the 40 per cent increase you would have made if you had paid out £200,000. It is the possibility of buying on margin that makes futures risky for the speculators, since the margin means that prices are around ten times more volatile for speculators than they are for the hedgers, who actually trade in commodities themselves and do not use the margin to buy more than they otherwise would. The futures markets have grown massively as more and more speculators have become involved, and this has increased short-term volatility.

# Financial futures – hedging versus speculation

Shares, bonds and currencies can be treated as if they were commodities, and futures contracts can be made on them. Earlier we looked at forward contracts and options on foreign currencies, which are just two of a wide range of financial futures, and new ones are being invented all the time.

Most futures are tied to important currencies or a stock market index such as the FT-SE 100. They can also be tied to interest rates and bonds.

The margins on financial futures can be considerably less than the 10 per cent or so required as a deposit on commodity futures, which means that speculators can take even greater risks than they do in commodities.

 **Example**

Suppose you manage your company's investments, and are dealing in futures based on 'long gilts' (long term bonds issued by the British Government); in this case, the contract size is £50,000. Suppose that the price when you buy is 100-28 (this means 100 28/32: gilts move in 32nds of 1 per cent; each 32nd is called a 'tick'). The margin you must deposit is £500.

If you believe that gilts are going to go up and you want to buy gilts at a future date when money becomes available, you might buy the futures contract now to hedge against the expected higher cost of the gilts when you have the cash to buy them. If you are wrong, all is not lost, because the lower cost of gilts will roughly balance the loss you make on the futures contract. You can close out a futures contract either by delivering the gilts on the due date or by selling an identical contract; most people do the latter.

If you are speculating, however, the situation is rather different. Suppose the underlying value of your gilts contract dropped by 50 per cent; you would not have lost £250, but £25,000, all on your £500 initial deposit. The rules of the system say that investors' contracts have to be checked daily for losses and profits; if you are losing, you will get a 'margin call' for more money to cover the losses, and you can close out the contract to stop any further losses.

---

# Other financial risks

There are many other risks which can impact an organisation. These include:

- interest rate risk
- liquidity risk
- credit risk
- operating risk.

## Interest rate risk

Interest rates vary due both to market forces and to the intervention of the Bank of England, which sets the basic interest rates at which banks can borrow and lend money in the UK. The rates directly affect the cost of borrowing and investing funds, and companies can protect themselves against sudden changes by buying and selling a wide variety of financial products based on interest rates.

The type of financial product used will depend on the individual circumstances of the company, and the view that the company adopts on how interest rates will move in the future. The variety of derivatives available ranges from those that can give you certainty, such as forward contracts and interest rate swaps, to more exotic arrangements where only parts of the risk are hedged.

An example of interest rate risk might include a contractor bidding for a large contract under the new PFI (Private Finance Initiative) rules. Here the government will often look for a fixed price over an extended period of several years.

This will clearly expose the contractors bidding for the contracts to a substantial degree of risk should interest rates rise (cost of borrowing increases) or inflation increase (cost of labour and material rises). The prudent bidder will need to hedge these risks before finally bidding for such work.

## Liquidity risk

A company may have, say, £10 million worth of assets, but if it has no cash it cannot pay its bills, and might have to be wound up, which would inevitably involve serious loss. Managing the company's cash flow is essential to its survival, which is why strict regular budgeting is so important. Expanding companies are particularly prone to liquidity risk through 'overtrading', which is where a rapid increase in sales and purchases leads to firms running out of cash.

The alternative is to maintain committed credit lines (*see Chapter 10*) which will enable the company to borrow up to a pre-set lending limit at pre-agreed rates of interest.

## Credit risk

This is simply the risk that your customers do not pay their bills. There are many ways to control this, in particular by careful and frequent checks on customers' financial status and by imposing limits on the amount of credit you allow them, as we saw in Chapter 2.

## Operating risk

This covers risks associated with the day-to-day running of your company, and includes:

- fraud
- computer breakdown
- bad weather
- 'force majeure', such as wars and political crises.

Operating risk can be insured against to some degree, but also must be anticipated and managed carefully. Judgement, caution and experience are necessary – three human qualities that are impossible to measure.

# Longer-term risk

The above instruments are excellent at managing the risk profile of an organisation over the shorter term – a thriving market exists in options and forward contracts at terms of up to a year – and these instruments can also be arranged for periods of several years for larger amounts, albeit usually at somewhat higher relative cost.

There may also exist a structural risk – whereby the organisation is manufacturing in one country for sale in another. Consider the case of the German motor industry. BMW, for instance, manufacturing in Germany, with a substantial proportion of its sales in to the US, can hedge the short-term risks if it wishes through the above tools. Longer term though, it is seriously exposed to a potential long-term decline in the value of the dollar against the mark. It can of course increase the prices of its vehicles in the market to maintain margins, but this will reduce competitiveness and probably reduce sales levels. Essentially there is a structural imbalance giving surplus dollar income and surplus D-Mark costs.

This could be addressed by purchasing a US company with a dollar cost base, which exports to Germany. Or the company could increase the proportion of components it buys from the US for installation in all its production, subject of course to cost issues.

Understanding these issues, it was not a great surprise to note the site of BMW's newest production facility: in the United States, with cars to be exported into Europe. The net effect – to increase European income and US dollar costs – reducing the company's structural exposure. That they may also gain from reduced labour costs will also have played a part in the equation.

# The risk/reward relationship and the stock market

The prime motive for being in business is to make money, and in order to do this investors, whether they are individuals or companies, must take risks.

The amount of risk you take is usually, but not always, closely linked to the size of the return you may make. One of the great arts of investment is the analysis of risk, and we will look at some ideas about risk below. Before doing so, we should examine some important points about risk:

- diversification
- there is no such thing as no risk
- 'trees don't grow up to the sky'.

## Diversification

As we saw earlier, diversification simply means not putting all your eggs in one basket. If you spread your wealth amongst different assets, you reduce risk to some degree, because if a disaster happens to one group of assets or businesses, the others may escape.

## There is no such thing as zero risk

There really isn't! If a nuclear war broke out, all bets would be off! The fashionable business strategies of one decade often become no-nos a few years later, so although it is tempting to think that what has been safe and secure in the recent past will continue to be so in the future, history shows us that this is not the case.

> There is always a tiny chance that unlikely events can affect investments adversely: even the most copper-bottomed, gilt-edged guarantee does not assure you of zero risk.

## 'Trees don't grow up to the sky'

This famous saying is often applied to investments in rapidly growing companies. The point is that there are limits to how far anything will grow. Just as a tree will stop growing higher after a number of years, so will a business.

# The 'equity risk' of a listed company

Equity risk means the risk that any investor, including a company, faces that their collection of shareholdings (their 'portfolio') will not perform as well as the general average of the market. For publicly quoted companies, a drop in the value of their shares can adversely affect their ability to borrow money, and, in some cases, to win large contracts.

The variability of the stock market as a whole, known as the 'market risk', is different from the variability of individual shares. There will be particular influences on a particular company that cause it to rise or fall, such as labour problems or an increase in market share, but all shares tend to rise and fall with the market overall.

To compare the movements of a particular share with the stock market overall, we say that the 'beta' (the Greek letter 'b') of the market risk is 1. A share with a beta of 2 will swing twice as much as the market does in either direction, and a share with a beta of 1.5 will swing only one and a half times as far. Thus, the higher the beta of a portfolio or individual share, the more risky it is.

A listed company might want to reduce its equity risk by buying shares in many other businesses which would be likely to do well at times when the company's own enterprises were doing badly. The trouble is that this kind of diversification cannot eliminate the 'market' risk. In other words if, say, a worldwide recession or economic disaster occurs, almost all shares will drop. What a company can try to do, though, is to bring the risk of its portfolio down to a beta of 1, the same as the market risk beta.

## The 'Capital Asset Pricing Model' (CAPM)

CAPM is a theory which tells us that it is only the overall market risk that is relevant for valuation of a stock, since the part of the risk that is peculiar to an individual share, the 'unsystematic risk', can be eliminated by diversification. As a rough and ready rule, CAPM says that a portfolio of as few as 20 diversified shares should be enough to eliminate almost all of the unsystematic risk.

'Beta' is an officially approved way of measuring risk, and you can obtain estimates of the beta of a stock from brokers and investment advisers.

Giving the overall market risk a beta value of 1, and a 'risk-free' investment, such as a bank deposit, a beta value of 0, CAPM uses the following formula to work out the expected return on a diversified portfolio:

Expected return on a share =
  'Risk-free' interest rate + [Beta of the share ×
                (Expected return on the market
                − 'Risk-free' interest rate)].

The reason for calculating the expected return is that CAPM states that if, in the long term, you want to get a higher rate of return than the market average, all you have to do is to increase the beta value of your portfolio.

**Example**

A company has £1 million to invest. It decides to work out the expected return from four choices:

**1** A 'risk-free' investment in a bank deposit.

**2** An investment of half its money in the stock market and the other half 'risk-free'.

**3** Investing the whole sum in a portfolio with a beta in line with that of the market average.

**4** A high-risk portfolio.

Suppose the company finds that it can get 5 per cent interest after inflation from the bank deposit, and that the market average return is currently 8 per cent per annum after inflation:

**Choice 1**  Your expected return is the interest rate the bank gives you, 5 per cent, or £50,000. Remember that no investment is completely risk-free, but short of a major crisis it is reasonable to describe such an investment as risk-free, although inflation will eat into the capital and the interest.

**Choice 2**  You decide to put £500,000 in a portfolio with a beta of 1, and the rest in a bank. Using the expected return formula, the expected rate of return = 5 per cent + 0.5(8% – 5%) = 6.5%. Note that although the portfolio has a beta of 1, you have only invested 50 per cent of your money, so you must halve the beta value.

**Choice 3**  You invest all the money in a portfolio with a beta of 1; your expected rate of return will therefore be in line with the market average, 8 per cent.

**Choice 4**  You invest in a portfolio with a beta of 2.5, which should generate higher returns; expected rate of return = 5 per cent + 2.5(8% – 5%) = 12.5%.

A portfolio of investments with a beta of 0 should, according to CAPM, produce the same return as a risk-free investment outside the stock market which also, by definition, has a beta of 0 too. Studies have shown, however, that over the medium term share portfolios with a beta of 0 have done better than risk-free investments, contradicting the theory. In addition, in the 1980s investment funds in the US produced returns that had no correlation to their beta values. There have been objections to the way that beta values are measured, and it has been shown that betas for individual shares fluctuate significantly over time.

It has been said that you cannot measure the overall market risk accurately; if this is so, then CAPM is untestable. Many stock market professionals do continue to use CAPM, however, and claim that they have good results and are refining their techniques.

# Conclusion

Risks come on many levels for a commercial organisation, which is one of the reasons why companies are so interesting. It is important to understand where a company stands in terms of its risk profile and to have plans and policies in place to address them.

Forward swaps and derivatives can play an important part in managing short and medium term risk, while structural imbalances can only be addressed with structural adjustments.

Strategic and market risks must be understood fully in order that plans can be developed to keep the company moving forward.

# Financial controls – who, where, when and how

Proper internal controls have a tremendous effect on reducing loss due to error and theft. In this appendix we will look at a checklist for these control systems in detail.

The Auditing Practices Committee defined internal controls as:

the whole system of controls, financial and otherwise, established by the management in order to carry on the business of the enterprise in an orderly and efficient manner, ensure adherence to management policies, safeguard the assets and secure, as far as possible, the completeness and accuracy of the records.

The needs of every company will be different, but it is worthwhile examining the details of a general set of financial controls; most of it should apply to your own company.

The main points that a system should have are:

- an appropriate and properly integrated system of accounts and records

- a system of financial supervision by managers using budgets, regular interim accounts and special reports on problem areas

- a proper system for safeguarding important records, if necessary storing duplicates separately

- adequate training of employees to ensure that they are competent for their duties, and rotation of the duties.

One source of weakness in schemes is where certain people are excepted from the rules; a blanket rule should apply to all members of the firm.

General matters that probably apply to most firms include the following:

# Keys

Keys, especially to business premises, are often a status symbol which many people want to possess. They can be easily lost or copied. Overdistribution of keys often leads to irregularities.

There should be a good key system with a register of all key holders. The company should install good quality locks and make sure that keys are not easily copied. When making enquiries, check:

- who has the keys, originals and duplicates, and
- have employees who have departed returned their keys?

# Using figures

Data from records can be extremely revealing when investigating a problem: often a close examination can throw up clues as to the cause.

- In retail outlets, are the number of returns, rejections or sales proceeds too consistent or do they have regular spikes?
- Are there regular delays when money is handed over from refunds and cash sales?
- Which employees have had loans from the company, what are the outstanding balances and have there been any slow payers?
- If your company offers special terms for sales to staff, have you investigated these records to see who is using the facility?
- Do some employees consistently work the most overtime?

Simple calculations and reconciliation often point up excessive claims for materials, mileage allowances and fuel.

# Cash and cheques received

Companies need systems to:

- Restrict the number of people allowed to handle cash and cheques.
- Define their responsibilities in writing.

- Ensure that the parts of each transaction are divided between different individuals for security.
- Ensure independent checks and proper supervision.
- Ensure that cash is paid into the bank quickly.
- Keep proper safeguards to stop postal cheques being intercepted after they have arrived at the company.
- Have an independent supervisor of the opening of postal cheques.
- Keep a list of cash and cheques received each day for checking against subsequent accounting records.
- Cross all money orders and cheques when first received.
- Ensure that only individually authorised people can handle cash and cheques – these could include sales staff, marketing managers and delivery staff.
- Keep a close check on cash sales receipts by the use of tills.

## Keeping cash safe

- Named individuals should be responsible for cash and cheques at each stage before they are banked.
- Money should be collected from tills and offices frequently by an independent person.
- Cash and cheques received should be recorded as soon as possible using receipt forms, counterfoils, cash registers and/or post lists.
- A named person should be responsible for cash records. This person should ideally have no other accounting duties. Make sure that there is a named substitute when the responsible person is absent (even during lunch hours).

## Bank payments

- It is preferable to make sure that cash and cheques received are paid into the bank every day.
- The person who makes out the paying-in slips should be separate from the cashier who records the receipts.

- The person who pays the money into the bank should not be the person who makes out the paying-in slips.

- If not all payments are banked, there should be a special system to control what happens to the rest of the money.

- Keep limits on cash floats at cash desks and registers.

- How are cash floats repaid?

- Make frequent independent checks on the size of cash floats in registers and offices.

- How is cash that is left on the premises overnight kept safe?

- Take out special insurance for cash kept on the premises and when it is in transit.

- An independent person should reconcile bank statements.

## Cash and cheques paid out

- Keep a system for controlling the issue of blank chequebooks and keeping spare ones safe.

- A named person should be responsible for preparing cheques.

- Companies will have different rules on the number of signatories on cheques. Ideally, a cheque should have at least two signatories and be independently authorised.

- If some accounts only require one signatory, put a limit on the amount that can be drawn, and prohibit cheques from being made out in favour of the person signing them.

- If your cheques have printed or stamped signatures, you need a system for keeping the stamps and printing machines secure.

- Make sure that signed cheques are despatched promptly, and take precautions against them being intercepted.

- The person who prepares cheques should not be an authorised signatory.

- For cash payments, institute a system for authorising payments, with a record of who has authorised them.

- Institute a system to prevent vouchers authorising cash payment from being presented twice.

- Keep a maximum limit on cash payments to individuals.

- Make written rules on cash advances, IOUs and cashing employees' cheques.

- The cashier should be separate from other accounting jobs.

## Debtors and sales

- Make checks to see that your goods and services are sold at the correct price, including discounts and exchanges.

- Have independent supervision of the granting of credit terms.

- Supervise customer orders, despatch orders and production orders.

- Have a named person responsible for invoices, credit notes, and the safekeeping of blank invoices.

- Keep special control on special terms and free goods.

- A named person should authorise despatch, and there should be a system to prevent forgery of this authority.

- An independent person should record and examine goods out – this person should have no other accounting duties and no control over stock.

- Regularly reconcile the records of goods out with customer orders, despatch notes and invoices.

- Ideally, people who are responsible for dealing with sales should not have access to cash, cash books or stock, or be responsible for invoicing.

- Institute a special system for sales within your own group of companies.

- Institute a system for issuing statements to customers, and take care to prevent the unauthorised alteration of statements.

- Supervise the granting of discounts.

- Supervise the review and pursuit of overdue accounts.

- A named person should be responsible for writing off bad debts, and each decision should be justified.

# Purchases

There are three main types of control:

**1** authorising

**2** receiving the goods

**3** record keeping.

 When buying, there should be the following controls:

- a system for ordering stock replacement
- a system for authorising purchase orders, including obtaining competitive quotes
- purchase order forms should be kept safe
- a system for checking that goods delivered match the purchase order
- a named person should be responsible for accepting and recording goods in
- regular reconciliation of the 'goods in' record against purchase orders
- keep the functions of checking invoices, recording purchases and returns, checking suppliers statements and authorising payment as the separate responsibilities of different individuals
- a system for making sure that before a supplier's invoice is paid, the goods or services have been received and match the purchase order, and the invoice, in price, quality and quantity
- a special system for returns and special credits
- a special system for purchases from other companies in the group
- a special system for employee purchases at a discount
- an independent check of suppliers' accounts against their statements.

# Wages

 Wages and salaries are usually the responsibility of a special team or department (the Payroll Department in most organisations).

Divide responsibilities so that:

- there is an authorised person in charge of firing and hiring
- changes in the level of an employee's pay are authorised
- there is a system to control how changes to personnel and pay rates are recorded
- there is a system to control how deductions from pay are authorised
- there is a system for recording hours worked, piecework done, and overtime earned; an independent person should authorise payments
- you keep written rules on advances against wages, how they are authorised and how the advances are paid back
- you keep written rules on holiday pay
- a named person is responsible for dealing with pay queries
- there is a system for authorising and calculating pay
- there are special procedures for dealing with absence from work and short notice departures.

If employees are paid in cash:

- plan how the cash is collected from the bank and distributed to staff
- have an independent person pay over wages
- verify the identities of employees when they collect their pay
- keep a system for dealing with uncollected wages.

If employees are paid by cheque or bank transfer:

- have separate people to prepare cheques and sign them
- have a proper system for deducting statutory items such as PAYE, National Insurance, and pension contributions.

## Other controls on wages

- Make random counts of cash held in wages departments.
- Compare pay totals with budgets and investigate any discrepancies.
- Keep separate pay lists for employees and check them against the wages department's records.
- Find the explanations for discrepancies in totals and deductions between one pay day and the next.

# Stocks

Stock can be as vulnerable to irregularity as cash is, and can often be a source of much larger losses. Stock control procedures should ensure that stocks are properly protected against loss or misuse, are properly used in the business and are properly accounted for.

The basic types of stock are:

- raw materials
- components
- work in progress
- finished goods
- consumable stores.

The main controls should be:

- systems for receiving, checking and recording goods
- a named person should be responsible for safeguarding stocks and taking precautions against theft, misuse and deterioration
- there should be maximum and minimum stock limits
- the keeper of stock records should be separate from the people who have access to stocks and from sales and purchase records
- reconcile stock records with financial accounts
- have a system for authorising the removal of stocks out of store
- keep accounting control over company stocks held by third parties, such as goods on consignment, at a warehouse or undergoing some process, and a system of goods belonging to others which are held by the company
- a named person should be responsible for physical stock checks and the frequency of checks; this should not be the store keeper
- a named person should have full authority for preventing unauthorised entry into stock rooms; sometimes storekeepers are not given the power to prevent senior staff or customers from entering the stores
- have a consistent rationale for calculating the value of stocks in the accounts
- have a regular review of the condition of stocks, and a system for dealing with damaged and obsolete stocks

- have a system for dealing with scrap and waste, and how any money received from its sale is received and recorded.

## Fixed assets and investments

- Who authorises capital expenditure, and what evidence is needed to prove the authorisation?
- Who authorises the sale, scrapping and transfer of fixed assets?
- What are the arrangements for controlling and dealing with receipts from disposals?
- A named person should be responsible for keeping accounting records for fixed assets.
- There needs to be a written policy on how to ensure that the proper distinction between capital and revenue expenditure is kept.
- Keep registers of plant and property and regularly reconcile them with the accounts and a physical check of the items.
- Make regular checks on the maintenance, operation and location of all fixed assets.
- Have a written policy on how depreciation rates are authorised and evidenced, and a named person to calculate the amounts.
- Have a named person responsible for authorising purchases and investments. This person should preferably not have custody of cash and title documents.
- Keep a detailed investment register, a system for verifying title documents (such as share certificates) and reconcile it regularly with the investment account.
- Institute a system for checking stockbrokers' contract notes against purchase and sales instructions. Check the calculation of charges.
- A named person should be responsible for dealing with share transfers, and the delivery and collection of share certificates. A different person should account for dividends, interest and bonuses.
- Keep a list of all title documents including property title deeds and share certificates.
- A named person should be responsible for insuring title documents.
- Ideally, only two people should have access to title documents, and they should only be allowed to inspect or withdraw them together.

# Information technology

The increasing reliance on computerised systems in all aspects of business means that increasing importance in audits is placed on checking and verifying computer records and controls. On an operational basis, at the very least all managers should ensure that there are plans in place to protect the ongoing integrity of computer systems by establishing procedures to ensure regular backups of data and the availability of stand-by equipment to maintain continuity in the event of failure of critical systems.

The complexity and variety of information technology mean that the controls should be designed by software specialists. Often a company will operate mainframes on networks as well as a large number of specialised machines for different tasks, and desktop personal computers. Here are some points that should be borne in mind when devising controls in the office to prevent hacking and theft:

- A 'data-thief' often needs physical access to a workstation or PC – so office security needs to be tight. Visitor sign-in systems, and badges for visitors and staff are necessary in large offices.

- If a PC has no password, the intruder can take copies of relevant files – such as spreadsheets – rapidly onto a disc.

- If the PC is connected to a network or a mainframe, there will usually be passwords required before accessing the larger facilities. If an intruder comes during the day, at lunch-time or during breaks, the computer may already be switched on and logged in.

- Data-thieves will look around for passwords written in books or on desks near the computer. If they visit the legitimate user regularly, they may be able to read the password when the user types it in.

- An intruder with a laptop may be able to bypass security packages by direct file transfer through attaching a cable to the communication port on the target machine.

- Internal networks which are connected to external public networks such as the Internet can be vulnerable to attack. Ensure that such networks are protected by appropriate physical or software devices.

# Internal audit

The above checks and balances should all be incorporated into policies and procedures throughout the company. These procedures should be subject to internal audit at regular intervals.

# Some numerical tools

In this chapter we will look at some basic mathematical concepts, and probability, which is the science of chance and forms the basis of statistics.

While no one knows the future, companies need to make calculated guesses about what will happen. To do this, they need to be able to interpret figures accurately, and to judge whether or not the figures themselves are correct.

## Three kinds of average

Averages express the middle point in a set of numbers, and there are three main ways of calculating them. Each method produces a number with a different meaning, so when you are presented with an average, you should always check how it was calculated.

### The arithmetic mean

This is the most commonly used average. To calculate it, add together all the numbers in the set and divide the sum by the number of numbers.

**Example**

You have six regular customers. You know how much each one has spent this year. To find the mean annual spend of these customers,

**Step 1.** Add the amounts together:

| | |
|---|---|
| Customer 1 | 25,001 |
| Customer 2 | 34,340 |
| Customer 3 | 100 |
| Customer 4 | 25,003 |
| Customer 5 | 100 |
| Customer 6 | 112,890 |
| Total spent | 197,434 |

**Step 2.** Divide the total by the number of customers, which is 6. 197,434/6 = 32,905.66.

The mean annual spend per customer is £32,905.66. This doesn't mean that most of the customers spent around £32,905.66. Looking at the figures, you can see that the majority spent less – big-spending Customer 6 made the average higher.

---

## The median average

You can find the median by putting your numbers in order of greatest value, and taking the middle number. If there is no middle number, take the two in the middle and divide by 2.

 **Example**

---

**Step 1.** Using the same example as above, rank your customers by how much they spent:

| | |
|---|---|
| Customer 3 | 100 |
| Customer 5 | 100 |
| Customer 1 | 25,001 |
| Customer 4 | 25,003 |
| Customer 2 | 34,340 |
| Customer 6 | 112,890 |

**Step 2.** Add the 2 middle numbers in the series, Customer 1 and Customer 4:

| | |
|---|---|
| Customer 1 | 25,001 |
| Customer 4 | 25,003 |
| Total | 50,004 |

**Step 3.** Divide the total by 2. 50,004/2 = 25,002.

The median annual spend by customers is £25,002. This tells you that half your customers spent more than £25,002 and half spent less.

## The mode

The mode tells you the most commonly appearing, or 'popular', number.

**Example**

Using the same example, list your customers:

| | |
|---|---|
| Customer 3 | 100 |
| Customer 5 | 100 |
| Customer 1 | 25,001 |
| Customer 4 | 25,003 |
| Customer 2 | 34,340 |
| Customer 6 | 112,890 |

Customers 3 and 5 both spent £100, so the mode (the most commonly appearing number) is 100. This would be misleading in our example where two thirds of the customers spend much larger sums, but where you have a large collection of customers, the mode is more likely to reflect 'popularity' accurately, although you may find that you get more than one mode occurring on occasion.

## Which average to use?

The arithmetic mean is usually the best way to get an average, but sometimes you can't get a mean from your data.

**Example**

You conduct a customer survey to find out preferences for different products:

| | No. of responses |
|---|---|
| Product 1 | 1000 |
| Product 2 | 3200 |

271

| | |
|---|---|
| Product 3 | 2010 |
| Product 4 | 1100 |
| Product 5 | 1500 |

You can say that the mode of preferences is for Product 2 but calculating the mean will not tell you anything because the categories are of different things that can't be added together.

## Weighted averages

We came across weighted averages in Chapter 7, page 134, in the context of the weighted average cost of capital (WACC).

### Example

Suppose your company sells only two products. Product 1 gives a return on sales of 5 per cent and Product 2 gives a return of 15 per cent on sales. If you want to find out the average return on total sales you might simply add the percentages together and divide by the number of products:

$$(15 + 5)/2 = 10$$

But what if Product 1 accounted for 95 per cent of your company's sales? It would be wrong to say that average return on sales was 10 per cent, since almost all of the sales produced a 5 per cent return. To work out the right answer, you need to give the two figures for return a 'weight' to reflect their relative importance:

| | Return on sales | % of total sales |
|---|---|---|
| Product 1 | 5% | 95% |
| Product 2 | 15% | 5% |

To give Product 1 its correct weight, we multiply the return (5%) by its percentage of total sales:

$$5 \times 0.95 = 4.75$$

Doing the same for Product 2, we get:

$$15 \times 0.05 = 0.75$$

Adding the two together,

$$4.75 + 0.75 = 5.5$$

Thus, the weighted average return on total sales is 5.5%.

---

Most commonly, weighted averages are used to calculate an index.

## Indices

An index number is a summary of a large quantity of data. They are widely used in finance and investment in a similar way to averages. In other words, as a number which represents a mass of other figures. For instance, if you want to know how the stock market as a whole is doing, you would look at an index – such as the FT-SE All Share Index – instead of looking at the figures of hundreds of companies and performing the calculations yourself.

Many indices give their constituents different 'weights' in order to reflect the greater importance of some of their constituents – many stock market indices are weighted, for example.

### Weighting an index

Suppose you want to compare the relative values of four basic food items: milk, bread, mincemeat and potatoes, in 1995 and 1980. Figure A.1 shows notional prices and quantities. To get the total value of the 'basket' of four foods in each year, you just add the value of each food together, as has been done in the table. The total value in 1990 is £121.59, and the total value in 1995 is £400.86, so the percentage change in 2005 from 1990 is $[(400.86/121.59) \times 100] - 100 = 229.68\%$.

| Food | Quantity | 1980 Price | | Quantity | 1995 Price | |
|------|----------|-------|-------|----------|-------|-------|
| | Q0 | P0 | Value | Q1 | P1 | Value |
| Bread | 60 lb | 0.67 | 40.20 | 53 lb | 1.95 | 103.35 |
| Mince | 31 lb | 0.99 | 30.69 | 70 lb | 2.20 | 154.00 |
| Potato | 70 lb | 0.51 | 35.70 | 61 lb | 1.20 | 73.20 |
| Milk | 100 ltr | 0.15 | 15.00 | 79 ltr | 0.89 | 70.31 |
| | | | £121.59 | | | £400.86 |

Figure A.1

273

This kind of index is called a 'weighted index' because each price has been multiplied by a weight, in this case, quantity consumed per capita. Its full name is 'weighted aggregate index' because it considers the 'aggregate', or total, of several items.

### The Retail Prices Index (RPI)

Perhaps the most important index in the UK today is the General Index of Retail Prices, or RPI, which you can use as a measure of inflation. The RPI is published by the Central Statistical Office as a guide to the changes in the cost of living. It also publishes a Monthly Digest of Statistics which contains indexes of many facets of the economy. These publications are of great use to companies.

Here's how the RPI works. It attempts to show changes in the cost of living for the average person, and is based on the prices of a large number of goods and services, compared with the prices for the same things at a previous period.

When comparing, say, annual price levels, one particular year is taken as the 'base' year, and other years are compared with it. The convention is to write the base year as P0 and the year you are comparing it with as P1. If just one item is in the index, such as petrol, the difference, or 'price relative', is calculated as:

$$\text{Price relative} = (P1/P0) \times 100$$

**Example**

If your base year is 1990, and the price of petrol then was 0.75 a litre, and in 2005 it is 1.85 a litre, the price relative is $(1.85/0.75) \times 100 = 246.66$.

Subtracting 100 from the price relative gives you the percentage increase over the period. The percentage increase in the price of petrol in our example of the 15 year period between 1990 and 2005 would be $246.66 - 100 = 146.66\%$.

In some widely published indices, the average of several consecutive years is used as the base year; so it would be more correct to describe it as a base period.

## Spotting errors and misleading statements

It is a good idea to get into the habit of looking critically at figures and doing the calculations, where possible, for yourself. Since managers use figures to make decisions, they need to make sure that the figures are correct. In this section we will look at some common mistakes and misuses of statistical information.

## Which average?

The three kinds of averages – the arithmetic mean, the median and the mode – often give very different values; the fact that they can all be called 'the average' offers enormous scope for misleading statements. Consider the following: '*The median age of area sales managers is 42 and their average income is £42,000*'.

Does this mean that the median income is £42,000? We don't know, and there is no way of finding out without seeing the raw data.

Suppose that the person making this statement is trying to make the income seem as big as possible and the age of managers seem as small as possible. He or she calculates the three possible types of average, and finds, say, that the medians of both age of managers and their income is smaller than their arithmetic means.

He or she then chooses the median for the income figure, to make it larger, and the arithmetic mean for the age to make it look smaller. We read 'the median age', and, unless we are careful, we assume that the average income is also the median.

## Decimal points in the wrong place

As a child, were you ever told that spinach was good for you because it has lots of iron in it? Remember the cartoon character Popeye eating spinach for strength? The idea that spinach has a relatively large amount of iron in it stems from an analysis of vegetables that was done early this century, which showed that spinach had higher traces of iron in it than other vegetables.

It was recently discovered that the value for the iron content in spinach in this analysis had the decimal point one digit to the right of where it should have been; in other words, the figure quoted was ten times more than it should have been!

## Are they correlated?

We are often told things like 'there is a close correlation between being a full time student and buying CDs'; it is important to realise that correlation never implies a cause and effect. Nevertheless, one often comes across statements to the effect that since x and y are positively correlated, x caused y. But couldn't y have caused x? Or could x and y have been caused by other factors? Correlation alone does not tell us.

Correlation that occurs by chance can be found everywhere, especially when using small samples of large amounts of data. Often when you take more samples, the correlation disappears.

Another kind of positive correlation is where there is a real relationship, but there is no way of knowing which variable is causing which. For example, suppose that there is a correlation between an individual having a high income and owning shares in the stock market; does this mean that the more shares you have the higher your income, or that the higher your income is, the more you buy shares? You can't say that one has caused the other.

## Shifting the base

Consider the following statement:

*'Our market share dropped last year by 33 per cent from the year before. This year our market share has increased by 11 per cent, clawing back a third of last year's loss.'*

This may appear to be true, but it isn't. If the market share in Year 1 was 60 per cent, and in Year 2 it dropped to 40 per cent (a loss of 33 per cent), the 11 per cent increase in Year 3 is 11 per cent of 40 per cent, which is 4.4 per cent, bringing the market share back to 44.4 per cent.

This is not the same as 'clawing back' a third of the loss of Year 2, which is a third of 20 per cent = 6.67 per cent, and would make the Year 3 share 46.67 per cent, not the real figure of 44.4 per cent.

What has happened is that the statement has confused two different bases. The Year 2 decrease uses the Year 1 market share as the base. The Year 3 increase uses the Year 2 market share as a base, which is a smaller number.

People shift the base all the time without realising it; so remember, when comparing figures from different years, make sure that you take one year as your benchmark, or base, and compare all the other figures with it.

## General points to check

Here are six basic points you should bear in mind when you are looking at figures which are being used to support an argument:

1   Is there any sign of conscious bias? Are any of the statements ambiguous or clearly untrue? Do the results talk about averages in some cases and then switch to a specific kind of average (mean, median or mode) in other cases? Check the other averages to see if they make the results different.

**2** Check the source of the data. Surveys are often 'sponsored' by organisations who have a vested interest in the outcome of the survey.

**3** Is there any sign of unconscious bias? For instance, estate agents generally want to show that the market in private homes is improving. They may honestly be trying to be objective with their figures, but nevertheless they often overlook certain factors. The same goes for customers, suppliers, politicians, special interest groups, economists and many others.

**4** In a reported correlation, how big was the sample? If it is stated that A caused B, could B have conceivably caused A? Is the standard error given (this tells you how much the answer might be out by)? In many cases, the answers to these questions are enough to reject inferences regarding cause and effect as unproven.

**5** Reported figures may not be the same as actual figures. Economic data from many developing countries, for instance, are often highly unreliable. Problems also occur when people are asked survey questions that they do not wish to answer truthfully; what they say they do is not the same as what they actually do.

Suppose that a survey found that no one who was asked said that they disliked their boss. Would you be entitled to assume that it showed that no one dislikes their boss? The survey may have polled 'new' employees only – or perhaps the boss was present during the survey!

**6** All economic forecasts and extrapolations should be regarded with caution. In the early seventies we were told that oil would have run out by now; it hasn't. Predictions about the future are guesses, not facts. This is as true for government predictions as it is for the estimates you use in your own business.

## An introduction to probability

Consider the following two statements:

*'This investment is too good to miss; the benefits are so great that even if it has only a tiny chance of success, it would be madness to pass it up.'*

*'Our company has decided not to open a branch in Britain because of all the bombs.'*

Both these statements display a misunderstanding of probability. Let's examine them in turn.

The first statement ignores the possibility that other investment opportunities of equal risk exist. It does not estimate the probability of failure, but implies that this is high. If we wanted to take a chance, we could invest, but in order to hedge our bets it would be safer to invest in a wide range of schemes. If the risk were very high, though, we would run out of money before we had a reasonable chance of covering our bets.

The second statement refers to a phenomenon that most travellers are familiar with; the news about a country usually makes it sound more dangerous than it really is. This is because news tends to focus on dangerous events.

Think about your own neighbourhood. How many terrible things happen there in a year? There is probably more bad news in a year about your town than your neighbourhood, more bad news about your part of the country than your town, more bad news about your country than your part of the country, and more bad international news than home news.

We tend to forget that other countries are just like our own; they are made up of districts, towns and neighbourhoods just as ours is. The company would be reasonably safe from bombs in almost every district in Britain.

## Defining probability

Life is full of uncertainty, and so is business. The mathematics of probability help us to understand uncertainty better, and to reduce risk. Mathematicians studying probability were first prompted to do so by wealthy gamblers, so many of the problems they have worked on are stated in terms of games of chance, using cards, coins and dice.

Figure A.2 shows a probability scale. If we give absolute certainty a value of 1, and impossibility a value of 0, it is easy to see that the probability of all uncertain events will fall between 0 and 1. A 0.75 chance of an event occurring is the same as a 3 in 4 chance, and is readily converted into a percentage – in this case, 75 per cent.

 **Example**

You flip a coin. What is the chance that it will land showing heads? There are only two possibilities, heads or tails, so the chance of flipping heads is 1 in 2, or 50 per cent, assuming that the coin is 'fair', in other words, that the coin is not weighted or shaped to favour a particular side. If you have to predict the outcome before you flip the coin, you will either be right or wrong, but if you flip the coin many times, you will be able to guess how many times heads will turn up with some accuracy. In fact, the more times that you flip the coin, the smaller your percentage of error in your overall prediction will get; if you flip the coin 10,000 times, and guess that you will get heads 5,000 times, you will probably be out by a very small percentage.

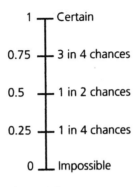

Figure A.2

The 'law of large numbers' states that if you flipped the coin a very large number of times, you would get heads almost exactly 50 per cent of the time overall. The trouble is that you can't flip the coin an infinite number of times, so you will probably always be a little bit out in your predictions.

In business, however, being slightly out on a prediction is much better than not being able to predict at all, so probability is extremely useful.

## Measuring probability

If you can work out all the possible results of a problem, you can express the probability of a particular result quite easily. Suppose you want to know the probability of getting exactly one head when you flip a fair coin twice. The possible results are:

HH   TT   TH   HT

There are 4 possible outcomes, all equally likely, of which 2 give you one head, so the probability is 2 in 4, or 50 per cent. Suppose you want to know the probability of getting exactly 2 tails when you flip a coin three times. The possible results are:

HHH   HTH   HHT   THH   TTH   THT   HTT   TTT

There are 8 possible outcomes, of which 3 give you two tails. Thus, the probability is 3 in 8, or 37.5 per cent. Another way of calculating the probability is to say that since there are 8 possible outcomes, all equally likely, the probability for any one of them occurring is 1 in 8. Since three of the outcomes give you two tails, the probability is 12.5 + 12.5 + 12.5 = 37.5 per cent.

Working out the probability of exactly two tails not occurring is easy – just subtract the previous result from 1, if you are using fractions, or 100 per cent if you are using percentages:

$$1 - \tfrac{3}{8} = \tfrac{5}{8}$$
$$100 - 37.5 = 62.5\%$$

If you have to work out the probability when there are many possible outcomes, writing them all out and counting them can be very laborious, so it is better to use a formula. To work out the probability, called P, of a particular event, called A, the formula is:

$$P(A) = n(A)/n$$

$n(A)$ represents the number of outcomes when A occurs, and $n$ represents the total number of outcomes.

## Example

You have a pack of playing cards and you want to know the chances of drawing any court card in spades. There are 52 cards in a pack, and 3 court cards in spades (Jack, Queen and King), so using the formula you can work out that:

P(any court card in spades) = 3/52 = 5.77 per cent

So far, so good, but what if you can't easily spot the number of possible outcomes?

## Example

You run a computer software company, and you have just developed a new program for business PC users. You estimate that the probability of showing a profit in the first year is 80 per cent, but only if your major competitor does not come out with a similar product. If the competitor does introduce a similar product, you think that the probability that you will make a profit will fall to 40 per cent. You also estimate that the chance that the competitor will indeed introduce a rival program is 1 in 2, or 50 per cent. Say that:

Event A is the competitor introducing the rival program, and

Event B is your program showing a profit in the first year if A occurs.

You want to know the probability of A and B occurring together.

| | |
|---|---|
| P(A) | = 50%, or 0.5 |
| P(B given that A occurs) | = 40%, or 0.4 |
| P(B given that A doesn't occur) | = 0.8 |

Using the formula, we see that:

$$P(A\ B) = 0.5 \times 0.4 = 0.2$$

There is a 20 per cent probability of showing a profit in the first year and your competitor introducing a rival product.

---

## Probability trees

If you want to work out the probability of several events occurring, it often helps to draw a tree of all the possible events. Figure A.3 shows a probability tree for all the possible events when you flip a coin twice. There are four possible events:

> Heads on the first flip (H1)
> Tails on the first flip (T1)
> Heads on the second flip (H2)
> Tails on the second flip (T2)

There are four possible outcomes:

> Heads, heads (H2 H1)
> Heads, tails (T2 H1)
> Tails, heads (H2 T1)
> Tails, tails (T2 T1)

Probability trees are more useful in more complicated problems.

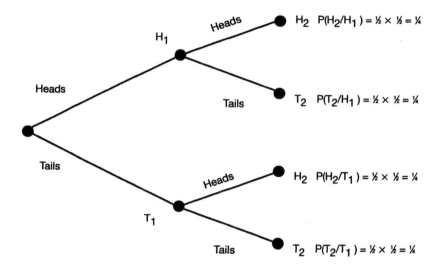

$H_2$  $P(H_2/H_1) = \frac{1}{2} \times \frac{1}{2} = \frac{1}{4}$

$T_2$  $P(T_2/H_1) = \frac{1}{2} \times \frac{1}{2} = \frac{1}{4}$

$H_2$  $P(H_2/T_1) = \frac{1}{2} \times \frac{1}{2} = \frac{1}{4}$

$T_2$  $P(T_2/T_1) = \frac{1}{2} \times \frac{1}{2} = \frac{1}{4}$

Figure A.3    Probability tree

## Example

You are the manager of a department store, and you are examining the buying patterns of customers in the shoe section. You know that the probability of a customer buying a pair of shoes (S) after entering the section is $0.4 = P(S)$. If a customer buys a pair of shoes, there is a 0.5 chance that shoe cream (C) will also be purchased, $P(C\,S) = 0.5$. If the customer does not buy a pair of shoes, there is a 0.1 chance that shoe cream will be purchased, $P(C\,\bar{S}) = 0.1$. Find the probability of the following:

Purchase of a pair of shoes $P(S)$
Purchase of a pair of shoes and shoe cream
Purchase of either a pair of shoes or shoe cream
Purchase of shoe cream

We know that

$$P(S) = 0.4,\ P(C\,S) = 0.5 \text{ and } P(C\,\bar{S}) = 0.1.$$

where $\bar{S}$ means the customer doesn't buy shoes.

Starting with the unconditional event that a customer buys a pair of shoes, we can now draw the tree in Figure A.4.

282

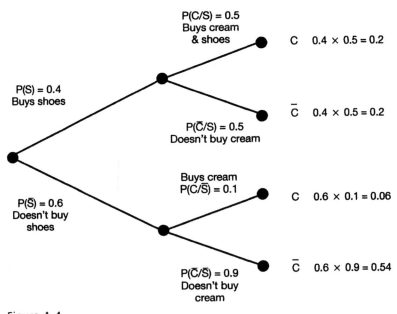

Figure A.4

In Figure A.4, we calculated P($\overline{C}$ S) by subtracting P(C S) = 0.5 from 1 and we calculated P($\overline{C}$ $\overline{S}$) by subtracting P(C $\overline{S}$) = 0.1 from 1.

Now we can work out that:

The probability of the customer buying shoes and cream is 0.4 × 0.5 = 0.2
The probability of the customer buying cream is 0.2 + 0.06 = 0.26
The probability of the customer buying shoes or cream is 0.2 + 0.2 + 0.06 = 0.46
The probability of the customer buying cream only is 0.06

## Estimating probability

It is often not possible to know as much about a problem of chance as we do when we
flip a coin, so we have to guess. If you are supplying computer chips, and you test a
batch of 1000 and find that 60 are faulty, you can guess that the probability of any
individual getting a faulty chip from you is 60 in 1000, or 6 per cent – you are making
a guess about all your chips, although you have only tested 1000 of them. This is called
sampling and is the basis of most statistical tests.

283

# The Greenbury report

Following increased concern amongst the public and shareholders about the way in which directors of some listed companies have behaved, a 'Study Group' of industrialists and investors was set up under the chairmanship of Sir Richard Greenbury, the Chairman of Marks and Spencer plc. The Study Group investigated the following topics:

- The accountability of directors to their stakeholders.

- The responsibilities of directors.

- The standards for disclosure of information.

- How the interests of shareholders and directors are, and should be, 'aligned'.

- How the performance of companies might be improved.

In 1995 the group produced a document, *The Greenbury Report*, which sets out a 'code of best practice' embodying proposals for standards of behaviour to conform with contemporary ideas about companies as having 'stakeholders' to whom they are responsible.

The group identified the main concerns of the public and shareholders as being:

- Concern about large increases in the remuneration of some executives at a time when more junior staff were suffering lay-offs and pay restrictions, and increases in the prices of products and services.

- Concern that some directors left companies with very high compensation packages.

- Concern that some companies whose businesses are in 'less competitive environments' might have boards which were not properly accountable to stakeholders.

The group opined that:

- most UK companies behave responsibly in their remuneration of directors but that
- there have been some 'mistakes and misjudgements' in this regard;
- there is a potential conflict of interest when boards set their own remuneration;
- proper remuneration of directors is essential to attract individuals of the highest quality to industry.

The group is against the introduction of statutory controls, and believes that boards can be made more accountable to stakeholders by voluntarily increasing their accountability and 'transparency', and by appointing a committee in each company to decide on executive remuneration who do not themselves have a financial interest in that remuneration. The group also is in favour of performance-related remuneration for directors, and has recommended that profits made by directors from exercising share options should be taxed as income rather than as capital gains, which would lower the tax paid.

# Disclosing directors' remuneration

The group recommended that:

- There should be a 'remuneration report' in the annual report of every listed company which sets out company policy on:
  - remuneration levels,
  - share options and performance related pay,
  - executive directors accepting directorships and payments from outside the company,
  - directors' employment contracts, retirement and pension arrangements

 ■ The 'remuneration report' should include details of the remuneration packages, pensions and share options of each executive director by name, and that these should be audited.

# Company policy on remuneration

The group recommended that:

- boards of directors and remuneration committees should be given flexibility in setting policy;

- companies should not pay directors more than is needed to attract people of the right competence;
- companies should not pay their directors more than the 'average' unless performance justifies this;
- bonuses should not be guaranteed, but performance related, with an upper limit;
- share option schemes should be phased to prevent directors benefiting unduly from volatile conditions in the stock market, and that such schemes should be subject to shareholder approval;
- directors should be encouraged to hold their shares in their companies for the long term.

## Directors' employment contracts

The group recommended that:

- there is a 'strong case' for making contracts renewable once a year, or even more frequently;
- if directors leave, their compensation should reflect their performance as individuals.

## Committees for the remuneration of directors

The group recommended that:

- such committees should consist of non-executive directors (NEDs) who know the company well and are properly trained, but who have no personal financial interest in remuneration decisions except as shareholders;
- to make sure that the NEDs do not have a personal financial interest in these decisions, they should receive set fees for their work which are fixed by the executive board.

**Note:**
Although they are not mandatory, many of the UK's largest companies are adopting the Greenbury recommendations in full.

For full details of the Greenbury recommendations, buy *Director's Remuneration. Report of a Study Group chaired by Sir Richard Greenbury 17 July 1996*, published by Gee at £10.

# Present value tables

These tables give the PV of a one-off payment you receive between 1 and 50 years in the future at a given discount rate of up to 20%.

## Example

A payment of £1,000 in 10 years' time at a discount rate of 5% has a PV of 0.6139 or £613.90.

| Years | 1% | 2% | 3% | 4% | 5% | 6% | 7% | 8% | 9% | 10% |
|---|---|---|---|---|---|---|---|---|---|---|
| 1 | 0.9901 | 0.9804 | 0.9709 | 0.9615 | 0.9524 | 0.9434 | 0.9346 | 0.9259 | 0.9174 | 0.9091 |
| 2 | 0.9803 | 0.9612 | 0.9426 | 0.9426 | 0.9070 | 0.8900 | 0.8734 | 0.8573 | 0.8417 | 0.8264 |
| 3 | 0.9706 | 0.9423 | 0.9151 | 0.8890 | 0.8638 | 0.8396 | 0.8163 | 0.7938 | 0.7722 | 0.7513 |
| 4 | 0.9610 | 0.9238 | 0.8885 | 0.8548 | 0.8227 | 0.7921 | 0.7629 | 0.7350 | 0.7084 | 0.6830 |
| 5 | 0.9515 | 0.9057 | 0.8626 | 0.8219 | 0.7835 | 0.7473 | 0.7130 | 0.6806 | 0.6499 | 0.6209 |
| 6 | 0.9420 | 0.8880 | 0.8375 | 0.7903 | 0.7462 | 0.7050 | 0.6663 | 0.6302 | 0.5963 | 0.5645 |
| 7 | 0.9327 | 0.8706 | 0.8131 | 0.7599 | 0.7107 | 0.6651 | 0.6227 | 0.5835 | 0.5470 | 0.5132 |
| 8 | 0.9235 | 0.8535 | 0.7894 | 0.7307 | 0.6768 | 0.6274 | 0.5820 | 0.5403 | 0.5019 | 0.4665 |
| 9 | 0.9143 | 0.8368 | 0.7664 | 0.7026 | 0.6446 | 0.5919 | 0.5439 | 0.5002 | 0.4604 | 0.4241 |
| 10 | 0.9053 | 0.8203 | 0.7441 | 0.6756 | 0.6139 | 0.5584 | 0.5083 | 0.4632 | 0.4224 | 0.3855 |
| 11 | 0.8963 | 0.8043 | 0.7224 | 0.6496 | 0.5847 | 0.5268 | 0.4751 | 0.4289 | 0.3875 | 0.3505 |
| 12 | 0.8874 | 0.7885 | 0.7014 | 0.6246 | 0.5568 | 0.4970 | 0.4440 | 0.3971 | 0.3555 | 0.3186 |
| 13 | 0.8787 | 0.7730 | 0.6810 | 0.6006 | 0.5303 | 0.4688 | 0.4150 | 0.3677 | 0.3262 | 0.2897 |
| 14 | 0.8700 | 0.7579 | 0.6611 | 0.5775 | 0.5051 | 0.4423 | 0.3878 | 0.3405 | 0.2992 | 0.2633 |
| 15 | 0.8613 | 0.7430 | 0.6419 | 0.5553 | 0.4810 | 0.4173 | 0.3624 | 0.3152 | 0.2745 | 0.2394 |
| 16 | 0.8528 | 0.7284 | 0.6232 | 0.5339 | 0.4581 | 0.3936 | 0.3387 | 0.2919 | 0.2519 | 0.2176 |
| 17 | 0.8444 | 0.7142 | 0.6050 | 0.5134 | 0.4363 | 0.3714 | 0.3166 | 0.2703 | 0.2311 | 0.1978 |
| 18 | 0.8360 | 0.7002 | 0.5874 | 0.4936 | 0.4155 | 0.3503 | 0.2959 | 0.2502 | 0.2120 | 0.1799 |
| 19 | 0.8277 | 0.6864 | 0.5703 | 0.4746 | 0.3957 | 0.3305 | 0.2765 | 0.2317 | 0.1945 | 0.1635 |
| 20 | 0.8195 | 0.6730 | 0.5537 | 0.4564 | 0.3769 | 0.3118 | 0.2584 | 0.2145 | 0.1784 | 0.1486 |
| 21 | 0.8114 | 0.6598 | 0.5375 | 0.4388 | 0.3589 | 0.2942 | 0.2415 | 0.1987 | 0.1637 | 0.1351 |
| 22 | 0.8034 | 0.6468 | 0.5219 | 0.4220 | 0.3418 | 0.2775 | 0.2257 | 0.1839 | 0.1502 | 0.1228 |

# APPENDIX D: PRESENT VALUE TABLES

| Years | 1% | 2% | 3% | 4% | 5% | 6% | 7% | 8% | 9% | 10% |
|---|---|---|---|---|---|---|---|---|---|---|
| 23 | 0.7954 | 0.6342 | 0.5067 | 0.4057 | 0.3256 | 0.2618 | 0.2109 | 0.1703 | 0.1378 | 0.1117 |
| 24 | 0.7876 | 0.6217 | 0.4919 | 0.3901 | 0.3101 | 0.2470 | 0.1971 | 0.1577 | 0.1264 | 0.1015 |
| 25 | 0.7798 | 0.6095 | 0.4776 | 0.3751 | 0.2953 | 0.2330 | 0.1842 | 0.1460 | 0.1160 | 0.0923 |
| 26 | 0.7720 | 0.5976 | 0.4637 | 0.3607 | 0.2812 | 0.2198 | 0.1722 | 0.1352 | 0.1064 | 0.0839 |
| 27 | 0.7644 | 0.5859 | 0.4502 | 0.3468 | 0.2678 | 0.2074 | 0.1609 | 0.1252 | 0.0976 | 0.0763 |
| 28 | 0.7568 | 0.5744 | 0.4371 | 0.3335 | 0.2551 | 0.1956 | 0.1504 | 0.1159 | 0.0895 | 0.0693 |
| 29 | 0.7493 | 0.5631 | 0.4243 | 0.3027 | 0.2429 | 0.1846 | 0.1406 | 0.1073 | 0.0822 | 0.0630 |
| 30 | 0.7419 | 0.5521 | 0.4120 | 0.3083 | 0.2314 | 0.1741 | 0.1314 | 0.0994 | 0.0754 | 0.0573 |
| 35 | 0.7059 | 0.5000 | 0.3554 | 0.2534 | 0.1813 | 0.1301 | 0.0937 | 0.0676 | 0.0490 | 0.0356 |
| 40 | 0.6717 | 0.4529 | 0.3066 | 0.2083 | 0.1420 | 0.0972 | 0.0668 | 0.0460 | 0.0318 | 0.0221 |
| 45 | 0.6391 | 0.4102 | 0.2644 | 0.1712 | 0.1113 | 0.0727 | 0.0476 | 0.0313 | 0.0207 | 0.0137 |
| 50 | 0.6080 | 0.3715 | 0.2281 | 0.1407 | 0.0872 | 0.0543 | 0.0339 | 0.0213 | 0.0134 | 0.0085 |

| Years | 11% | 12% | 13% | 14% | 15% | 16% | 17% | 18% | 19% | 20% |
|---|---|---|---|---|---|---|---|---|---|---|
| 1 | 0.9009 | 0.8929 | 0.8850 | 0.8772 | 0.8696 | 0.8621 | 0.8547 | 0.8475 | 0.8403 | 0.8333 |
| 2 | 0.8116 | 0.7972 | 0.7831 | 0.7695 | 0.7561 | 0.7432 | 0.7305 | 0.7182 | 0.7062 | 0.6944 |
| 3 | 0.7312 | 0.7118 | 0.6931 | 0.6750 | 0.6575 | 0.6407 | 0.6244 | 0.6086 | 0.5934 | 0.5787 |
| 4 | 0.6587 | 0.6355 | 0.6133 | 0.5921 | 0.5718 | 0.5523 | 0.5337 | 0.5158 | 0.4987 | 0.4823 |
| 5 | 0.5935 | 0.5674 | 0.5428 | 0.5194 | 0.4972 | 0.4761 | 0.4561 | 0.4371 | 0.4190 | 0.4019 |
| 6 | 0.5346 | 0.5066 | 0.4803 | 0.4556 | 0.4323 | 0.4104 | 0.3898 | 0.3704 | 0.3521 | 0.3349 |
| 7 | 0.4817 | 0.4523 | 0.4251 | 0.3996 | 0.3759 | 0.3538 | 0.3332 | 0.3139 | 0.2959 | 0.2791 |
| 8 | 0.4339 | 0.4039 | 0.3762 | 0.3506 | 0.3269 | 0.3050 | 0.2848 | 0.2660 | 0.2487 | 0.2326 |
| 9 | 0.3909 | 0.3606 | 0.3329 | 0.3075 | 0.2843 | 0.2630 | 0.2434 | 0.2255 | 0.2090 | 0.1938 |
| 10 | 0.3522 | 0.3220 | 0.2946 | 0.2697 | 0.2472 | 0.2267 | 0.2080 | 0.1911 | 0.1756 | 0.1615 |
| 11 | 0.3173 | 0.2875 | 0.2607 | 0.2366 | 0.2149 | 0.1954 | 0.1778 | 0.1619 | 0.1476 | 0.1346 |
| 12 | 0.2858 | 0.2567 | 0.2307 | 0.2076 | 0.1869 | 0.1685 | 0.1520 | 0.1372 | 0.1240 | 0.1122 |
| 13 | 0.2575 | 0.2292 | 0.2042 | 0.1821 | 0.1625 | 0.1452 | 0.1299 | 0.1163 | 0.1042 | 0.0935 |
| 14 | 0.2320 | 0.2046 | 0.1807 | 0.1597 | 0.1413 | 0.1252 | 0.1110 | 0.0985 | 0.0876 | 0.0779 |
| 15 | 0.2090 | 0.1827 | 0.1599 | 0.1401 | 0.1229 | 0.1079 | 0.0949 | 0.0835 | 0.0736 | 0.0649 |
| 16 | 0.1883 | 0.1631 | 0.1415 | 0.1229 | 0.1069 | 0.0930 | 0.0811 | 0.0708 | 0.0618 | 0.0541 |
| 17 | 0.1696 | 0.1456 | 0.1252 | 0.1078 | 0.0929 | 0.0802 | 0.0693 | 0.0600 | 0.0520 | 0.0451 |
| 18 | 0.1528 | 0.1300 | 0.1108 | 0.0946 | 0.0808 | 0.0691 | 0.0592 | 0.0508 | 0.0437 | 0.0376 |
| 19 | 0.1377 | 0.1161 | 0.0981 | 0.0829 | 0.0703 | 0.0596 | 0.0506 | 0.0431 | 0.0367 | 0.0313 |
| 20 | 0.1240 | 0.1037 | 0.0868 | 0.0728 | 0.0611 | 0.0514 | 0.0433 | 0.0365 | 0.0308 | 0.0261 |
| 21 | 0.1117 | 0.0926 | 0.0768 | 0.0638 | 0.0531 | 0.0443 | 0.0370 | 0.0309 | 0.0259 | 0.0217 |
| 22 | 0.1007 | 0.0826 | 0.0680 | 0.0560 | 0.0462 | 0.0382 | 0.0316 | 0.0262 | 0.0218 | 0.0181 |
| 23 | 0.0907 | 0.0738 | 0.0601 | 0.0491 | 0.0402 | 0.0329 | 0.0270 | 0.0222 | 0.0183 | 0.0151 |
| 24 | 0.0817 | 0.0659 | 0.0532 | 0.0431 | 0.0349 | 0.0284 | 0.0231 | 0.0188 | 0.0154 | 0.0126 |
| 25 | 0.0736 | 0.0588 | 0.0471 | 0.0378 | 0.0304 | 0.0245 | 0.0197 | 0.0160 | 0.0129 | 0.0105 |
| 26 | 0.0663 | 0.0525 | 0.0417 | 0.0331 | 0.0264 | 0.0211 | 0.0169 | 0.0135 | 0.0109 | 0.0087 |
| 27 | 0.0597 | 0.0469 | 0.0369 | 0.0291 | 0.0230 | 0.0182 | 0.0144 | 0.0115 | 0.0091 | 0.0073 |
| 28 | 0.0538 | 0.0419 | 0.0326 | 0.0255 | 0.0200 | 0.0157 | 0.0123 | 0.0097 | 0.0077 | 0.0061 |
| 29 | 0.0485 | 0.0374 | 0.0289 | 0.0224 | 0.0174 | 0.0135 | 0.0105 | 0.0082 | 0.0064 | 0.0051 |
| 30 | 0.0437 | 0.0334 | 0.0256 | 0.0196 | 0.0151 | 0.0116 | 0.0090 | 0.0070 | 0.0054 | 0.0042 |
| 35 | 0.0259 | 0.0189 | 0.0139 | 0.0102 | 0.0075 | 0.0055 | 0.0041 | 0.0030 | 0.0023 | 0.0017 |
| 40 | 0.0154 | 0.0107 | 0.0075 | 0.0053 | 0.0037 | 0.0026 | 0.0019 | 0.0013 | 0.0010 | 0.0007 |
| 45 | 0.0091 | 0.0061 | 0.0041 | 0.0027 | 0.0019 | 0.0013 | 0.0009 | 0.0006 | 0.0004 | 0.0003 |
| 50 | 0.0054 | 0.0035 | 0.0022 | 0.0014 | 0.0009 | 0.0006 | 0.0004 | 0.0003 | 0.0002 | 0.0001 |

# Glossary

**A**

**Absorption costing** – a method of costing that makes each product 'absorb' a portion of the company's overhead.

**Accruals** – debts which have been incurred, but not yet paid for, are recorded as 'accruals'.

**Activity Based Costing (ABC)** – an alternative to standard costing which identifies 'cost drivers' with the aim of allocating costs to products accurately. ABC allocates indirect costs more accurately than do traditional costing methods.

**Actuary** – a specialist who calculates risk data and prices for insurers and pension funds.

**Advance corporation tax (ACT)** – A basic rate tax paid by companies on dividends distributed to shareholders, who can sometimes set ACT tax credits against other tax liabilities.

**Advance Pricing Agreements** – agreements between companies and tax authorities on how transactions will be taxed in advance of incurring the liability.

**Arbitrage** – buying something in one market and selling it immediately in another for a higher price.

**Arm's length rule** – when related businesses sell products and services to each other, tax authorities often insist that they set prices at the level which unrelated businesses would pay.

**Asset** – anything which has a monetary value.

**Associate company** – a company which is part-owned by another; normally a shareholding of 20–50% makes the company an associate.

**Audit** – inspection of a company's accounts by independent accountants known as auditors.

**Average return on book value** – a rule-of-thumb measure of a proposed investment. The average book value of the investment is divided by the average forecast net profits.

## B

**Balance sheet** – a statement of a company's assets and liabilities at a given moment in time.

**Beta** – a measurement of the risk of a share relative to the stock market overall.

**Bills of exchange** – documents in which a borrower promises to repay a lender a sum of money at a fixed date in the future (often three months). They are usually guaranteed by banks, and may be sold on in the financial markets before they become due.

**Blue chip** – The top 100 or so companies on the stock market, reputedy stable investments.

**Bonds** – a loan to a large company, government or quasigovernmental organisation, usually paying a fixed rate of interest.

**Bonus issue** – the issue of additional shares by a company to its shareholders at no cost; also called a 'scrip issue' or a 'capitalization issue'.

## C

**Call option** – the right to buy shares at an agreed price within a certain time.

**Capital Asset Pricing Model (CAPM)** – a theory for assessing the relative risk and potential return on the shares of a listed company.

**Capital Gains Tax (CGT)** – a tax on the increase of value of assets realised in a particular year.

**Capital rationing** – a method of limiting the amount of capital available for investment by the divisions of a company.

**Capitalisation** – the total value at the market price of securities issued by a company, industry or market sector.

**Cash flow statement** – a statement in published accounts which show the pattern of cash inflows and outflows during the period.

**Commodities** – any raw material.

**Consistency** – a principle of accounting that transactions are treated according to a consistent method except when there is a genuine need for a change in method.

**Consolidated accounts** – the published accounts of a group of companies.

**Convertible bonds** – a security paying a fixed rate of interest which may be changed in the future for ordinary shares.

**Corporate governance** – the systems used to ensure that a company is properly run, in accordance with 'best practice' as well as the law.

**Cost centre** – the smallest unit for which costs are collected separately.

**Coupon** – the nominal interest rate on a fixed-interest security (bond), or a warrant which is detached from a bearer bond or bearer share certificate to be used to claim interest.

**Currency hedging** – trying to reduce or eliminate exchange rate risks by buying forward, using financial futures or borrowing in the exposed currency.

**Current ratio** – current assets divided by current liabilities. The result should normally be more than 1.

## D

**Debt financing** – obtaining money for use in a business by creating debt, such as obtaining bank loans or leasing.

**Depreciation** – the process of 'writing down' the value of an asset during its useful life.

**Derivative** – an investment which is tied to an 'artificial' concept, like a stock index, rather than to stocks and shares or tangible assets.

**Discounted cash flow (DCF)** – a method of calculating the estimated value of an investment, based on adjusting future cash inflows and outflows to their 'present value'.

**Dividends** – a regular payment out of profits by companies to their shareholders. Currently taxed in the UK at 20%.

**Double entry** – a basic accounting principle in which every transaction is recorded twice, once as a credit and once as a debit.

**Double taxation treaties** – treaties between countries to prevent companies and individuals being taxed twice on the same income or profits.

**Due diligence** – the process of checking that the details of a company's business are as has been claimed, usually done on behalf of a prospective purchaser.

## E

**Earnings** – the net profit of a company which is distributed to its shareholders.

**Earnings per share (EPS)** – the profits of a company after tax, divided by the number of its shares.

**Equity financing** – obtaining capital for a business by issuing shares.

**Eurobond** – a bond which is issued by a syndicate of banks and is usually bought and sold outside the country in whose currency it is denominated.

**Eurocurrency** – deposits of a currency which are held outside its own country.

**Eurodollar** – US dollars held outside the US.

### F

**Factoring** – where companies sell their unpaid invoices at a discount to a specialist company (called a 'factor') which collects the money itself. This improves cashflow.

**Feedback/feedforward** – terms taken from systems design, and used to refer to processes in organisational control cycles.

**Financial accounting** – accounting processes leading to the production of published accounts.

**Fixed cost** – business costs that do not change significantly if sales/production volume changes.

**Force majeure** – a supplier usually has a clause in delivery contracts allowing him to break the contract when there is force majeure, which is a major external event such as a strike, war or major catastrophe.

**Forward exchange contract** – an agreement to buy an amount of a currency at an agreed exchange rate on a fixed date.

**FT Actuaries All-Share Index** – a stock market index, divided into forty sections, covering all shares quoted in the UK.

**FT Industrial Ordinary Share Index** – an index of the ordinary shares of thirty top companies.

**FT-SE 100 Index** – A.K.A. the 'Footsie', the principal index for the price of shares quoted on the London stock market. The 100 companies whose shares are represented in the FT-SE 100 Index are generally regarded as blue-chip.

**Future** – the right to buy or sell a product or a financial instrument at an agreed price at some future time.

### G

**Gearing** – the ratio between a company's share capital and its borrowings. High-gearing means a proportionately large amount of debt, and low-gearing means a small amount of debt.

**Going concern** – a business which, it is assumed, is going to continue trading and not go bust.

**Goodwill** – the difference between the purchased value of a company and the book value of its assets.

**H**

**Hedging** – the act of reducing risk by 'laying off bets', for example by buying a forward contract.

**Holding company** – a company which has controlling shareholdings in its subsidiary companies.

**Hurdle rates** – a required rate of return on any investment. If a company sets a hurdle rate of, say, 20%, then any proposed project must be expected to produce an annual return greater than 20%.

**I**

**Inflation** – a general increase in prices.

**Insider trading** – trading in shares when in possession of price-sensitive information which is not known to the stock market. Illegal to some degree in most markets.

**Interest cover** – the amount by which profits exceed the amount of interest due to be paid.

**Interim accounts** – six monthly accounts, usually not audited.

**Internal audit** – methods for checking the effectiveness of internal controls.

**Internal control** – systems to ensure the proper running of a company, including measures to prevent error, wastage and theft.

**Internal rate of return (IRR)** – a way of calculating estimating the profitability of an investment by forecasting future benefits compared with the capital required now. The IRR is the rate or return at which Net Present Value is 0. See also DCF and NPV.

**Investment bank** – called a 'merchant bank' in the UK, a bank which works as a financial intermediary, offering such services as take-over and merger assistance, and the placing of new share and bond issues.

**Invoice discounting** – a type of factoring where the factor advances a proportion of the value of a company's invoices, but the company still collects the payments itself. See 'Factoring'.

**J**

**Junk bonds** – company bonds which are not rated by credit-rating agencies; they are 'low quality', and offer a higher rate of interest than other bonds.

**L**

**LIFFE** – the London International Financial Futures and Options Exchange.

**London Interbank Offered Rate (LIBOR)** – the rate of interest offered by commercial banks to other banks on the London interbank market.

**Liquidity** – the speed at which assets can be turned into cash. Cash is very liquid, but plant and buildings may not be.

## M

**Management accounting** – accounting processes designed to provide information to managers for decision-making purposes.

**Materiality** – the amount below which an item is considered too small to bother with.

## N

**Net Asset Value (NAV)** – the net assets of a company divided by the number of shares it has issued gives the NAV per share.

**Net present value (NPV)** – the total of all future cash inflows from an investment less all future cash outflows, with an adjustment for inflation and, sometimes, for the 'discount rate', which is a rate of return required by the investor.

**Non-executive directors (NEDs)** – a director who is not part of the day to day management of the company. Their importance has increased following the recommendations of the Cadbury and Greenbury reports.

## O

**Off-balance sheet financing** – types of financing that are not required to be shown on a company's balance sheet. These include operating leases.

**Operating activities** – cash generated in the normal course of trading.

**Operating profit** – net profit after administration costs but before financing charges.

**Option** – the right to buy or sell a security at an agreed price within an agreed time span.

**Ordinary share** – the most usual type of share, called 'ordinary' to distinguish it from other kinds, such as 'preference' shares which pay a fixed dividend.

**Overtrading** – when a company does not have enough working capital to fund increased sales, it is said to be overtrading.

## P

**Par value** – the nominal value of a share or bond, as stated on its certificate. This is not its market value.

**Payback** – a way of assessing an investment by estimating how long it will take to recoup the sum invested.

**Portfolio** – a collection of securities held by one investor or fund.

**Preference shares** – fixed dividend shares giving preference as a creditor over ordinary shareholders, but behind bond-holders.

**Price earnings ratio (PE)** – the market price of a share divided by its earnings (eg profits) gives the p/e ratio, which is a commonly used investment measure of a share.

**Profit centre** – the smallest unit in a business which is made responsible for its profits.

**Profit and loss account** – in published accounts, a statement of profits or losses for the period.

**Provisions** – a charge against profits for a possible future expense, such as a pending court case or bad debts.

**Prudence** – a principle of accounting that items should be treated conservatively – in other words, to err on the safe side.

## R

**Rating** – of bonds is done according to risk; the least risky bonds are rated AAA and the highest risk rated is D. Junk bonds are too risky to be rated.

**Realisation** – when the money from sales is actually received.

**Residual income** – the controllable contribution of a division less a capital charge.

**Return On Capital Employed (ROCE)** – operating profit divided by capital employed.

**Revaluation reserve** – the revaluation of assets whose value has increased, as shown in a balance sheet.

**Rights issue** – when a company offers new shares pro rata to its own shareholders, usually at a discount.

## S

**Securities** – any financial instrument traded on a stock exchange, such as shares and bonds.

**Share premium account** – shares which are issued by a company at more than their normal value are said to be issued at a premium, and the difference between their nominal value and issued value is shown as the 'share premium account'.

**Special value programme (SVP)** – variations on a product with enhanced perceived value.

**Stakeholder** – anyone with an interest in a company, including its customers, suppliers, shareholders and employees.

**Standard cost** – the cost of a product under standard conditions.

## T

**Takeover** – the purchase of one company by another.

**Tap stock** – in the UK, the name for an issue of government bonds that is not fully subscribed. In such cases, the broker keeps the remainder and 'dribbles' it into the market slowly.

**Throughput accounting** – the measurement of total plant performance through the identification of the plants' bottlenecks and the ranking of products by their contribution per unit of bottleneck resource.

**Tombstone** – a newspaper advertisement that sets out the details of a bond issue or major loan, and the banks who have underwritten it.

**Transfer pricing** – the internal prices set by a group of companies when transferring services and goods internally.

**Treaty shopping** – the attempt by a group to incorporate a subsidiary or holding company in a country which has advantageous double taxation treaties.

**Turnover** – annual revenue.

## V

**Variable cost** – costs which change with volume of output of products and services – for example, direct labour and raw materials.

## W

**Warrants** – a certificate, usually attached to a bond, which gives the holder the right to buy shares at a given price and date.

**Weighted Average Cost of Capital (WACC)** – the average of the cost of equity (the return required by the shareholders) and the cost of debt (the interest on loans, usually lower than the former) to a company. WACC is usually lower when a company is high-geared.

**Withholding tax** – tax witheld by tax authorities before the money goes overseas.

**Working capital** – net current assets. It represents the capital needed to fund operations between the payment for inputs and the time that customers settle their invoices.

# Index